D1761182

27 FEB 2012

23/08

07/09.

Withdrawn from Sto

The Honan Chapel

Withdrawn from Stock

The Honan Chapel
A Golden Vision

EDITED BY

VIRGINIA TEEHAN AND
ELIZABETH WINCOTT HECKETT

Photography by Andrew Bradley
Design by Christian Kunnert

CORK UNIVERSITY PRESS

First published in 2004 by
University College Cork
Ireland

© Cork University Press 2004
Photographs © The Honan Trust 2004

All rights reserved. No part of this book may
be reprinted or reproduced or utilized in any
electronic, mechanical or other means, now
known or hereafter invented, including
photocopying and recording or otherwise,
without either the prior written permission of
the Publishers or a licence permitting
restricted copying in Ireland issued by the Irish
Copyright Licensing Agency Ltd, The Irish
Writers' Centre, 19 Parnell Square, Dublin 1.
British Library Cataloguing in Publication Data
A CIP catalogue record for this book is
available from the British Library.

ISBN 1-85918-346-8

Designed and Typeset by Kunnert & Tierney,
Information Design, Riverstick, Cork

Printed by Butler & Tanner Ltd., Somerset

Contents

LIST OF ILLUSTRATIONS

Foreword

The Board of Governors of the Honan Chapel is delighted to be associated with this publication and the conference it records. This book fulfills the original vision of the promoters and founders of the Honan Chapel – the Honan Family, Sir John O' Connell, and Sir Bertram Windle.

By developing new knowledge and interpretations of this unique spiritual and artistic resource, the Chapel and its collection of liturgical art are being made accessible to wide and diverse audiences as envisaged by the founders of the chapel. Although legally separated from University College, Cork, the Honan Chapel and the University are inextricably linked. Universities dedicate their vision to fostering innovation and creativity. Historically, both the Governors and the University shared this vision, as manifested in the Honan Chapel, and now again, mirrored in this book.

This publication is important in that, for the first time, the Honan collection of Liturgical art is fully documented. By providing a unique record of the work of the many designers, artists and craft workers – whose work might otherwise have been overlooked – a testimony to their contribution to Irish artistic development has been created. This new assessment of the Honan collection brings fresh knowledge and appreciation of Irish design, art, craft and architecture.

In supporting the publication of this book, the Governors hope that the Honan Chapel and Collection will be made more accessible to the wider community. We also hope that this volume will contribute to our spiritual patrimony. Finally, we remember and celebrate the memory of Fr. Gearoid Ó Súilleabháin (1924–2001), Dean of the Honan Chapel and contributor to this publication.

Professor G. T. Wrixon
Chairman
Board of Governors, The Honan Trust
President
University College, Cork

September 2004

Editor's Preface and Acknowledgements

In January 2000, the Heritage and Visual Arts Office, University College Cork, with support from the Trustees of the Honan Chapel organized a conference entitled 'The Craftsman's Honoured Hand', which focused on exploring the richness and variety of the Honan Chapel and Collection. The objective of the conference was to develop greater awareness of the importance of the Honan Chapel and Collection as a unique cultural resource. The conference was most successful and attracted 230 participants. The popularity of the conference was a manifestation of the great esteem in which the chapel and collection are held, not only locally but also nationally and abroad. Participants came from Oxford, Belfast, Dublin and other places to attend.

The conference comprised eight papers, which are all reproduced in this book. They embrace all aspects of the chapel, its collection and the philosophy underpinning its foundation. In addition to the conference papers, it was decided to build on earlier work and include in the book an inventory of the collection that we had previously compiled. Mairéad Dunlevy, who was unable to attend the conference, has contributed the introduction, setting the collection in context. The resulting publication sets out permanently to record the importance of the chapel and its collection. It is of vital interest to those studying Irish architecture, art, visual and social culture and the design process. This book, like the collection that it records, is our contribution to the growing recognition of the importance of Irish art and design in an international context.

Initially we were invited by Professor Finbarr Holland, the Warden of the Honan Hostel in 1990, to compile a short list of extant items from the collection, which were, at that time, stored in various parts of the Honan Hostel and the Warden's House. The process of compiling the list opened our minds and hearts to the wonderful splendour

FIG. 1: *Replica of the Cross of Cong, (detail back)*

xiii

that is the Honan Collection. From that time onwards we worked to understand the collection and its relationship with the chapel building and its wider resonance in the context of Irish visual, art-historical and social culture. After a long cold winter locating, identifying and recording each item that we could find both in the Chapel and other locations, an unpublished Inventory was produced in limited number. From this time forward we agitated and cajoled to ensure that the beauty and significance of the collection would be communicated to wider audiences.

There are many people who helped and supported this work over the years. We would like to extend to them our warmest thanks and acknowledge their support here. Those who set us on this track over ten years ago – Professor Finbarr Holland and Mrs Holland, Professor Séan Teegan and Mrs Teegan – provided considerable help, support and hospitality. The university chaplains, the Revd Fr Finbarr Corkery, Dean Gearóid Ó Suilleabháin, the Revd Fr Michael Regan and the Revd Fr Joseph Coughlan, and the staff at the Chaplaincy were considerate and supportive of our work.

Our thanks are extended to staff at University College Cork, and must start with President Gerald T. Wrixon, Vice-President Michael O'Sullivan and the many wonderful people who have worked at the College Archives and subsequent Heritage and Visual Arts Office. Margaret Lantry provided much valuable support and IT skills. Professor Peter Woodman, Dr Elizabeth Shee Twohig and staff at the Department of Archaeology provided help and advice. We gratefully acknowledge support received from Michael F. Kelleher, Vice-President for Administration, Michael Farrell, Administrative Secretary, and the staff at the Secretary's Office; Professor Michael P. Mortell, President, UCC (1989–99), Katherine Weldon and the staff at the President's Office during Professor Mortell's tenure; Tony Perrott, Tomás Tyner and the staff at the Audio-Visual Services; Edward Burke and the staff at the Printing Office; the staff at General Services and the Works Departments who have carefully and cheerfully moved and lifted boxes of artefacts and undertaken numerous other tasks, often at a moment's notice; staff at the Boole Library, UCC, including Helen Davis and all our colleagues and friends at UCC. The interest and support of the university's Heritage Committee under the chairmanship of Professor John A. Murphy and Dr Tom Cavanagh, respectively, are also gratefully acknowledged.

Stella Cherry, Curator at Cork Public Museum generously supported this work and kindly hosted an exhibition of some of the collection in 1995. Journalists Mary Leland and Letita Polland and the photographer the late Brian Lynch brought the collection to wider audiences. This support was greatly appreciated.

The book received financial support from the Trustees of the Honan Chapel, under the chairmanship of Professor G.T. Wrixon, and the Heritage Council through the professional offices of Ms Beatrice Kelly, Publications Officer. We are deeply grateful to both the Trustees and the Council for their kind generosity.

We were privileged to meet and get to know two extraordinary people during the course of this project: Dr Madoline O'Connell, whose grandfather Sir Bertram Windle was one of the visionaries behind the original commission, and the late Mr John Sisk, whose family firm, then run by his father, built the chapel and made many of the furnishings. Both shared with us their memories of their families' involvement with the Honan Chapel. The pleasure of their company, their interest and support and their attendance at the conference in 2000 will always remain in our minds.

Regrettably, the production of the book was often interrupted by unforeseen personal and professional events (one of which was the birth of twins). The patience required from the contributing authors as well as the publishers was therefore very great indeed. Accordingly, we would like to thank the contributors for their forbearance and we are deeply indebted to all for their professionalism, care, diligence and friendship. Equally, we are very grateful to Sara Wilbourne at Cork University Press for her calm acceptance of these many delays and her continued interest, support and friendship. Our thanks are also due to Professor Tom Dunne and Caroline Somers of CUP for their helpful contribution to the publication of the book. Designers Chris Kunnert and Elaine Tierney and photographer Andrew Bradley are thanked for the personal and sustained interest which they took in this project, their wonderful expertise and also their friendship.

Our real debts are to our families for making the space in all our lives that allowed us progress this work over the past decade. To them, most particularly Cian Ó Mathúna and Euan, Edward and Alannah Ó Mathúna, Ruth and Jim Teehan and Louisa Heckett, we say a deep and heartfelt thank you.

This book is dedicated to the memory of the Revd Fr G. Ó Suilleabháin (1924–2001), Dean of the Honan Chapel and contributor to this volume.

Any errors in this text we claim as our own.

Virginia Teehan
Elizabeth Wincott Heckett

The Honan Chapel
A Visionary Monument

The Honan Chapel was made possible through the generosity of a merchant family to its city and university, a family who appreciated the academic standards of the university president and who trusted a zealot to develop a fitting living monument in their memory. They expected that every aspect – intellectual, liturgical, architectural and historical – would be fully researched and that the building would be built to the highest standards using the best local materials. The contributors have shown how this was achieved and that, in being built with a passion for order and a pride in Ireland, it followed the ambition of being

> *furnished free from all exuberance of ornament (but) as a whole – design, building, decoration, site – harmonious and suited to the needs of the people for whom it is built, and also for the place in which it is erected.*[1]

The chapel should be judged also by the fact that a treasure-house was created of works from Ireland's 'golden age' of modern craftsmanship, works that in 1916 sought to express the new Ireland.

DESIGNED AS AN ENTITY

The Honan Chapel is remarkable in Irish church architecture as it was completely designed, both externally and internally, by a single architect.[2] This contrasted with the generality of contemporary Irish churches which, as Fr Gerard O'Donovan angrily told the Maynooth Union, were the products of 'incompetent architects and pushful

FIG. 1: *Replica of the Cross of Cong, (detail front)*

1

commercial travellers from Birmingham and Munich'.[3] A planned entity approach was indeed new. Throughout the centuries, architects had confined their work to the architectural envelope and occasionally to some fittings. Apart from the fact that many large buildings took decades to complete, it was accepted that the upholsterer could fit out the interiors in the current fashion, taking instructions from the owners. On occasions architects may have designed key pieces of furniture, but the principles of architecture did not begin to control interior design until after the 1780s. Even then the upholder remained dominant, although criticized as being 'entirely ignorant of the most familiar principles of visible beauty, wholly uninstructed in the simplest rudiments of drawing [and] totally destitute of those attributes of true elegance'.[4] Even as late as 1903, the desirability of a close collaboration between architect and interior designer was indifferently appreciated.[5] Change was hastened by the questioning of the accepted attitudes of the past particularly by art movements in the mid to late nineteenth century. Movements such as Impressionism revolutionized the approach to fine art while from the 1880s architecture, furniture and furnishings were influenced by the principles of art nouveau, which held that, while art should be logical and well constructed, it should also observe the limitations imposed by the materials used. Because of this, every element of a room was expected to blend together.[6] Parallel with this was the Arts and Crafts movement in England, which was developed further by a younger generation who from about 1890 designed entire buildings with interiors usually exhibiting a new lightness of tone and clarity of outline.

In Glasgow, from 1897, Charles Rennie Mackintosh and his colleagues developed a unique and short-lived art nouveau style, which had linear, geometric and sinuous lines, and was described as a synthesis of Gothic, old Scottish and 'other ideas'.

The art nouveau influence on Irish architecture was less spectacular, but the proponents of these various international art movements would surely have understood and applauded the Honan Chapel and would have admired the integrity in which the building and its furnishings were designed and created in architectural unison and with a profound appreciation of symbolism.

CELTIC REVIVAL DESIGN IN ARCHITECTURE

That the Honan Chapel was designed and furnished in an overall Celtic Revival style is a reflection of the attitude of many in contemporary Ireland who saw such designs as representing Ireland's glorious past.[7]

As Teehan and Lamb have pointed out (pp. 23, 53), Sir John O'Connell believed that the chapel 'would not win its way to the hearts of those for whom it was intended unless, in its inspiration and design, it was truly and sincerely Irish'. He knew that his audience was proud of that period when Cormac Mac Carthaig, King of Munster, encouraged the building of Romanesque churches and became the patron of his royal chapel at Cashel and church at Roscrea.[8] He disagreed with the recently published theory of the architectural authority A.C. Champneys, which said that the Romanesque style came to Ireland through England. Instead he argued that the Hiberno-Romanesque was the product of an age of national progress and exceptional activity and vigour.[9]

Paul Larmour has shown that to achieve this 'most complete example of a Hiberno-Romanesque revival church' they studied a number 'of important early Irish churches' (pp. 37–51). Others had already taken this approach. A.W.N. Pugin (1812–52) studied Dunbrody Abbey and Kilkenny Cathedral when he was building churches in Ireland.[10] Benjamin Woodward (1816–61), a member of the Cork architectural firm of Woodward & Deane, studied and drew details of Holy Cross Abbey and the Rock of Cashel, possibly contributing to the firm's success in winning the commission for Queen's College, Cork (1847–9).[11] In about 1867, the leading Aesthetic movement architect-designer E. W. Godwin (1833–86) measured and studied the construction of at least a dozen old castles as well as the Rock of Cashel before producing his plans for the Earl of Limerick's pile at Dromore. Although considered 'the most archaeologically correct' of modern Irish castles, that built by Godwin was modified to suit contemporary living.[12]

This approach to archaeological accuracy applied not just to Celtic Revival architecture but also to interpretations of neo-Gothic buildings: in both Celtic and Gothic there was an aspiration to be archaeologically correct. A 'freer historicism' was developed in both by about the 1860s–70s and subsequently both styles suffered from an eclectic approach.[13] The Honan Chapel departed from this trend by returning to a careful interpretation. Part of its honesty was the selection of a site close to that of St Finbarr's early school, a site therefore worthy of reverence for historical reasons.

NEW CELTIC FURNISHING

Ostensibly the Honan Chapel was built and furnished in a Celtic Revival style showing

> the spirit and work of the age when Irishmen built churches and nobly adorned them under an impulse of native genius. It was desired to put before the eyes of the Catholic students of Munster a church designed and fashioned . . . as those which their forefathers had built for their priests and missioners all over Ireland nearly a thousand years ago.[14]

However, the Celtic Revival style presented at the Honan Chapel was, as O'Connell said, not a 'slavish reversion to ancient forms however beautiful' but, following the study of the spiritual and aesthetic forces of national art, an attempt to present an interior which was traditionally Irish, and yet which would be appreciated by contemporary society. This search for a modern expression of early Irish art paralleled the quest undertaken by other 'old' societies throughout Europe at the turn of the twentieth century, in which distinctive art and architectural styles were sought to symbolize national heritage, ancient history, geography and climate.[15] This was particularly true in lands that were controlled by other powers, such as Poland and Hungary. Usually these European architects and designers had academic backgrounds and were familiar with the current international art movements – Impressionism, Symbolism, Japonisme, art nouveau and Fauvism – which tended to question the established order and encouraged an openness of mind. The distinctive art and architectural styles that evolved derived from an idea of a national past, mixed with an appreciation of contemporary styles.[16]

This recourse to the past for stability and inspiration occurred not just in subjugated lands but also in countries such as Russia and Britain. Indeed, in the latter, the Gothic style was seen as a true expression of British history and national identity, which led to the restoration and refurbishing of many medieval churches, to the enactment of a medieval tournament (1839) and to Queen Victoria and Prince Albert wearing medieval dress at historically themed balls.

At the time of the building of the Honan Chapel, writers such as Æ sought a new 'signature of the Irish mind', while the art movements in Paris taught that art does not merely imitate what previous ages have achieved but also interprets the present.[17] Works created for the Honan Chapel show this mindset. O'Connell enthused that the Mass cards and bookbindings showed interpretations of early Irish work; yet Joseph Tierney's watercolours show less of the influence of an Irish manuscript illumination than of Renaissance art. Similarly, the beauty of Eleanor Kelly's interpretation of the Tullylease cross symbol lies in its modernity. Even Edmond Johnson Ltd, famed for faithful reproduction of early Irish metalwork, carefully marshalled authentic-style motifs and then juxtaposed them with idiosyncratic *Book of Kells* animals, as well as enamelled strapwork on the altar card frames. A similar use of Celtic designs with a freedom of interpretation is seen in Barry Egan's work. His family had a long and respected tradition in silversmithing, watch-making and jewellery and also sold vestments and church plate from at least 1875.[18] To improve the business along the most advanced contemporary lines, Barry Egan was trained in Paris and Belgium.[19] In the development of his embroidery workshops he had the advantage that embroidery classes were held in the Cork School of Art from at least 1897.[20] Moreover, before that formal course began, James Brennan had nurtured training in lace design at the school to the extent that the prominent lace schools of the country ordered designs from Cork. Egan was able, therefore, to draw on graduates of a school with trained artists and skilled embroiderers who understood colour and subtle shading.

THE ARTS AND CRAFTS MOVEMENT

The Arts and Crafts movement, which developed in England from the 1830s, was based on A.W.N. Pugin's and John Ruskin's theories of a belief in a truthfulness to structure, function and material and that human labour was essential to creative work.

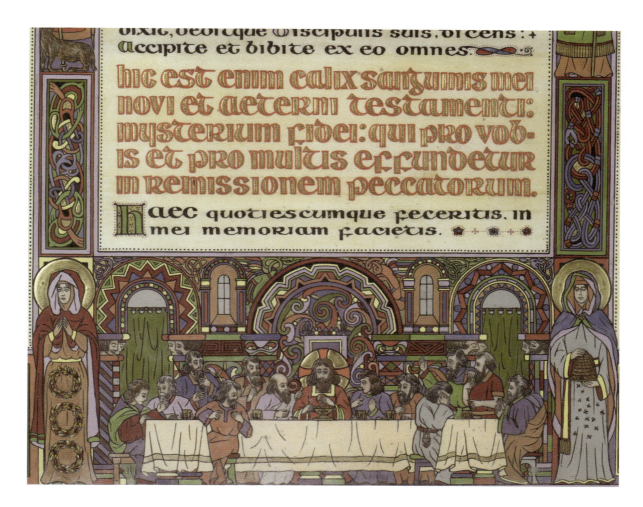

hic est enim calix sanguinis mei
novi et aeterni testamenti:
mysterium fidei: qui pro vob-
is et pro multis effundetur
in remissionem peccatorum.

Haec quotiescumque feceritis, in
mei memoriam facietis.

Fig. 2: Altar card
(detail)

Fig. 3: Gold altar
frontlet (detail)

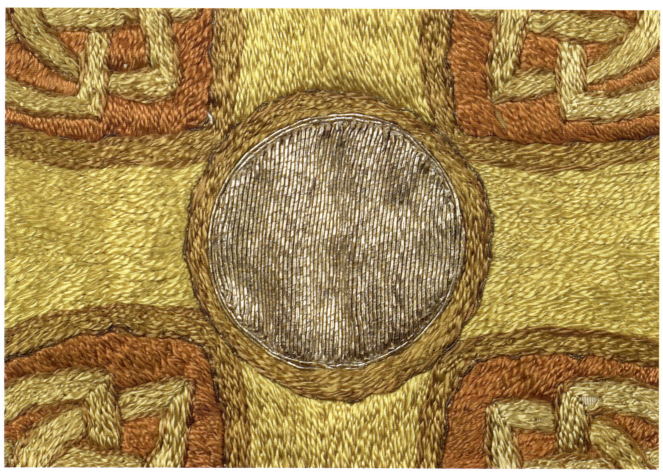

William Morris (1834–96) developed that idea and held that the handcraft worker should be central to such work. Accepting this, but deviating from Morris's preoccupation with the medieval, the next generation of architect-designers sought a style that was original, British and had clarity of outline. Consequently, with an anti-establishment fervour and a dedication to creativity, the English Art-Workers' Guild was established in 1884. Subsequently, those anxious for a forum in which to exchange ideas and to hold exhibitions of their work, formed the Arts and Crafts Society and held their first exhibition in London in 1888.[21] The Cork School of Art appreciated their approach and in the following year, 1889, dedicated funds to get either of the two prominent members of the society, William Morris or Walter Crane, to address their annual meeting.[22] With equal enthusiasm, a number of progressive Irish artists worked directly with English School members. This link was so close that at the time of the Cork Exhibition, 1902, Evelyn Gleeson had a fireplace by C.A. Voysey for sale.[23]

By contrast, when the Irish Arts and Crafts Society was established in Dublin in about 1894, it was composed principally not of practitioners but of collectors, amateurs and admirers. Another contrast with the English society is that the first Irish exhibition in 1895 was criticized as having an 'over-inclusion of amateur work' with a high representation of lace and crochet, work which was infrequently that of an individual designer/worker.[24] This clearly outweighed the number of quality works by Irish-born artists Mary G. Houston and Phoebe Traquair, the ironwork by J. & G. McGloughlin and the bookbindings by Edward Sullivan.

However, there were forces working to improve standards in Ireland. Among the members of the first executive committee of the Irish Arts and Crafts Society was the energetic Director of the new Dublin museum, Col. G.T. Plunkett.[25] The principal aim of that museum was to provide to all 'students, artisans and others – an opportunity of improvement – by the study of approved models and objects'. To that aim the museum collected works by such renowned artists as Réne Lalique and Alexander Fisher as well as glass by Gallé, Tiffany, Léveillé, Lobmeyr, Rousseau and Loetz. There were also displays of medieval carved wooden panels, Italian majolica and Spanish lustreware. After a visit to Nürnberg and Cologne in November 1901, Col. Plunkett dedicated one room to temporary exhibitions of 'articles made by living artists or manufacturers' from Irish, English, European and American firms.[26] Consequently there were changing displays of quality contemporary enamel-work, glass, jewellery, furniture, ceramics, brass-work and bookbindings.[27]

Such museum activities and other developments in the School of Art focused attention on design and handcraft production and contributed to a greater appreciation of the artist.[28] Consequently, when the Irish Arts and Crafts Society was reorganized in 1909, a guild was established for art-workers. In the next wave of revision in February 1917, John O'Connell was elected Chairman of the Society's executive committee. That period, 1909–17 was arguably one of the greatest flowerings of Irish designed and handcrafted work.

Quality Handwork

The fundamental approach to the design of the Honan Chapel lies in the belief that

> *no church can be regarded as a beautiful and worthy whole unless all those things which are needed for the service of the altar are designed and fashioned for it as parts of a thought-out scheme based on one guiding ideal – the same idea which appears in the building and the decoration also inspires and moulds all the furniture, the altar plate and the vestments and everything which is used in the service of the chapel.*[29]

The success of the furnishing at the Honan Chapel is clearly related to a control of design and symbol and to the selection of artists who 'enthusiastically seconded his efforts to make this chapel an expression of the best work that can be produced in Ireland'.[30] It is no coincidence that the artists were of such calibre that virtually all of them served on the reformed executive and Munster committees of the Irish Arts and Crafts movement. The chapel's success is related too to the fact that O'Connell would seem not to have been hampered by financial constraint and so the best work was able to be commissioned.

One such outstanding piece of artwork is the tabernacle door and tympanum by P.O. Reeves.[31] It is striking in its luminosity and strength of colours, in the power of the prominent Lamb of God 'pouring forth His blood for the life and nourishment of His people' and in the silver 'tree of life' background. The awesome host of angels with elongated bodies, hands and feet, their faces forming a protective sky, show, as does the whole composition with its organization of form and colour, that Reeves was not only a great enamellist but that he was an avant garde artist. Here he shows that he was as conversant with the most recent artistic developments in Paris as was, for example, Eileen Gray who lived there and whose comparable lacquer panel was hailed in 1917 as an outstandingly original work of art.[32]

Harry Clarke's windows, with their luminosity, symbolism and integrity were clearly (as discussed by Nicola Gordon Bowe) the creations of a remarkable genius who richly deserved the immediate international acclaim he received.[33] Bowe discusses how he drew on and interpreted from an extremely large repertoire of medieval, academic and contemporary art.

The best of the Irish Arts and Crafts Societies is represented by Evelyn Gleeson. As William Morris had been an advisor on textiles to South Kensington, so Gleeson fulfilled that role to the Dublin Museum. She would have been aware of the late fifteenth-century Waterford vestments on display there and of the Kenmare mitre acquired at the Cork Exhibition. An artist rather than a businesswoman, when she was commissioned to weave a copy of the Huntingdon Verdure tapestry that was on loan to the museum in 1908, she did so much research and copied the original so faithfully that she lost money.[34] It is not improbable that she lost money at the Honan Chapel too. The lustrous silk suggests that it was of that quality which the guild boasted was spun from cocoons raised in Greyabbey, Co. Down. The densely worked embroidery, with its rich background and linear figures, is reminiscent of *Opus Anglicanum*, embroidery that was worked to order by professionals in the medieval period. Similarly, the much less detailed Celtic embroidery that was worked at Kenmare was, according to Sr Bonaventure, 'such slow work even slower than needlepoint', that prepayment was required for work undertaken.[35]

There is a suggestion of the influence of the successful Cork architect Thomas Newenham Deane, yet it is probable that that influence was only through W.A. Scott, who worked in his office for a time. Both Deane and his father were the architects of the Dublin Museum (1890) and were proud of achieving an Irish building with pertinent symbolism. There they employed the firm of J. & G. McGloughlin, who made the spectacular gates and railings for the complex. There too Ludwig Oppenheimer of Manchester laid the floors, which were designed with appropriate motifs. W.A. Scott, who has been described as 'architect by appointment to the Celtic Revival', was also a great apostle of the English Arts and Crafts doctrines. His designs at the Honan Chapel show these influences which, because they range from candlesticks to carpets, give the building a remarkable unity.[36] The importance of his influence can be seen in his design for McGloughlin's iron grille. It is an exciting presentation of Celtic design in art nouveau mode which contrasts greatly with their usual work as illustrated in the Arts and Crafts exhibition catalogues.

COMPARISONS

The two churches most regularly compared with the Honan are St Brendan's, Loughrea, and the Oratory of the Sacred Heart, Dominican Convent, Dún Laoghaire. These comparisons are made because of the quality of the contemporary art fittings and furnishings at Loughrea and the Celtic Revival designs at Dún Laoghaire. However, neither building was designed as an entity, neither had similarly generous funding and neither benefited from so much preliminary research. Neither Gerard O'Donovan, who was curate and later administrator at Loughrea, nor his mentor, Edward Martyn, a local landlord and leading figure in the Irish national literary and artistic revival, could influence the architectural shell of St Brendan's Cathedral, of which the foundation stone was laid in March 1897. There was little argument when the sculptor John Hughes described it as 'worn out Puginism'. However, with the aid of the bishop, Dr Healy, O'Donovan and Martyn were later able to involve prominent Irish craft workers as well as W.A. Scott in much of the furnishing design. There was, still, no single unifying influence as the furnishing was controlled by successive bishops who expressed their personal preferences and who continued with the furnishing after O'Donovan had left the diocese in 1904 and after Martyn's death in 1924. Loughrea is, nevertheless, an undoubted treasure-house of designed Irish handcraft, particularly of the 1901–10 period.[37]

FIG. 4: *White antependium (detail)*
FIG. 5: *Altar card (detail)*

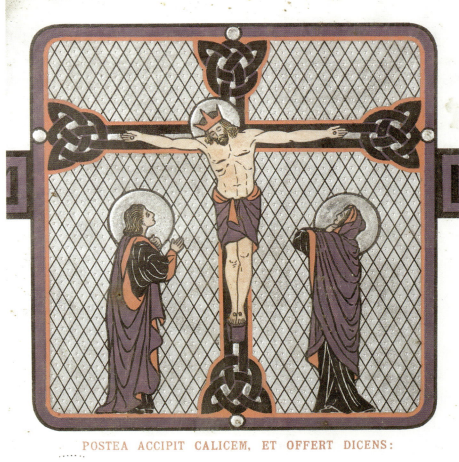

POSTEA ACCIPIT CALICEM, ET OFFERT DICENS:

The Dún Laoghaire oratory, which was built to celebrate peace after the First World War, is architecturally a plain little building. The interior was not completed until 1958 when Sr M. Theodora added a parquet floor and an altar carpet.[38] Its tour de force is the wall painting by Sr Concepta Lynch. Trained by her father as an illuminator, she worked in the oratory between 1920 and 1936. Her interpretation of early manuscript motifs is original, fluid, vibrant and truly worthy of the recent conservation and protection programme.

READABILITY/LANGUAGE PROBLEMS

After decades of bad interlacing and tawdry images of early Irish metalwork, the people of post-nationalist Ireland are conditioned to expect no intellectual messages from the generality of Celtic interlacing. Indeed, since the establishment of the state, with some outstanding exceptions, many amateur Celtic Revival designs were used to communicate nationalism. This was the case as early as 1923, when, at an exhibition of contemporary church art, Canon Willis Moyne bemoaned the fact that men like himself who had tried to revive the 'spirit of their ancient Church' were now regarded as 'faddists'. In criticizing that same exhibition, Dermot O' Brien, PRHA, described it as a 'snare of Celtic designs' and recommended that the clergy get 'a great deal of education in the ecclesiastical arts'.[39] The naivety of much of those Celtic Revival designs has been interpreted as satisfaction with shoddy standards in an age when poets, talkers and dreamers won comfort from mythological stories of Ireland's past. Because of this baggage it can be suggested that in this modern age few are now inclined to try to understand the thrust of the Celtic Revival images at the Honan Chapel or stand in awe at the quality of the work.

Apart from this difficulty, other imagery in the Honan Chapel is more obscure now because of the Second Vatican Council (1962–5), which revised the Church's role in modern society. Sadly, as a result, many of today's visitors are not aware of the rich liturgical symbolism in church architecture, vestments and literature, which extends from the tripartite window to the simple triple twist of the girdle. That of the Honan Chapel is explained in this book superbly by Jane Hawkes (pp. 105–131).

SUMMARY

The Honan Chapel was designed and built at a time some Irishmen were fighting for national freedom at home and others were fighting 'in defence of right, of freedom and of religion' on the fields of Europe. It was a time too when articulate and principled men like John O'Connell argued for freedom for the poor from the evils of slum management and when thinkers, writers and activists – as with their equals elsewhere – sought to develop a unique cultural language which would express a new nation.[40]

It was a watershed period in art development too as internationally there was experimentation, the trend towards the standards of the machine age meaning a new approach to contemporary craft and design. John O'Connell was a man fired with idealism who was funded by a family who respected his standards, so for this project he was able to select artists of the highest calibre, most of whom were conversant with the most recent thinking in international art circles. Their commitment to the project was such that they overcame the difficulties of supply in wartime and many of them achieved the greatest works of their creative lives. Built and furnished in a short period of about three years, the chapel shows a pride in Ireland's past and hope for its future. Built to accommodate and to inspire university students, it is an apt monument for a city with such a long art-education history.

Notes and References

1   Sir John R. O'Connell, *The Honan Hostel Chapel, Cork* (Cork: Guy & Co., 1916), pp. 19–20. This work appeared in a second edition as *The Collegiate Chapel, Cork: Some notes on the building and on the ideals which inspired it*, 2nd edn (Cork University Press, 1932).

2   Whether the architect was McMullen alone or McMullen working with O'Connell or Scott is not entirely relevant as the instructions were channelled as one.

3   'Address to the Maynooth College Union', *The Irish Builder*, 18 July 1901, p. 809.

4   Thomas Hope, *Household Furniture and Interior Decoration: classic style book of the Regency period with a new introduction by David Watkin* (New York: Dover, 1971), p. 1.

5   Peter Thornton, *Authentic Décor: The Domestic Interior 1620–1920* (London: Seven Dials, 2000), pp. 9–10, 142–3.

6   Alastair Duncan, *Art Nouveau* (London: Thames & Hudson, 1994), pp. 8, 33.

7   Luke Gibbons, *Transformations in Irish Culture* (Cork University Press, 1996), p. 81; Richard Kearney, *Post-nationalist Ireland: Politics, Culture, Philosophy* (London: Routledge, 1997), p. 122.

8   Tadhg O'Keeffe, 'Lismore and Cashel: Reflections on the Beginnings of Romanesque Architecture in Munster', *Journal of the Royal Society of Antiquaries of Ireland*, vol. 24, 1994, pp. 118–52.

9   Arthur C. Champneys, *Irish Ecclesiastical Architecture, with some notes of similar or related work in England, Scotland or elsewhere* (London: G. Bell & Sons, 1910), pp. 121–32; O'Connell, op.cit. p. 21.

10 Maurice Craig, *The Architecture of Ireland from the Earliest Times to 1880* (London: Batsford, 1989), pp. 289–93.

11 Frederick O'Dwyer, *The Architecture of Deane and Woodward* (Cork University Press, 1997), pp. 46–51.

12 Mark Bence-Jones, *A Guide to Irish Country Houses* (London: Constable, 1988), pp. 110–12; Craig, op.cit. p. 318.

13 P. Larmour [pp. 37–51, in this volume] and Jeanne Sheehy, *The Rediscovery of Ireland's Past: the Celtic Revival, 1830–1930* (London: Thames & Hudson, 1980), pp. 60–63, 121–3; Peter Cormack, 'Recreating a Tradition: Christopher Whall (1849–1924) and the Arts & Crafts Renascence of English Stained Glass', in Nicola Gordon Bowe (ed.), *Art and the National Dream: the search for vernacular expression in turn-of-the-century design* (Blackrock: Irish Academic Press, 1993), p. 15.

14 J.J.Horgan, 'The Honan Hostel Chapel, Cork' [review], *Studies*, vol. 5, 1916, pp. 612–14.

15 János Gerle, 'What is Vernacular? or, The Search for the 'Mother-tongue of Forms'', and Wendy Kaplan, 'The Vernacular in America, 1890–1920: Ideology and Design', in Bowe, op. cit., 1993, pp. 53, 143–5; Nicola Gordon Bowe, 'The Irish Arts and Crafts Movement (1886–1925)', *Irish Arts Review*, 1990–91, pp. 172–85.

16 Katalin Gellér, 'Romantic Elements in Hungarian Art Nouveau', in Bowe, op. cit., 1993, p. 117.

17 G.W. Russell (Æ), *The National Being, a design for developing Ireland* (1916), re-issued 1982, pp. 110, 122–5.

18 Francis Guy, *County and City of Cork Directory for the years 1875–76* (Cork: F. Guy, [1875]), adv. p. 24.

19 Elizabeth Heckett [pp. 133–62, in this volume]; Mairéad Dunlevy, *Jewellery, 17th to 20th Centuries* (Dublin: National Museum of Ireland, 2001), p. 25.

20 Cork School of Art, Minutes of Department Committee, 3 November 1896 and 29 March 1897.

21 Michael Snodin and John Styles, *Design and the Decorative Arts: Britain, 1500–1900* (London: V&A, 2001), pp. 363–5, 391.

22 Cork School of Art, Minutes of Department Committee, 11 November 1889.

23 Rough notes on the material for the Cork Industrial Exhibition, 1902, in the Art & Industrial Division archives. Voysey is considered one of the founding fathers of the Modern Movement.

24 Arts & Crafts Society of Ireland, *Catalogue of the Fourth Exhibition*, 1910 (Dublin: The Hall, 35 Dawson St, 1910), p. 21; *Catalogue of the First Exhibition, at the Royal University Buildings, Dublin, 1895* (Dublin: Arts & Crafts Society of Ireland, 1895).

25 On the executive also were the architects of the museum, T.M. Deane, who donated ironwork and jewellery to the collections, George Coffey, who, although he lectured on art and industry, usually confined his interest to the Royal Irish Academy's collection, and Horace Plunkett, whose main interest was rural revival and related industries. Plunkett was to become later the powerful secretary of the Department of Agriculture and Technical Instruction.

26 National Museum of Ireland, Art & Industrial Division correspondence, 1905, 1907.

27 As material was not purchased but only taken on loan from the exhibitor, some firms such as Belleek declined invitations. The 1904–5 exhibition, though, dis-

played works by Lobmeyer, Powell, Hicks, Strahan, Doulton, Minton and the Cork Brick and Tile manufacturing company, Dún Emer, Johnson, West and enamels by Mrs Nelson Dawson and P.O. Reeves. NMI A&I archives, 1905, 1032.

28 Paul Larmour, *The Arts and Crafts Movement in Ireland* (Belfast: Friar's Bush Press, 1992), pp. 90–104.

29 O'Connell, op. cit., p. 55.

30 ibid., p. 55.

31 Paul Larmour, 'The Works of Oswald Reeves (1870–1967), Artist and Craftsman: an interim catalogue', *Irish Architectural and Decorative Studies: the Journal of the Irish Georgian Society*, vol. 1, 1998, pp. 35–59; Nicola Gordon Bowe, 'Evocative and Symbolic Memorials and Trophies by Percy Oswald Reeves', *Irish Arts Review*, vol. 16, 2000, pp. 131–8; Larmour, op. cit., 1992, p. 134; Nicola Gordon Bowe and Elizabeth Cumming, *The Arts and Crafts Movements in Dublin and Edinburgh, 1885–1925* (Dublin: Irish Academic Press, 1998), pp. 173–7.

32 Peter Adam, *Eileen Gray: Architect / Designer: A Biography* (London: Thames & Hudson, 1987), re-issued 2000, p. 72.

33 Nicola Gordon Bowe, *The Life and Work of Harry Clarke* (Dublin: Irish Academic Press, 1989).

34 National Museum of Ireland, Art & Industrial Division archives 671/833 and 1019, 1908.

35 Sr Bonaventure writing to James Brenan, National Museum of Ireland, Art & Industrial, 1901, 1150.

36 The design of the Dún Emer carpets was attributed to Scott in *Irish Builder & Engineer*, 16 September 1916, p. 455; Sheehy, op. cit., pp. 134–42.

37 Patrick K. Egan, *St Brendan's Cathedral, Loughrea, Co. Galway*, Irish Heritage Series: 56 (Dublin: Eason, 1986); Thomas Mac Greevy, 'St Brendan's Cathedral, Loughrea, 1897–1947', *The Capuchin Annual*, 1946–7, pp. 353–73.

38 Etienne Rynne, *A Shrine of Celtic Art: The Art of Sr M. Concepta Lynch in the Oratory of the Sacred Heart, Dominican Convent, Dún Laoghaire* (Dublin: C.J. Fallon, 1977); Theo Snoddy, *Dictionary of Irish Artists: 20th Century* (Dublin: Wolfhound Press, 1996), pp. 271–2.

39 Exhibition held in Molesworth St, Dublin, *The Irish Independent*, 17 May 1923, p. 11.

40 Fintan Cullen, *Visual Politics: The Representation of Ireland, 1750–1930* (Cork University Press, 1997), pp. 166–8.

BIBLIOGRAPHY

'ADDRESS TO THE MAYNOOTH COLLEGE UNION', *The Irish Builder*, 18 July 1901.

ADAM, PETER, *Eileen Gray: Architect / Designer: A Biography* (London: Thames & Hudson, 1987), re-issued 2000

ARTS & CRAFTS SOCIETY OF IRELAND, *Catalogue of the First Exhibition, at the Royal*

University Buildings, Dublin, 1895 (Dublin: Arts & Crafts Society of Ireland, 1895)

ARTS & CRAFTS SOCIETY OF IRELAND, *Catalogue of the Fourth Exhibition: 1910*
(Dublin: The Hall, 35 Dawson St, 1910)

BENCE-JONES, MARK, *A Guide to Irish Country Houses* (London: Constable, 1988)

BOWE, NICOLA GORDON, 'The Irish Arts and Crafts Movement (1886–1925)',
Irish Arts Review, 1990–91, pp. 172–85

BOWE, NICOLA GORDON, *The Life and Work of Harry Clarke* (Dublin: Irish Academic
Press, 1989)

BOWE, NICOLA GORDON, AND ELIZABETH CUMMING, *The Arts and Crafts
Movements in Dublin and Edinburgh, 1885–1925* (Dublin: Irish Academic Press, 1998)

BOWE, NICOLA GORDON, 'Evocative and Symbolic Memorials and Trophies by
Percy Oswald Reeves', *Irish Arts Review*, vol. 16, 2000, pp. 131–8

CHAMPNEYS, ARTHUR C., *Irish Ecclesiastical Architecture, with some notes of similar or
related work in England, Scotland or elsewhere* (London: G. Bell & Sons, 1910)

CORMACK, PETER, 'Recreating a Tradition: Christopher Whall (1849–1924) and the
Arts & Crafts renaissance of English Stained Glass', in NICOLA GORDON BOWE
(ed.), *Art and the National Dream: the search for vernacular expression in turn-of-the-century
design* (Blackrock: Irish Academic Press, 1993)

CRAIG, MAURICE, *The Architecture of Ireland from the Earliest Times to 1880* (London:
Batsford, 1989)

CULLEN, FINTAN, *Visual Politics: The Representation of Ireland, 1750–1930*
(Cork University Press, 1997)

DUNCAN, ALASTAIR, *Art Nouveau* (London: Thames & Hudson, 1994)

DUNLEVY, MAIRÉAD, *Jewellery, 17th to 20th Centuries* (Dublin: National Museum
of Ireland, 2001)

EGAN, PATRICK K., *St Brendan's Cathedral, Loughrea, Co. Galway, Irish Heritage Series: 56*
(Dublin: Eason, 1986)

GELLÉR, KATALIN, 'Romantic Elements in Hungarian Art Nouveau', in
N. GORDON BOWE (ed.), *Art and the National Dream: the search for vernacular
expression in turn-of-the-century design* (Blackrock: Irish Academic Press, 1993)

GERLE, JÁNOS, 'What is Vernacular? or, The Search for the 'Mother-tongue of
Forms'', in N. GORDON BOWE (ed.), *Art and the National Dream: the search for vernacular
expression in turn-of-the-century design* (Blackrock: Irish Academic Press, 1993)

GIBBONS, LUKE, *Transformations in Irish Culture* (Cork University Press, 1996)

GUY, FRANCIS, *County and City of Cork Directory for the years 1875–76*
(Cork: F. Guy, [1875])

HORGAN, J.J., 'The Honan Hostel Chapel, Cork' [review], *Studies*, vol. 5, 1916, pp.
612–14

HOPE, THOMAS, *Household Furniture and Interior Decoration: classic style book of the
Regency period with a new introduction by David Watkin* (New York: Dover, 1971)

KAPLAN, WENDY, 'The Vernacular in America, 1890–1920: Ideology and Design', in N. Gordon Bowe (ed.), *Art and the National Dream: the search for vernacular expression in turn-of-the-century design* (Blackrock: Irish Academic Press, 1993)

KEARNEY, RICHARD, *Post-nationalist Ireland: Politics, Culture, Philosophy* (London: Routledge, 1997)

LARMOUR, PAUL, *The Arts and Crafts Movement in Ireland* (Belfast: Friar's Bush Press, 1992)

LARMOUR, PAUL, 'The Works of Oswald Reeves (1870–1967), Artist and Craftsman: an interim catalogue', *Irish Architectural and Decorative Studies: the Journal of the Irish Georgian Society*, vol. 1, 1998, pp. 35–59

MAC GREEVY, THOMAS, 'St Brendan's Cathedral, Loughrea, 1897–1947', *The Capuchin Annual*, 1946–7, pp. 353–73

O'CONNELL, SIR JOHN R., *The Honan Hostel Chapel, Cork* (Cork: Guy & Co., 1916); *The Collegiate Chapel, Cork: Some notes on the building and on the ideals which inspired it*, 2nd edn (Cork University Press, 1932)

O'DWYER, FREDERICK, *The Architecture of Deane and Woodward* (Cork University Press, 1997)

O'KEEFFE, TADHG, 'Lismore and Cashel: Reflections on the Beginnings of Romanesque Architecture in Munster', *Journal of the Royal Society of Antiquaries of Ireland*, vol. 24, 1994, pp. 118–152

RUSSELL, G.W. (Æ), *The National Being, a design for developing Ireland* (1916), re-issued 1982

RYNNE, ETIENNE, *A Shrine of Celtic Art: The Art of Sr M. Concepta Lynch in the Oratory of the Sacred Heart, Dominican Convent, Dún Laoghaire* (Dublin: C.J. Fallon, 1977)

SHEEHY, JEANNE, *The Rediscovery of Ireland's Past: the Celtic Revival, 1830–1930* (London: Thames & Hudson, 1980)

SNODIN, MICHAEL, AND JOHN STYLES, *Design and the Decorative Arts: Britain, 1500–1900* (London: V&A, 2001)

SNODDY, THEO, *Dictionary of Irish Artists: 20th Century* (Dublin: Wolfhound Press, 1996)

THORNTON, PETER, *Authentic Décor: The Domestic Interior 1620–1920* (London: Seven Dials, 2000)

A Golden Vision
John O'Connell, Bertram Windle and the Honan Bequest

(In memoriam Eamon Teehan, 1922–99; Maura Teehan, 1923–2004)

INTRODUCTION

In his classic fantasy *Gulliver's Travels*, Jonathan Swift satirized the division between those who work with their minds and those who work with their hands – the 'philosophers' as against the 'mathematical practitioners'. Swift's comments through Gulliver on the people of his fantasy land, Laputa, emphasize the traditional divisions between theorists and users.

Their houses are very ill built, the Walls bevil, without one right Angle in any Apartment; and this Defect ariseth from the Contempt they bear for practical geometry; which they despise as vulgar and mechanick, those Instructions they give being too refined for the Intellectuals of their Workmen; which occasions perpetual Mistakes.[1]

It is what is considered the 'Vulgar and Mechanick' aspect of the scholarship of art – the work of the craftsperson – that is commemorated in this book.

FIG. 1.1: *The Honan Chapel, interior view*

The aim of the book is to develop greater awareness of the Honan Chapel and the associated collection of ecclesiastical artefacts. The outstanding achievement of the craftsmen and women who worked under the supervision of Sir John O'Connell and Sir Bertram Windle has not previously been recognized. This book is an effort to redress this.

Conceived and executed at the height of the early-twentieth-century Celtic Revival, the collection is a unique expression of this renaissance. It contains items in silver, wood, cloth, paper and stone, each contributing to the very particular concept of the union of function and design. In its entirety the Honan Collection includes the work of the finest craftsmen and women of the time and provides a unique record of their creativity and skill.

In an Irish context the Arts and Crafts movement had strongly regional aspects. In relation to the Honan Chapel, Cork contributed the silversmiths, William Egan & Sons, who were responsible for many items of altar plate, furnishings and vestments; John Lees designed the vestments and the seamstresses were local women; the oak pews and other furnishings, carved in Irish Romanesque style with many fine details, were the work of John Sisk & Son, who were responsible for building the chapel; and local architectural firm McMullen & Associates designed the chapel. The stone capitals of Munster saints were carved by Henry Emery of Dublin assisted by apprentices from the Cork Technical School. Other craftsmen and women who worked on this commission were Evelyn Gleeson at the Dún Emer Guild, Dublin; Oswald Reeves, the enamel artist who made the tabernacle door; Eleanor Kelly of Dublin, who was responsible for the tooled bindings of the missals; and Joseph Tierney, who designed and illuminated a set of altar cards. The chapel is renowned for its stained glass windows. Of the nineteen lights, eight were made by members of the Sarah Purser Studio, Dublin, the remaining eleven by An Túr Gloine (The Tower of Glass) Studio, which included the work of Harry Clarke, then a young artist.

Although the collection is composed of work by various artists working in a wide range of differing designs and techniques, all are, nonetheless, in sympathy. It provides a valuable and unique record of the best of Irish ecclesiastical art at the time. Fortunately for Cork, most of the collection remains within the context of its original home, the Honan Chapel, where it most appropriately belongs. Items that are no longer required for liturgical use are in storage.

As the chapel and collection are a testimony to the work of the Irish Arts and Crafts renaissance, they are the legacy of the unique vision of two remarkable men – Sir John O'Connell (1868–1942), a lawyer and in later life a priest, and Sir Bertram Windle (1858–1929), President of Queen's College, Cork/University College Cork

1904–19. The means by which they realized their dream was through the Honan bequest.

THE HONAN BEQUEST

The Honan family was active in the commercial life of Cork since the late eighteenth century. The last members of the Honan family (Robert, Matthew and Isabella) established links with University College Cork in 1909 through Isabella, who, after the death of her last remaining brother, Robert, presented £10,000 to the College for the purpose of funding scholarships.

In essence there are three elements to the Honan bequest to UCC: firstly, the funds awarded for scholarships in 1909, as mentioned above; secondly, funds awarded in 1914 and used to establish the Honan Hostel and to build the Honan Biological Institute and the hydraulics laboratories, Department of Civil Engineering; thirdly, funds, also awarded in 1914, to build and furnish the Honan Chapel.

The first element of the Honan bequest, the scholarship fund, was an exciting new initiative in a contemporary educational and social context. Until this time, university education was not available to those without the means to pay for it. These scholarships were intended for those who could not otherwise afford a university education and thus marked the beginning of a whole new mix of students into the university system. Munster, excluding Clare, was stipulated as the area of benefit – students from other provinces were excluded from applying for a scholarship. The first awards were made in 1910–11. The scholarships were, and remain, unrestricted denominationally, unlike the Kelliher scholarships which are confined to members of the Roman Catholic faith. Today, the Honan scholarship remains a prestige award and is competitively sought by many Munster students.

FIG. 1.2: *The Foundation Stone, Honan Chapel*

FIG. 1.3: *The Honan Hostel and Warden's House, now demolished*

FIG. 1.4: *The Honan Biological Institute, northern perspective, now demolished*

The second element of funding was awarded to UCC in 1913 after the death of Isabella Honan, who bequeathed funds, which represented the residue of the property of her late brother, Robert, in trust, to the lawyer Sir John O'Connell. The terms of the bequest were that they were 'to be applied in my discretion for charitable purposes in Cork'.[2] O'Connell decided to direct this money to UCC. In a letter to the President of the college, Sir Bertram Windle, dated 4 April 1914, O'Connell stated that he proposed, in view of the previous Honan interest in UCC, to reconstitute St Anthony's Hall as a hall of residence for Catholic male lay students.

St Anthony's Hall was, at that period, a hall of residence for clerics and Roman Catholic students, managed by the Franciscan brothers, which was about to close. O'Connell saw the conversion of the premises as a development which 'would be of immense benefit to the church and to the entire Catholic population of Munster'.[3] The new hall of residence would be known as the Honan Hostel. O'Connell envisaged a married warden (Roman Catholic) chosen from among the academic staff to run the hostel. This second award of funding also enabled the construction of the Honan Biological Institute[4] and the development of hydraulics laboratories in the Department of Civil Engineering.[5]

Thus, as envisaged, Honan Hostel opened in 1916 and remained active as a hall of residence for male students until its closure in 1991, when the demand for this type of accommodation had diminished. The building was bought by UCC in 1991 and subsequently demolished. Part of the newly completed O'Rahilly and Árus na Mhac Léinn building now stands on the site of the former hostel (FIG. 1.8).

As well as the establishment of the Honan Hostel, O'Connell stipulated that there would also be a 'proper chapel, suitable to the dignity of a university with a chaplain resident in the hostel . . . provided for by endowment'.[6] This endowment represents the third and final element in the Honan bequest. To Windle it was the most significant, for UCC is, by law, a non-denominational college; this bequest awarded the means to provide a place of worship for the students, a desire very close to Windle's heart.[7]

PUBLIC RESPONSE TO THE HONAN BEQUEST

The general response to the Honan bequest was strongly appreciative, not only of the generosity of the Honan family but also of the way in which the money was to be employed by O'Connell for the promotion of many social and religious values. *The Cork Examiner*, detailing the bequest, carried a leading article on 6 April 1914, which recalled the regret expressed at the time of the Irish Universities Act (1908) that the government had made no residential provisions for students. *The Cork Examiner* replicated the view, held in many quarters, that the Honan money would be used in a way which compensated for the perceived deficiencies in the recent university legislation. The article outlined the opinion that it was fortunate for the Catholic public of Munster that the Franciscans had converted the 'derelict but excellent' Berkeley Hall into St Anthony's Hall, which had housed lay students as well as its own novices and which would now become the Honan Hostel. The *Examiner* looked forward to seeing the new chapel in 'the Celtic Romanesque' style, and expressed the hope that other wealthy people 'and there are much more in Munster than perhaps would like to be known would emulate the Honan example'.[8] The Munster Roman Catholic bishops, when they heard the news, naturally expressed approval[9] and Windle, as

FIG. 1.5: *The Honan Chapel pier and entrance gates, completed 1916, are complemented by the adjacent Áras na Mhac Léinn, and Devere Hall, completed 1997 and augmented in 2003*

FIG 1.6: *St. Fin barr carved by Sheppard*

FIG. 1.7: *The Honan Chapel, interior, bare of all ornament, photographed upon completion in 1916*

recorded in his biography, had always dreamed of a generous sponsor whose aspirations and values coincided with his own.[10]

LEGAL FRAMEWORK

The management of the Honan funds was vested in a trust. The constitution of this trust is clearly the work of John O'Connell, whose considerable legal skills are evident in every aspect of its detail. The Honan Hostel and Chapel were vested, by O'Connell, in a statutory body of governors, which were established by royal charter called the Honan Trust (granted in 1915).[11] Windle, in his position as President of UCC, was the first Chairman of the Trust and O'Connell was, by statute, made a lifelong member of the Trust. In 1915, the trust applied for and was awarded a grant of arms by the Ulster King at Arms. The resulting crest and motto are frequently used as a form of decoration on many items of the chapel details and furnishings. This trust continues to remain active today and

the responsibility for decisions about all matters relating to the management of the chapel and its collection resides in the hands of the trust. Even though the chapel is intimately associated with UCC, it was established as a completely separate legal entity and remains so today. It is located on its own land, separate from the university grounds, bounded by railings and gates designed in 1915 by William Scott, first professor of architecture at University

College Dublin. The management of the chapel and associated collection of artefacts have remained the exclusive legal responsibility of the trust since 1915.

THE HONAN CHAPEL: FOUNDING VISION

O'Connell's strongly held beliefs in the promotion of Irish and, more specifically, local resources are explicitly laid out in the terms of the bequest. In a letter to Windle, O'Connell wrote:

... all work was to carried out in Ireland, and so far as possible carried out in Cork, by Cork labour and with materials obtained from the City or County of Cork. It is an additional gratification to me, and will, I am

sure, be to you, that the expenditure of the necessary monies will lead to a considerable amount of employment for Cork workmen ...[12]

It is recorded on 5 December 1914 in *The Irish Builder and Engineer* that 'Messrs. John Sisk and Son, of Cove St., Cork have been awarded the contract for the new memorial chapel at University College Cork, at the cost of over £8,000. The architect being Mr. J. F. McMullen of Cork'.[13] *The Freeman's Journal* records the laying of the foundation stone on 18 May 1915.[14]

The guidebook which O'Connell published to coincide with the opening of the chapel[15] outlined his thoughts on the many details of its construction and design. The

FIG. 1.8: *The Honan Chapel, western façade, photographed upon completion in 1916*

chapel was founded in the belief that it is essential for a college to meet both the spiritual and academic needs of students. Coupled with this belief was O'Connell's contention that to win the hearts of its congregation the chapel's design must be truly Irish in inspiration and representative of insular ecclesiastical art. In both the design and construction of the building this purpose has been achieved. Similarly, the internal decoration of the chapel is based on fundamental principles held by O'Connell. His philosophy was that all ornament be applied with restraint and severity so as to achieve that solemn dignity which he believed desirable in a house of God. O'Connell argued that :

. . . simplicity in decoration is essential since it does not disturb the thoughts of the congregation thus leaving the mind free to concentrate. The achievement of this simplicity calls for patience and enthusiasm from the craftworkers whose exceptional skills were inspired by this single purpose. Those few essential items which furnish the chapel are the best and most suitable for their purpose. They are in themselves items of extraordinary beauty and therefore fall into place naturally as part of a harmonious whole . . .[16]

The chapel and its collection also benefited from the patriotic pride of its founders – a pride which in the volatile context of Ireland in 1915–16 very much represents the views of cultural nationalists. O'Connell's views are explicit in his belief that Irish workers and materials had to be used in the design and construction of the chapel: this is stipulated very clearly in the terms of the bequest. The philosophy as outlined by O'Connell in his guidebook that '. . . no building – especially a chapel, the people's Mass-house – can be so worthy as when it is built of the stone of the land in which it is set, and when it is made by the labour of the men who will worship

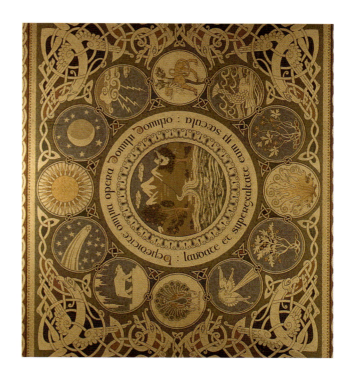

FIG. 1.9: *Floor mosaics in the chancel, depicting in the central medallion a world that is paradise in the Book of Genesis and the eternal paradise that will be restored at the end of time. Around this world are images of the seasons, the elements, the forces of nature and the lion and peacock, images of the resurrection*

FIG. 1.10: *Red chasuble (detail)*

and pray in the church which their own hands have helped to build . . .' was not uncommon at the time.[17]

The promotion of Irish industries and improvements in technical education, as expressed by others, such as Sir Horace Plunkett and the Recess Committee, directly mirrored the ideals embraced by O'Connell and Windle. Such ideals were freely outlined in a range of journals, publications and in the national press. For example, *The Irish Builder and Engineer* published articles on topics such as 'The Present State of Irish Industries', 'Irish Arts and Industries', 'Technical Education in Ireland' and 'Art Instruction in Technical Schools' and many other such articles and letters on this general topic.[18] Prominent figures such as Lord Mayo and Lady Aberdeen were personally associated with the Irish Industries Association, their patronage affording considerable prestige to what was often considered lowly craft and industry.[19]

Undoubtedly Windle used his position as university president to promote his keen personal interest in Irish industrial development. His belief in industrial self-reliance and the promotion of Irish skills and crafts is outlined in clear detail in his inaugural address as Chairman of the Irish Industrial Conference of 1905.[20] At the public meeting of the Cork Industrial Development Association in 1916, Windle, proposing the adoption of the Association's report, expressed disappointment at the exclusion of the Honan Chapel from the report saying:

. . . *for perhaps some of those who had admired the extraordinary beauty of the working that chapel had not reflected, as they should have done, on the artefacts, because with two comparatively small exceptions, everything in the chapel was built, fashioned, and made by Irish workmen and women . . . the chapel was*

proof positive that Irish workers were in no way deficient, but as ready now as in the past centuries to create such wonders as we admire in museums.[21]

Windle's personal conviction that Irish industrial development must be made manifest in actual results, thus providing evidence of the qualities of Irish skills and labour, is reflected in the Honan Chapel and collection. It is clear that he regarded this as one of the most significant achievements of his presidency.

A VISION REALIZED – THE OPENING CEREMONY

The opening of the chapel on 6 November 1916 was a tangible symbol of the realization of O'Connell's and Windle's vision. The opening ceremony was, predictably, a very important ecclesiastical, academic and civic occasion, with the sacred music performed by the much-lauded choir of St Mary's Cathedral, Cork, conducted by Herr Aloys Fleischmann (father of the future professor of music at UCC, Professor Aloys Fleischmann).

The ceremony was extensively covered in the local and national press, the most expansive coverage naturally being in *The Cork Examiner*.[22] In this long and detailed article, praise for the chapel was generous. The building is described in great detail, with particular emphasis on the Harry Clarke and Sarah Pursar windows. All involved were praised – the architect McMullen, builders John Sisk & Son, the silversmiths Egan's and other artists and craftworkers.

The lengthy homily delivered by Bishop Kelly of Ross had strong political undertones. The bishop clearly deplored the non-denominational status of the universities as defined by the Irish Universities Act (1908) and rejoiced in the new association between the college and

FIG. 1.11: *Sir Bertram Windle*

FIG. 1.12: *Sir John O'Connell*

the Church that that day symbolized. In this homily, the bishop used the symbol of St Fin barr as a unifying force between Church and college. Given the contemporary political context of 1916, Bishop Kelly drew the extraordinarily simplistic conclusion that:

. . . by opening this chapel, we restore St. Finn Barr's [sic] ideal; we link together once more the Church and the college. Henceforth the Catholic clients of St. Finn Barr will come into this House of God to perform the duties of their religion. The Protestant student clients of St. Finn Barr have St. Finn Barre's Cathedral on this same site for their religious exercises. Thus the whole community of this College, professors and students – Catholic and Protestant – can all rejoice today in the common joy that we have re-established the sanctity and indissolubility of the marriage of religion and education . . . [23]

The newspaper reports are interesting and, despite *The Cork Examiner's* own sectarian prejudice, which, it must be said, mirrored that of the bishop, the newspaper obviously understood the legal position – the chapel and hostel were technically and literally outside the grounds of the non-denominational college. And, as the newspaper put it, they were 'intimately associated, though not officially connected, with University College'.[24]

Sir Bertram Windle's description of the ceremony and associated comments, as recorded in his diary, provide evidence of the renowned acerbic aspect of his personality:

'*. . . procession (1) mayor etc (2) staff and governing body with mace and self, (3) clergy. Mass sung by Archbishop of Cashel. etc . . .*'[25], '*. . . chapel full and many students—a splendid ceremony with choir of sixty-five, everything done with dignity and order— lesson to the slip-shod. Lunch of fifty-five people* *at the Hostel—and speeches, not very good, King, Pope, O'Connell. Then Benediction—Bishop of Cork— a full chapel . . .*'[26]

PERSONAL CONTEXTS: WINDLE AND O'CONNELL

BERTRAM WINDLE

Bertram Windle was born in Staffordshire, England. His father was a Church of England clergyman and his mother, Sydney Katherine Coghill, was Irish. The Coghill family had close associations with Co. Cork, through the Coghills and Somervilles of Castletownshend. After studying medicine at Trinity College, Dublin, Windle began his career in Birmingham where he was central in the founding of the University of Birmingham. It was also in Birmingham that he converted to Catholicism and resultant Catholic associations brought him into contact with many Irish interests in the city. He had also begun to take an active interest in the wider aspects of education. These various activities together with his Irish associations led the Chief Secretary of Ireland, George Wyndham, to offer him the position of President of Queen's College, Cork, in 1904.

In Cork, Windle pursued a path which brought the college out of mediocrity and made it an institution more resembling a university. In 1908, after much agitation and negotiation in which Windle took part as one of the chief advisors to government, the Irish Universities Act was passed creating the National University of Ireland, of which Cork was a constituent college. As one of the special commission appointed to prepare the statutes and regulations, Windle was able to play a prominent and important part in laying the foundations of the new university.

FIG. 1.13: *Altar card (detail)*

FIG. 1.15: *Detail of enamel on the incense boat*

FIG. 1.14: *Sanctuary lamp (detail)*

FIG. 1.16: *Wrought-iron gate (detail)*

In parallel with this, Windle had for many years promoted the concept of an independent university for Munster. With the support of leading individuals in the province and backed by the resolutions of public bodies, a committee was formed in 1918 to further the project. Considerable progress was made, a draft bill was prepared, and the support of the government was obtained; but just as success was likely, the general election of 1919 swept away the old Irish Party and its policies of constitutional agitation at Westminster. This completely altered the situation. The new Sinn Féin party refused to support any scheme which required the passage of an Act of Parliament by the London government. The English government dropped the plan and Munster lost a university.

Windle had hoped to do for Cork what he had done for Birmingham but political circumstance prevented it. This situation caused him bitter disappointment, as revealed in a letter to an old friend, John Humphreys, written on 7 May 1919:

I can hardly write for the future is so black and uncertain. Desperate Sinn Féin opposition is on foot against the Munster University Scheme on the grounds – perfectly ridiculous – that nothing should be asked for from a British Parliament . . . If I do not get the University this year, I think I must resign; at present I see nothing else for it. I can't go on for ever standing the strain of low intrigue and the constant stream of abuse directed at me, as at anyone in this country who tries to do anything for it.[27]

FIG. 1.17: *St Declan window (detail)*

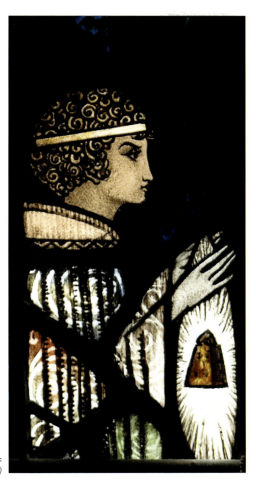

FIGS. 1.17A, 1.17B:
St Declan window (details)

At this moment he was offered a position as professor of philosophy at St Michael's College, Toronto, which, disappointed by his Cork experiences, he promptly accepted. He remained in Canada for the rest of his life, during which time he lectured and published many books and articles reflecting his wide range of interests until his death in February 1929.

As university President, Windle is recognized as having been an exceptionally gifted administrator and polymath, making extraordinary contributions to various scholarly disciplines, science, medicine and antiquities. His primary discipline was anatomy, for which he achieved the distinction of being elected a Fellow of the Royal Society. Windle was a great President, and to quote the history of University College Cork:

. . . he not only presided over, but was a primary contributor to, the transformations of Queen's College into University College Cork. Over the period of his presidency, and in a large part because of his *leadership, the college was restored from being little more than a glorified medical school, and a mediocre one at that, to the makings of a real university.*[28]

JOHN O'CONNELL

Personal conviction and belief drove John O'Connell's life. Born in Dublin on 12 February 1868, O'Connell was educated at Belvedere College and Trinity College, Dublin, where he was awarded a BA in 1889 followed by the degrees of MA and LLD in 1894. Thereafter, he pursued a successful career in law and ran the firm T.F. O'Connell & Son, solicitors in Dublin, which had a very extensive practice. A well-known civic figure in the city, he was also very active in artistic and cultural life. He held many positions reflecting his sense of civic responsibility: he was a governor of Belvedere College, a committee member of the Irish Arts and Crafts Association, a member of the senate of the University of Dublin and a member of the governing body of University College Cork.

FIG. 1.18: *An ensemble of altar plate on the altar of the Honan Chapel, which is dressed with the gold antependium (altar frontal)*

He was also a Fellow of the Royal Society of Antiquaries of Ireland and a member of the Royal Irish Academy. O'Connell was knighted in 1914 and was created Knight Commander of the Order of St Gregory the Great by Pope Pius XI.

After the death of his wife in 1925, O'Connell decided to retire from business and to enter the Benedictine Order at Downside Abbey, England. He left the Order after some time and continued his preparation for holy orders at Collegia Beda in Rome. O'Connell was ordained a priest in 1929, becoming curate at the Church of St Patrick's, Soho, London. After his ordination to the priesthood, he edited *Lyra Martyrym, an Anthology of the Poetry of the English Martyrs*; his *Life of St Thomas More* was published in 1935. O'Connell served as a priest in the London diocese of Westminster until his death in December 1943.

Within an Irish context, O'Connell is best remembered for his philanthropic approach to his legal responsibilities. The disbursement of the Honan monies reflect his personal beliefs in the promotion of Irish industrial development, and in particular the Arts and Crafts movement, as outlined in his guidebook published to mark the opening of the Honan Chapel. Unlike Windle, O'Connell had no known political associations; his life and writings indicate deep spirituality, underscored with a steely sense of purpose, which he used to great effect in realizing his ideals. O'Connell's convictions, together with his role as executor of a very significant estate, ensured that Irish craftworkers were provided with a rare opportunity to express their various talents within one artistically harmonious unit – the Honan Collection. The resulting legacy is one of the most significant expressions of the Irish Arts and Crafts movement.

LEGACIES

It is regrettable that the correspondence between Windle and O'Connell does not appear to have survived. It is definite that all the papers relating to the Honan bequest and Chapel, including correspondence with the artists, were kept in the offices of O'Connell's law firm, O'Connell, Rooney & Co., Kildare St, Dublin, at the time of O'Connell's death in 1943 and for some years afterwards.[29] In the absence of this material it is difficult to reconstruct or fully understand the nature of the relationship between the men. Individually, they had similar characteristics and were both devout Roman Catholics. Both were possessed of creativity and vision and had the determination to realize their aims. However, any attempt to understand their personalities is conjectural in the absence of detailed personal papers. That said, factual information about their backgrounds is reasonably well recorded.[30]

Amongst Windle's and O'Connell's many achievements, the Honan Chapel is probably one of their greatest. The chapel and collection are recognized as being the jewel in the crown of the Irish Arts and Crafts renaissance. The vision and creativity of both founders are reflected in every aspect of this collection from the detailed artwork of individual artefacts to the legal and financial provisions that support the long-term protection of this remarkable resource. It is timely that their importance is recognized as their vision has created one of the greatest legacies of the Irish Arts and Crafts movement, one which can never be described as either 'Vulgar' or 'Mechanick'.

FIG. 1.19 *Altar card (illumination detail)*

Notes and References

1   Jonathan Swift, 'A Voyage in Laputa', in *Travels into several remote nations of the world: Gulliver's Travels* (London: B. Motte, 1726).

2   Transcript of letter from Sir John O'Connell to Sir Bertram Windle, 4 April 1914, published in B.C.A. Windle, 'The Honan Benefactions', *University College Cork, Official Gazette*, vol. 4, no. 12, June 1914, p. 105.

3   ibid.

4   For a detailed description see B.C.A. Windle, 'The Honan Biological Institute', *University College Cork, Official Gazette*, vol. 5, no. 15, June 1915, p. 143.

5   For a detailed description see C.W.L. Alexander, 'The Hydraulics Laboratory', *University College Cork, Official Gazette*, vol. 5, no. 15, June 1915, p. 147.

6   Letter from O'Connell to Windle, published in Windle, op.cit., 1914, p. 105.

7   Monica Taylor, *Sir Bertram Windle, A Memoir* (London: Longman, Green & Co., 1932), p. 229.

8   *The Cork Examiner*, 6 April 1914.

9   ibid.

10 Taylor, op. cit., p. 228.

11 *The Royal Charter for Incorporating the Governors of the Honan Hostel, Cork*. The original charter is extant and administered by the University Archives, University College Cork.

12 Transcript of letter from Sir John O'Connell to Sir Bertram Windle, 12 February 1914, published in B.C.A. Windle, 'The Honan Benefactions', p. 106.

13 *The Irish Builder and Engineer, A Journal Devoted to Architecture, Archaeology, Engineering, Sanitation, Arts & Handicrafts* (hereafter *The Irish Builder and Engineer*), 5 December 1914.

14 *The Freeman's Journal*, 20 May 1915.

15 Sir John R. O'Connell, *The Honan Hostel Chapel, Cork* (Cork: Guy & Co., 1916).

16 ibid., p. 18.

17 ibid., p. 13.

18 *The Irish Builder and Engineer*, 21 November 1914; 11 November 1916; 20 September 1916; 23 December 1916.

19 See Paul Larmour, 'The Honan Chapel: the Artistic and Cultural Context' pp. 37–50. There are also many other publications detailing the development of the Irish Arts and Crafts movement, including Paul Larmour, *The Arts and Crafts Movement in Ireland* (Belfast: Friar's Bush Press, 1992); Nicola Gordon Bowe and Elizabeth Cummings, *The Arts and Crafts Movements in Dublin and Edinburgh: 1885–1915* (Dublin: Irish Academic Press, 1998); Jeanne Sheehy, *The Rediscovery of Ireland's Past: the Celtic Revival, 1830–1930* (London: Thames & Hudson, 1980).

20 See details in John J. Horgan, 'Sir Bertram Windle', *Studies*, vol. 21, December 1932, pp. 611–26.

21   *Report of the Proceedings of the Fourteenth Annual Public Meeting of the Cork Industrial Development Association* (Cork, 1917), p. 25.

22   *The Cork Examiner*, 6 November 1916.

23   *The Freeman's Journal*, 6 November 1916.

24   *The Cork Examiner*, 6 November 1916.

25   Taylor, op. cit., p. 254.

26   ibid.

27   Letter from Windle to Humphrys, published in Taylor, op. cit., p. 277.

28   John A. Murphy, *The College, A History of Queen's/University College Cork, 1845–1995* (Cork University Press, 1995), p. 210.

29   Correspondence between the warden of the Honan Hostel and Mr Meade of O'Connell, Rooney & Co., Kildare St., Dublin, at the time of Sir John O'Connell's death indicates that the files were extant at that time. However, O'Connell, Rooney & Co. states that it no longer has any material relating to Sir John O'Connell in its offices and that the material was possibly destroyed when the firm moved location.

30   Facts about Windle's life are well recorded in John J. Horgan, 'Sir Bertram Windle' (see note 20 above). Also see Taylor, op. cit. Information about John O'Connell is mainly recorded in obituaries, see *The Irish Times*, 30 December 1943; also 'Rev. Sir John O'Connell', *Cork University Record*, no. 1, 1944, pp. 14–15; for details of his estate see *The Cork Examiner*, 25 May 1944.

BIBLIOGRAPHY

Report of the Proceedings of the Fourteenth Annual Public Meeting of the Cork Industrial Development Association (Cork, 1917)

'REV. SIR JOHN O'CONNELL', *Cork University Record*, no. 1, 1944, pp. 14–15

ALEXANDER, C.W.L., 'The Hydraulics Laboratory', *University College Cork, Official Gazette*, vol. 15, June 1915

BOWE, NICOLA GORDON, AND ELIZABETH CUMMINGS, *The Arts and Crafts Movements in Dublin and Edinburgh: 1885–1915* (Dublin: Irish Academic Press, 1998)

HORGAN, JOHN J., 'Sir Bertram Windle', *Studies*, vol. 21, December 1932, pp. 611–26

LARMOUR, PAUL, *The Arts and Crafts Movement in Ireland* (Belfast: Friar's Bush Press, 1992)

MURPHY, JOHN A., *The College, A History of Queen's/University College Cork, 1845–1995* (Cork University Press, 1995)

O'CONNELL, SIR JOHN R., *The Honan Hostel Chapel, Cork* (Cork: Guy & Co., 1916)

SHEEHY, JEANNE, *The Rediscovery of Ireland's Past: the Celtic Revival, 1830–1930* (London: Thames & Hudson, 1980)

SWIFT, JONATHAN, 'A Voyage in Laputa', in *Travels into several remote nations of the world: Gulliver's Travels* (London: B. Motte, 1726)

TAYLOR, MONICA, *Sir Bertram Windle, A Memoir* (London: Longman, Green & Co., 1932)

WINDLE, B.C.A., 'The Honan Benefactions', *University College Cork, Official Gazette*, vol. 4, no. 12, June 1914

WINDLE, B.C.A., 'The Honan Biological Institute', *University College Cork, Official Gazette*, vol. 5, no. 15, June 1915

FIG. 1.20: *Altar card (illumination detail)*

tex

Qui
upi-
um;
um.

cca-
um,

uit:

ne

ego

neo

ini-

DIXIT, de
Accipite

hic est
novi et
myste
is et p
in rem

Haec
mei

The Honan Chapel
The Architectural Background

The chief interest in the Honan Chapel has always been in its fittings and furnishings which form a very fine record of the state of Irish applied arts of the early twentieth century, encompassing some of the finest textiles, stained glass, metalwork, illuminated painting and carved woodwork of the time. The role of the building itself should not, however, be overlooked, as it not only provides a suitable architectural setting for the treasures within but also itself serves to illustrate something of the artistic and cultural milieu of the time.[1]

The Honan Chapel was designed in 1914, the foundation stone laid in 1915 and the building completed in 1916, although the last windows were not fitted until early 1917. The architect was James F. McMullen of Cork and the builders were Messrs J. Sisk & Sons, of Cork. Although the architect was McMullen, it is clear that his guiding spirit was Sir John Robert O'Connell, the administrator of the Honan family bequest. McMullen was a well-known public figure, having been High Sheriff for the

City of Cork in 1907–8, but he appears to have had no special claim to fame as an architect, his most prestigious building having been the Eye, Ear and Throat Hospital in Cork, designed in 1895. It is unclear what his credentials as a church architect were for the Honan Chapel job, but it is possible that in this case he was little more than a functionary for Sir John O'Connell, who had a very clear idea of what he wanted and how it could be achieved, as was all set out in his detailed account of the building published in booklet form at the time of opening.[2] The booklet contains no statement by McMullen expressing his aims or explaining his approach to the work: O'Connell says it all and it is he who appears to have been the true 'architect' of the building, in the sense of having conceived it.

O'Connell's views on church building were very definite and his vision for the Honan Chapel very clear: 'It was felt that this chapel must call into life again the spirit and work of the age when Irishmen built churches and nobly adorned them under an impulse of native genius.'[3] For O'Connell this meant a necessity to 'be faithful to these early Celtic forms to be found in so many places in this country, which for want of a better term, are known as Hiberno-Romanesque'.[4]

In his compulsion to adopt the Hiberno-or Irish Romanesque style, O'Connell was following in the wake of a number of architects and patrons who had turned to the early Irish style in order to impart a native image to their buildings, doing so in a romantic nationalist spirit which affected some Irish architecture during the nineteenth and twentieth centuries. It may be useful briefly to outline the course of this Hiberno-Romanesque or Celtic Revivalist strand in Irish architecture before turning to the Honan Chapel itself, identifying its sources and describing some of its fixtures.

An emerging interest in native Irish architectural forms can be traced from the late eighteenth century on, very sporadic at first, but gaining some momentum in the mid to late nineteenth century, and then reaching its heyday around the turn of the century and the decades following that.[5]

Early nineteenth-century attempts to recreate some of the distinctive forms of early Irish architecture largely concentrated on the Irish round tower and include the freestanding belfries at the Roman Catholic churches at Whitechurch (c. 1830), and Waterloo (1836–43) both in Co. Cork and both conceived and built by the local parish priest Matthew Horgan. Of a similar period was Glenstal Castle, Co. Limerick (1837–41), designed by the English architect William Bardwell, with its Irish Romanesque dining-room doorway modelled on that of the doorway of Killaloe Cathedral. These were in comparatively isolated places and were not widely publicized at the time, but the first really prominent and well-known landmark of the Revival was the O'Connell Tower in Glasnevin Cemetery, Dublin, built in 1854 by the Dublin architect Patrick Byrne following a design by the artist and antiquary George Petrie, the 'father of Irish archaeology'. Appropriately, the tomb of Daniel O'Connell in the crypt below the tower also alluded to the Early Irish heritage of art in its carved Celtic interlaced ornamentation.

The 1860s saw the building of St Patrick's Church of Ireland church at Jordanstown, Co. Antrim (1865–8), designed by the Belfast architects Lanyon, Lynn & Lanyon in a Romanesque style that incorporated a round tower belfry, thus establishing a type which was to be followed for decades to come; we see a variant of this 'round tower style' at the Honan Chapel (FIG.2.1).

Aside from 'round tower' churches there were others of Romanesque type where the Irish identity depended on allusion to other specific historic features such as the 'tangent gable', as at Rathdaire Memorial Church of Ireland church, Ballybrittas, Co. Laois (1887–90), where the architect, J.F. Fuller, based the west front on that of the old church of St Cronan at Roscrea, thus establishing a precedent for the treatment of the west front at the Honan Chapel (FIGS, 2.3, 2.4 OPPOSITE).

The heyday of the Celtic Revival around the turn of the century saw such examples in Co. Cork as the little oratory at St Finbarre's Retreat, Gougane Barra (1900), designed by Samuel Hynes of Cork in the form of an Early Christian Irish single-cell church with a Celtic ornamented altar, and the Roman Catholic church at Timoleague (1906) by Maurice Hennessy, designed in a Romanesque style with an attached round tower belfry.

FIG. 2.2: *The Horan Chapel, west front, taken in 1916*

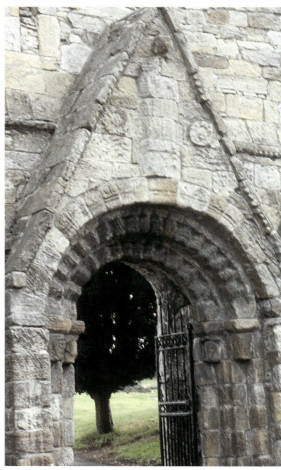

FIG. 2.3: *Entrance façade, Honan Chapel*

FIG. 2.4: *Entrance Façade, St Cronan's Church, Roscrea, Co. Tipperary*

This Irish or Hiberno-Romanesque revivalist strand of historicist architecture was to continue on to the 1930s and 1940s with some important examples appearing from time to time, but although it was a significant movement it was not as widespread as might have been expected. It was not as dominant for any prolonged period as was the classical tradition throughout the eighteenth century in Ireland, or the Gothic Revival throughout most of the nineteenth century. Indeed, the two most important buildings in the same area of Cork as the Honan Chapel bear testimony to the dominance of the Gothic Revival in Victorian Ireland. In the immediate vicinity of the chapel is University College, a fine example of Early Victorian Gothic, designed and built in the 1840s when English models were the rule; the architect was Sir Thomas Deane of Cork, assisted by his pupil Benjamin Woodward, and the style was based on the Tudor colleges of Oxford. Nearby is St Fin Barr's Church of Ireland Cathedral, a spectacular example of

High Victorian Gothic, built in the 1860s to the design of the English architect William Burges whose allegiance was to Early French Gothic.

The Gothic Revival persisted well into the twentieth century, and one observer, at least, seemed to feel that the Honan Chapel itself should have been built in a Gothic style in view of its close proximity and association with the main college building, and suggested the late Irish Gothic as appropriate.[6] Sir John O'Connell followed a different path, however, and although his chosen Romanesque was no more native than a number of other styles which had appeared in Ireland, it held the popular nationalist appeal of conjuring up a vision of a supposed golden age from the past; certainly the Irish Romanesque did relate to a particularly splendid period of art in Ireland.

In the spirit of the Celtic Revivalism of the time, O'Connell was also keen to emphasize not only the national qualities of the architecture of his new building but also its local character and relevance. The chapel was very fittingly dedicated to St Finn Barr because it stands on a site which was probably part of his original monastery. It also pays tribute to a number of other local saints in its stone carvings and stained glass windows, while many of the artists, craftworkers and other personnel who were employed on it came from Cork. The main building material was also local, the exterior walls being faced with punched ashlar of Cork limestone.

O'Connell was devoted to the Irish Romanesque and, between him and his architect, McMullen, a number of important early Irish churches were quoted in the compilation of details that were skilfully welded together to make the Honan Chapel, although the treatment was very free, and a number of elements are not strictly archaeologically correct. Some of the sources for the building were acknowledged by O'Connell in his book but others were not.

The building comprises a long nave and a deep square-ended chancel with a small sacristy and a circular belfry on the north side. The plan (FIG. 2.8) is typical of Irish Romanesque of the 'nave and chancel' type, as found at the likes of Kilmalkedar in Co. Kerry, but the size is bigger, about two to three times the size of the twelfth-century examples. The overall design of the west gable is based on that of St Cronan's church at Roscrea, Co. Tipperary, as O'Connell acknowledged (FIG. 2.4, P. 38). It provided the model for an arcaded wall treatment (FIG. 2.17, P. 45), with tangent gables over the central entrance and the flanking arcades, and 'antae' at the extremities. The Roscrea doorway even gave him the idea for the inclusion of a sculpted figure in the gable above – in the place of St Cronan at Roscrea we find St Finn Barr at the Honan Chapel, garbed in the raiment of a bishop, carved by Oliver Sheppard (FIG. 2.5).

To each side of the doorway are sculpted heads representing six well-known Munster saints: Colman, Patron Saint of Cloyne; Gobnet of Ballyvourney; Declan of Ardmore; Finn Barr of Cork; Ita of Limerick; and Brendan of Kerry (FIGS. 2.6, 2.7, 2.9, 2.10, P. 42) With their intertwining locks they appear to have been based on the carved doorway capitals at the old Romanesque church at Killeshin in Co. Laois, (FIG. 2.11, P. 42) and were sculpted by Henry Emery and a group of young stone-carvers selected by him from the Cork School of Art. The doors themselves are hung on large wrought-iron strapwork hinges of a Celticized art nouveau pattern, designed by William A. Scott, professor of architecture at University College Dublin, and made by the metalworkers J. and G. McLoughlin & Sons, of Dublin (SEE FIG. 3.37, P. 74). McLoughlin's also manufactured a pair

FIG. 2.5: *Honan Chapel, entrance detail, figure of St Finn Barr carved by Oliver Sheppard*

FIG. 2.6: *Honan Chapel, detail of carved capitals at entrance*

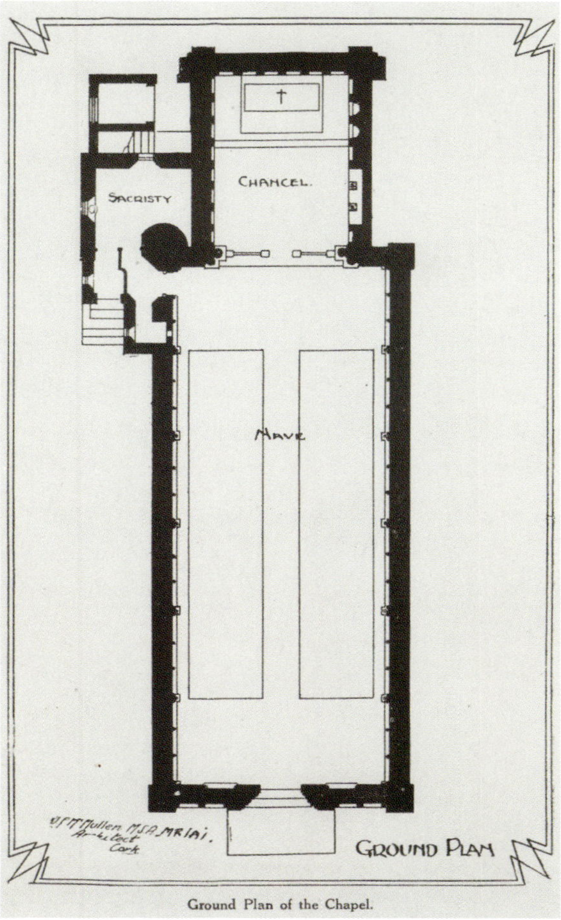

FIG. 2.7: *Honan Chapel, detail of carved capitals at entrance*

FIG. 2.8: *A plan of the Honan Chapel (from M.J. O'Kelly, The Honan Chapel)*

Ground Plan of the Chapel.

FIG. 2.9: *Carving at entrance façade, Honan Chapel (detail)*

FIG. 2.10: *Carving at entrance façade, Honan Chapel (detail)*

FIG. 2.11: *Church at Killeshin, Co. Leix, detail of entrance façade*

THE ARCHITECTURAL BACKGROUND

of wrought-iron grille gates designed by Scott in a freely treated Celtic style with interlaced panels and spiralled bosses and incorporating a full-width Celtic cross motif (SEE FIG. 3.35, P. 73). The grille was originally mounted in the doorway and permitted a view of the interior through the open doors while keeping the chapel locked, but it was removed sometime before 1969 for reasons that are unclear.

Elsewhere on the exterior the position of the belfry, in the angle between nave and chancel, and its form, a miniature Irish round tower, was influenced by Teampull Finghin at Clonmacnoise, Co. Offaly (FIG. 2.12), an Irish Romanesque ruin of the twelfth century, while the small circular window decorated by chevrons in the apex of the east gable was presumably derived from an example at Freshford in Co. Kilkenny (FIG. 2.13).

Notwithstanding the academic authority that its range of historical quotations seems to suggest, the building is not comprehensive in its adherence to Irish Romanesque precedent. The roof pitch is not quite steep enough to be archaeologically convincing and the antae at the west end are more in the form of clasping buttresses than simple projections of the side walls beyond the gable, as found in genuine Irish Early Christian and Romanesque buildings. The little angle turrets on the west front, in the form of conically capped arcaded drums of stone, are also not characteristic of the Irish Romanesque style (FIG 2.18, P. 45)but they do respond here to a theme suggested by the gate

FIG. 2.12: *Teampull Finghin, Clonmacnoise, Co. Offaly*

FIG. 2.13: *Church at Freshford, Co. Kilkenny, detail of small circular window*

THE ARCHITECTURAL BACKGROUND

piers at the front and expressed more fully else-where on the building (FIG. 2.14, P. 44), that is in the belfry at the north-east corner (FIG. 2.16). The form of the buttresses at the east gable (FIG. 2.15) also suggests a Gothic rather than a Romanesque model and from an archaeological point of view are therefore unsatisfactory, but oth-erwise the building is pleasing in its massing and compositional arrangement outside, not least when viewed from the north-east (FIG. 2.16).

The main west doorway leads to a lofty interior laid out as a simple nave and chancel, but obviously inspired by Cormac's Chapel at Cashel in its barrel-vaulted form of roof with transverse ribs, prominent chancel arch and arcading to the side walls, but whereas Cormac's Chapel is all of stonework, the ceiling

FIG. 2.14:
*Honan Chapel,
turret (detail)*

FIG. 2.15:
*Honan Chapel,
east gable*

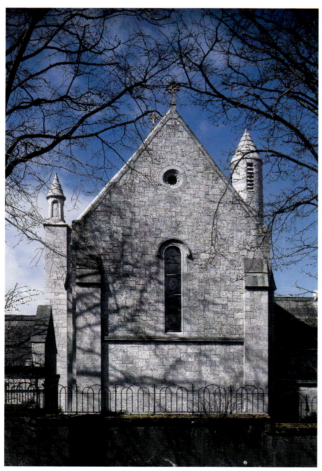

here is of plaster (FIGS. 2.9, 2.20, P. 46). The arcading to the sides contains Stations of the Cross in *opus sectile*, literally 'cut work' of richly coloured glass embedded in the plasterwork of the wall (FIG. 2.21, P. 47). O'Connell was keen on this method of creating Stations as it was a more permanent alternative to the conventional paintings that were usually used in Irish churches and often ended up hung or knocked askew, thus causing irritation to the more aes-thetically minded worshippers. The method had been employed in Ireland as early as 1908 by Sarah Purser's studio, An Túr Gloine, who were actually working on a set of similar Stations for Spiddal Church in Co. Galway dur-ing 1916, but O'Connell seems to have been unaware of the fact that *opus sectile* could be made in Ireland and went elsewhere with the commission for the Honan.[7] It was carried out for him by the firm of Oppenheimer, based in Man-chester, and was one of only two elements within the chapel that were not executed by Irish firms; the other was the mosaic flooring,

THE ARCHITECTURAL BACKGROUND

FIG. 2.16: *Honan Chapel, from a north-eastern perspective, showing belfry*

FIG. 2.17: *Honan Chapel, upper arcading, below roofline (detail)*

FIG. 2.18: *Honan Chapel, western façade, entrance pillars and railings*

also carried out by Oppenheimer's, although their role has never been publicized. Although he enthused about the floor itself, O'Connell did not identify the firm responsible in his book in 1916, presumably because such recourse to an outside firm would have been seen to be inconsistent with the aim to foster Irish arts and crafts (FIG. 2.22, P. 48).

Presumably as a result of O'Connell's reticence on the matter, other contemporary references also fail to identify the firm responsible for the mosaic floor and so, remarkably, its designer remains anonymous.[8] This is unfortunate as the floor is the most spectacular thing of its type in Ireland. The entire scheme, covering both the nave and the chancel, dwells on 'the Creation and the works of the Lord'.[9] On entering the chapel by the west door one first sees a large circular panel at the west end depicting the sun, surrounded by signs of the zodiac, with trees, plants and animals to each side. The central aisle depicts the 'river of life' containing fishes and other creatures, flowing eastward, and at the east end of the nave in front of the chancel is a design depicting animals, birds, fishes and trees, representing 'the work of God's Hands'. In the chancel itself is a multi-circled design showing such things as the sun and moon, stars and planets, wind and snow, rain and ice, trees and fruit, and birds and fishes, arranged around a central panel depicting the earth. The entire floor comprises a very colourful design, vigorously drawn, and bordered with Celtic interlaced and zoomorphic ornament.

FIG. 2.19: *Engraving of the interior of Cormac's Chapel, Cashel, Co. Tipperary (from Margaret Stokes, Early Christian Art in Ireland, 1887)*

FIG. 2.20: *Interior view, Honan Chapel, looking east*

The interior also contains a cleverly contrived confessional leading off the sacristy lobby and connected by a small grille to the nave on the north side, while within the chancel on the south side there is a small aumbry, or recess, taking the place of a credence table, with a triple-arched sedilia, or seating recess, adjacent to it. Originally the chancel was marked off from the nave by low arcaded communion rails of cut limestone, in the centre of which was an opening without a gate; these rails have now been removed. The gateway led to the altar, which is still intact, as designed by McMullen, consisting of a plain slab of limestone resting on five piers, each carved with a different pattern of Irish cross, and on the slab or table stands a tabernacle which fittingly takes the form of an early Irish oratory with a steeply pitched roof, and forms the focal point of the whole building (FIGS. 2.23, 2.24, P. 49).

The Honan Chapel stands as the most complete example of a Hiberno-Romanesque revival church in that all its fittings and furnishings were, in the words of O'Connell, 'designed and fashioned for it as parts of a thought-out scheme based on one recognised and guiding ideal'.[10] That special status that the chapel enjoys can, however, only be maintained so long as the building retains the integrity of its original layout and arrangement, and is neither denuded of any more of its essential furnishings and fittings nor encumbered by any further additions than have already been made.

FIG. 2.21: *Sixth Station of the Cross*

FIG. 2.23 *One of the altar piers (detail)*

FIG. 2.24 *Carving on altar slab*

FIG. 2.22: *Sun symbol at west end of Honan Chapel, floor mosaic (overview)*

Notes and References

1   References to the building subsequent to O'Connell's own description of it, include the following: *The Irish Builder and Engineer*, 28 October 1916, p. 529 and 31 March 1917, pp. 150–52, 154; M.J. O'Kelly, 'The Honan Chapel', *The Furrow*, vol. 1, no. 6, July 1950, pp. 290–96; Paul Larmour, 'Honan Hostel Chapel', in A. Becker, J. Olley and W. Wang (eds.), *20th-Century Architecture: Ireland* (Munich and New York: Prestel, 1997), p. 100.

2   Sir John R. O'Connell, *The Honan Hostel Chapel, Cork* (Cork: Guy & Co., 1916).

3   Revd Sir John R. O'Connell, *The Collegiate Chapel, Cork*, 2nd edn (Cork University Press, 1932), p. 9.

4   ibid., p. 21.

5   For the development of Hiberno-Romanesque Revival architecture, see P. Larmour, 'The Celtic Revival and a national style of architecture', unpublished Ph.D. thesis, The Queen's University of Belfast, 1977. See also Jeanne Sheehy, *The Rediscovery of Ireland's Past: The Celtic Revival 1830–1930* (London: Thames & Hudson, 1980).

6   See *The Irish Builder and Engineer*, 31 March 1917, p. 150.

7   An Túr Gloine went on to provide other sets of Stations of the Cross in *opus sectile* at Loughrea Cathedral, Co. Galway, in 1929–32, and St Anthony's Church, Athlone, Co. Westmeath, in 1934–6.

8   *The Cork Examiner*, 23 October 1916, p. 4, praised the floor but made no reference to the designer or firm responsible; *The Irish Builder and Engineer*, 28 October 1916, p. 529, merely stated 'the floor is inlaid with mosaic', while the same journal's long description of the chapel in its issue of 31 March 1917 made no reference to the floor at all.

9   As explained by O'Connell, op. cit., pp. 34–6.

10   O'Connell, op. cit., p. 58.

Bibliography

LARMOUR, PAUL, 'The Celtic Revival and a national style of architecture', unpublished Ph.D. thesis, The Queen's University of Belfast, 1977

LARMOUR, PAUL, 'Honan Hostel Chapel', in A. Becker, J. Olley and W. Wang (eds.), *20th-Century Architecture: Ireland* (Munich and New York: Prestel, 1997), p. 100

LARMOUR, PAUL, 'The Honan Chapel, Cork: A Shrine to the Irish Arts and Crafts Movement', in Irish Architectural and Decorative Studies: The Journal of the Irish Geogian Society, vol. V, 2002

O'CONNELL, SIR JOHN R., *The Honan Hostel Chapel, Cork* (Cork: Guy & Co., 1916)

O'CONNELL, REVD SIR JOHN R., *The Collegiate Chapel, Cork*, 2nd edn (Cork University Press, 1932)

O'KELLY, M.J., 'The Honan Chapel', *The Furrow*, vol. 1, no. 6, July 1950, pp. 290–96
SHEEHY, JEANNE, *The Rediscovery of Ireland's Past: The Celtic Revival 1830–1930*
(London: Thames & Hudson, 1980)

FIG. 2.25 *Carved arcading in the Sanctuary (detail)*

3

The Furnishings of the Honan Chapel, Cork, 1915–16

Sir John O'Connell's intention at the Honan Chapel was to re-create an Irish church from the golden age of Irish Christianity, complete with furniture and altar furnishings that would express Irishness down to the last detail. He also wished the interior to contain the very best work that Ireland could produce, unified by a common aesthetic. In his choice of makers and designers he achieved this aim triumphantly, and the chapel became a monument to the Irish Arts and Crafts movement and to the Celtic Revival.

Sir John outlines his aesthetic considerations clearly in his little book on the chapel published in 1916.[1] Firstly, as regards the Irish character of the church he states that 'such a building would not win its way to the hearts of those for whom it was intended unless, in its inspiration and design, it was truly and sincerely Irish'. So he chooses the 'Hiberno-Romanesque, of one thousand years ago' as the architectural style of the building, because it represents in his opinion 'the best age of Irish ecclesiastical art'.

Secondly, he states that 'no Church building can be regarded as a beautiful and worthy whole unless all those things which are needed for the service of the altar are part of a thought-out scheme, based on a recognised and guiding ideal', and unless the 'same idea which appears in the building and the decoration also inspires all the furniture'; and so we find Sir John's designers reinventing furniture and furnishings for the Honan Chapel in the Hiberno-Romanesque and the associated Celtic styles.

Thirdly, Sir John seeks to achieve an overall effect of simplicity and restfulness. He says: 'the sense of dignity and impressiveness of God's House can only be obtained by restraint and even severity', so, wishing to avoid 'warring elements and conflicting ideas', he resolves to keep the furnishings to a minimum, making sure that 'such few essential things that are allowed are the best and most suitable of their kind for the purpose – and are, in themselves, things of extraordinary beauty'. Also he is determined to exclude ruthlessly 'all unnecessary ornament' and make sure that 'all ornament that is necessary be marked with splendour and right feeling'.

Finally, he wants, where possible, the furnishing of the church to be carried out by Irish craftspeople so it would become 'an expression of the best work that can be produced in Ireland today', and he was fortunate that the Irish Arts and Crafts movement, which had been steadily developing over the preceding thirty years, had led to the 'availability of men and women who have both the knowledge and the skill to produce most beautiful, refined and appropriate work for the decoration of our churches'.

With these points in mind, and supervising every detail himself, Sir John succeeded in creating a church of striking simplicity and dignity, with a unified aesthetic linking the building and the contents, the whole being hallmarked as truly Irish, both in character and manufacture.

FURNITURE

Before we look at the furniture we might first glance at the architecture of the building. Looking at the west elevation one is immediately struck by the chief feature of the Hiberno-Romanesque style: the semi-circular arch, present here in the window openings, the arcades and the west door. We note that the door is decorated with three 'orders' or concentric bands of simple geometric decoration: a) lozenge and saltire (a form of zigzag); b) ball and pellet

FIG. 3.2: *The music stool*

FIG. 3.3: *Carved arcading in the Sanctuary*

FIG. 3.4: *Ceremonial chair and the University President's kneeler, with the University College Cork mace resting on specially designed brackets*

(a continuous line of dots); and c) chevron (another form of zigzag). Moving inside, we find the interior is also dominated by the semi-circular arch with its barrel vault, the window openings, the arcading and the chancel arch. Thus it is that the semi-circular arch becomes the chief element in the decoration of the furniture, conforming exactly to Sir John's specification (FIG. 3.3, P. 5). Simple oak pews fill the church, their ends composed of part-semi-circular arches, decorated in a simplified version of the orders of the west door, with concentric bands of geometric pattern. The same scheme is found in the oak music stool, only here it is a complete semi-circle (FIG. 3.2, P. 54), and in the credence table, which is similar but even more simplified.

The most interesting items of furniture are the two ceremonial chairs and their kneelers, located in the front row of the pews. These were used on special occasions by the Warden of the Honan Hostel and the President of the college, each chair featuring its appropriate carved coat of arms and motto (FIG. 3.4). Thus the Warden's chair bears the arms of the Honan Hostel and its motto, 'Do chúm gloire De agus honora na hEireann' (To the Glory of God and the Honour of Ireland), and the President's chair the arms of the college with its motto, 'Where Fin barr taught let Munster learn'. The use of coats of arms is a leitmotiv running through all the chapel furnishings and the building, reinforcing their common identity.

The ceremonial chairs are architectural in character, with the same part-semi-circular decoration, and they feature broad, double-curved arm-rests with spiral ends, which give them a certain art nouveau air (FIG. 3.5).

The kneelers are more overtly Celtic Revival in style, the President's one being provided with a pair of cast-bronze animal-interlace brackets upon which to rest the presidential mace during the service, and both the kneelers have a carved decorative panel, each a mirror image of the other. These feature an elaborate interlace pattern with Celtic borders, half concealed by a carved curtain hanging in folds from the top. This intriguing and attractive design becomes more intriguing when one realizes that the central interlace pattern, with its concentric circles linked by circular loops, is not really Irish at all: it is in fact Italian and is taken from a book first published in 1909, George Coffey's *Guide to the Celtic Antiquities of the Christian Period Preserved in the National Museum Dublin*. In his first chapter, Coffey writes about the origins of Celtic ornament which he shows to be a hybrid style composed of elements drawn from various sources: spirals from the La Tène style of Central Europe, animals from the animal art of Northern Europe, and interlace from the late classical art of the Mediterranean region. Examples of each source are given and therein shows examples of interlace from Rome and Ravenna of the sixth century, one of which (pierced marble screen from Ravenna) is the fragment upon which the panels of the kneeler are based.[2] The designer has turned the fragment upside down, surrounded it with a 'Celtic' interlace border and, instead of completing the geometry of the missing section, has simply drawn a curtain over it (FIGS, 3.7, 3.7A, P. 58).

One wonders who was responsible for designing the furniture. Interestingly, the architect J.F.Fuller, in designing pews for the Adair Memorial Church at Ballybrittas, Co. Laois, which is an earlier essay in the Hiberno-Romanesque style (1888), chose exactly the same solution to the problem, terminating his pews with semi-circular ends with decorative

FIG. 3.5: *Ceremonial chair (side view)*
FIG. 3.6: *Lectern*

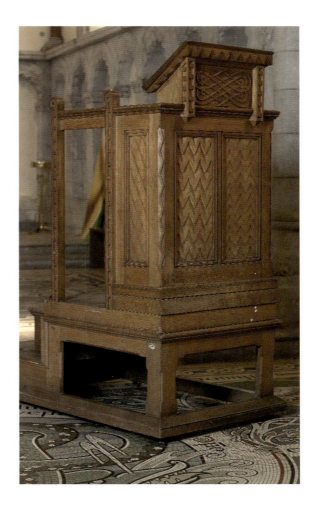

concentric bands. However, he was definitely not involved here. Might George Coffey have been involved? He had had a fascinating career as a leading nationalist in Dublin and a political activist. He was also an engineer, a lawyer and an archaeologist who ended up being the first Director of the National Museum of Ireland, and the author of several important books on Irish Stone Age and Bronze Age art. He had also been involved in the Arts and Crafts movement in Ireland from the beginning, and been one of the chief promoters of the revival of Celtic ornamentation, having lectured frequently on such subjects as 'The Use and Abuse of Celtic Ornament' and 'The Origin of Celtic Ornament'.[3] He had exhibited his own Celtic-style bookbindings in both London and Dublin,

but it seems unlikely that he was directly involved in the Honan project as he died in 1916 and had been physically incapacitated by a series of strokes from 1904 to 14. Another possible candidate is the architect W.A. Scott, who designed all the metalwork for the Honan Chapel and who had designed furniture for Loughrea Cathedral ten years earlier, and for Thoor Ballylee for W.B. Yeats (who described him afterwards as 'that late drunken genius Scott)'. However, he was a highly original designer, and probably too good to have been responsible for this furniture, which follows so closely the architecture of the building. In all probability the designer was the architect himself, J.F. Mc Mullen (1859–1933). [This theory was proved to be correct during the conference

FIG. 3.7: *Ravenna panel, from which the carved detail on the kneeler is derived*

FIG. 3.7A: *Detail of carved panel, ceremonial kneeler. The Celtic pattern is partly obscured by folds of drapery*

by information provided by John Sisk, one of the delegates, who is a grandson of the building contractor.]

The 'Irish' character of the woodwork was extended to the grille of the confessional set into the north wall (FIG. 3.8), and even to the ventilator panels (animal interlace) in the roof, so high over the congregation as to be almost invisible. The original furniture, which also includes a lectern (FIG. 3.6, P. 57), a reading-desk and a noticeboard, was made by the Cork building firm who built the chapel, John Sisk & Son, many of the items bearing their ivory label with name engraved in black letters (FIG. 3.9). The carvers who carved the furniture remain anonymous, as the Sisk firm, which was founded in 1859, no longer has

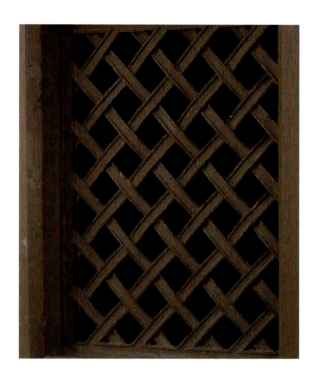

FIG. 3.8: *Confessional grille*

FIG. 3.9: *Maker's mark, John Sisk and Son, Builders, Cork, from one of the pews*

records of the commission. They may well have been trained in the Cork School of Art which instituted wood-carving classes in 1886, under John Linehan, and continued them under Michael Mc Namara between 1900 and 1925. Some time later, two extra kneelers were provided and labelled by the firm of M.J. Galligan, and later again, probably in the 1930s, a glass-topped display table for holding the book commemorating deceased collegians was supplied, in a watered-down Romanesque style, by The Quality Furniture Company, Pope's Quay, Cork. Additional furniture in the spirit but not in the style of the originals has been added from time to time up to the present, with some pieces of the original furniture being replaced.[4]

FIG. 3.10: *Ewer and Stand*

FIG. 3.11: *Candleholder*

THE FURNISHINGS OF THE HONAN CHAPEL

METALWORK

We turn now to the metalwork provided for the chapel which was designed by William A. Scott (1871–1921), professor of architecture in the National University of Ireland, and the leading Irish art-architect of the day. Having studied in the Metropolitan School of Art, Dublin, he trained for his profession under his father, the Drogheda architect Anthony Scott, and Sir Thomas Newenham Deane, from both of whom he gained his knowledge of early Irish architecture. He supervised the interior embellishment of Loughrea Cathedral in 1904–10, where he designed all the woodwork and metalwork. It was at Loughrea that the Dún Emer Guild and An Túr Gloine got their first major commissions, which helped to establish them – all his life Scott was an encourager of native Irish craftspeople. In 1906, he travelled to Ravenna with the art critic Robert Elliott (who was interested in the reform of Catholic Church art); they travelled on to Turkey to look at Byzantine churches there, and on their return Scott developed his unique 'Celto-Byzantine' style of architecture. At the Honan Chapel he supplied designs for the altar plate made in a variety of metals (silver, silver-gilt, brass, bronze and copper) and for the wrought-iron gate at the west door. In the Celtic Revival style, they display the designer's ability to reinvent the style in terms of both the decoration and the form of the objects. (FIGS. 3.10, 3.11, 3.12). The various items are linked also by the repeated

FIG. 3.12: Detail of candleholder, showing open-mouthed dragon at apex of handle

use of the motif of the ringed Celtic cross, which is the basis of the design of the gate and of several of the pieces of altar plate, and appears as a detail in others. The plate, for the most part, was made in Dublin by the firm of Edmond Johnson Ltd; two items, however, a chalice and a ciborium, were made under the direction of Barry Egan of Cork by his family firm of William Egan & Son, founded in 1823 (SEE FIGS. 3.21–3.23, PP. 67–8).

The missal stand is a good example of Scott's inventiveness. In form it consists of a flat rectangular brass book-rest supported on a short cylindrical shaft, with blue enamel bosses, standing on a flaring circular foot. Here he has adapted to his purpose the design of the early Irish book shrines, for example the eleventh

century *Soiscel Molaise*, dividing the rectangular space into four compartments by superimposing a ringed Celtic cross. The compartments are filled with animal-interlace patterns in cut-metalwork – a technique much used in the early work (e.g. the back of the Shrine of St Patrick's Bell). This technique makes the decoration highly visible from a distance because of the extreme contrast between the brightly polished metal and the blackness of the voids (SEE FIGS. 3.31–3.33, PP. 72–3).

The most magnificent item of the altar plate is the large silver-gilt monstrance. Its dominating circular top, of cut-work animal interlace and enamels, symbolizes a flight of doves, while its form subtly replays the Celtic cross motif, which is again repeated in the

FIG. 3.13: *A pair of benediction candlesticks*

FIG. 3.14: *Thurible*

FIG. 3.15: *Detail of decorative brackets connecting the suspending chains of the Sanctuary lamp*

details. The shaft, which tapers up to and down to a large central knop, with hemispherical blue enamel bosses, draws its inspiration from the tenth-century 'thistle brooches' found in Co. Kilkenny and elsewhere, and again illustrates W.A. Scott's ingenuity in reworking ideas from early metalwork in new ways. The foot of the monstrance is of flaring octagonal form with cut-work panels, blue enamel bosses and eight finely detailed enamel shields, featuring coats of arms connected with the chapel; a long inscription in Irish lettering records the names of designer, maker, patron and executor of the Honan estate[5] (SEE FIGS. 3.28–3.30A, PP. 70–71; FIG. 3.38, P. 74).

The altar candlesticks and altar cross, in brass and enamel, echo the shaft details of the

FIG. 3.16: Sanctuary lamp

FIG. 3.17: Detail of Sanctuary lamp showing hallmarks and maker's mark

FIG. 3.18: Partial detail of inscription surrounding Sanctuary lamp girdle

monstrance tapering towards central knops, embellished with blue enamel bosses (SEE FIGS. 3.39, 3.40, PP. 74–5). The benediction candlesticks, like the others, are supported on domed feet with cut-metal Celtic-style ribbon work, and their sloping arms are supported by very freely designed interlaced animals, with elaborately textured surfaces, involving gouging and beading, and with subtle contrasts of both materials and finish (copper, brass and silver plate; matt and polish) (FIG. 3.13, P. 62). This combining of metals of different colours is also a feature of the altar cross, which contrasts brass and copper with the bronze figure of Christ hanging against a red enamel background.

The largest silver item in the collection of altar plate is the mighty Sanctuary lamp, which

FIG. 3.19: Detail of engraving from the lid of the incense boat, depicting the Honan crest and motto

FIG. 3.20: Incense boat and stoup, Honan Chapel

FIG. 3.21: A ciborium showing the crest of University College Cork, made by William Egan and Sons, Cork

THE FURNISHINGS OF THE HONAN CHAPEL

weighs over 28 pounds (FIGS. 3.16–3.18, P. 64–5, 64–5; 3.15, P. 63). It consists of a large bowl decorated with animal interlace in cut-metalwork, birds with open beaks and blue enamel bosses; it formerly hung in the chapel by three silver chains from a silver ceiling dome decorated in similar vein, with the liveliest cut and engraved knotwork. Following developments in both liturgy and technology the chapel lighting has been modernized, and the Sanctuary lamp has been one of the casualties of the changes. Like the monstrance, it bears a long inscription. Related to it in design is the thurible and censer: a chalice-like bowl with pointed lid, linked by silver chains (FIG. 3.14 P. 63). The lid, with its double-curved profile, looking like a saracen helmet, features

FIG. 3.22: *Tray from cruet set, with support hold vessels*

FIG. 3.23: *A chalice and paten in an oak box, made by William Egan and Sons, Cork*

FIG. 3.24: *A chalice showing the crest of University College Cork, made by William Egan and Sons, Cork*

THE FURNISHINGS OF THE HONAN CHAPEL

FIG. 3.25: *Cruet set*

FIG. 3.26: *Custos (host carrier)*

FIG. 3.27: *Open custos, showing removable host carrier (lunette)*

diminishing bands of strapwork that bounce off the sides of their compartments with the greatest vitality and energy. Used with the censer are the silver gilt incense boat and stoup (a liturgical jug and spoon), which feature cast mounts, multicoloured enamel bosses and the engraved arms of the Honan Hostel (FIGS. 3.19, 3.20, P. 66).

Two sets of chalice and ciborium were made, both decorated with panels of repoussé knotwork, one set being embellished with garnets and armorial shields, the other with garnets and rock crystals. Both ciboria are topped with miniature Celtic crosses, and their forms contain references to the base and knop of the Ardagh Chalice (FIG. 3.21, P. 67). The associated cruets are a pair of glass bottles

FIG. 3.29:
Monstrance and
Thistle brooch detail

FIG. 3.30A:
Monstrance knop
(detail)

FIG. 3.28: Monstrance

FIG. 3.30: Monstrance
(detail)

mounted in silver-gilt Celtic cut-work, with a silver-gilt tray with engraved interlace decoration (FIGS. 3.24, 3.25, P. 68–9). The silver-gilt custos (with lunette) is a simplified miniature monstrance, with repoussé Celtic work and garnets (FIGS. 3.26, 3.27, P. 69).

This glittering treasure, which also includes a silver and enamel replica of the Cross of Cong, makes up the Honan Chapel altar plate and is probably the most complete collection of Celtic Revival ecclesiastical metalwork in the country (SEE FIGS. 4.1, P. 90; 4.4, P. 93).

Scott's other metalwork here comprises two bells based on those associated with the early Irish saints, one of brass, and the other of iron suspended from a cast-iron animal-interlace bracket. The most important item, however, is the great wrought-iron gate, which formerly hung outside the west door where it cast attractive shadows on the chapel floor when the doors were open. It is one of the most original items of the entire Irish Celtic Revival, and has now been in storage for many years (FIGS. 3.33, 3.35). The gate is divided symmetrically by a giant ringed Celtic cross forming compartments that are asymmetrically filled with wonderfully inventive interlace work, the iron rods of which it is composed twisting and turning in novel and modern ways. Not only is the iron wrought into patterns, it is also hammered and cut, producing varying widths of flat ribbon that form animal features and striking art nouveau shapes.

FIG. 3.31: *Missal stand*

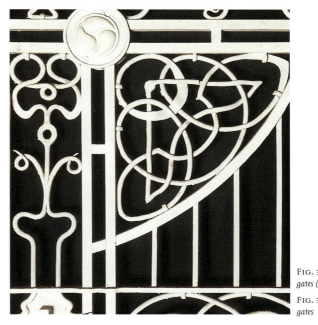

FIG. 3.33: Wrought-iron
gates (detail)

FIG. 3.35: Wrought-iron
gates

FIG. 3.32: Shire of St
Patrick's bell, showing
detail of early cut-metal
work

FIG. 3.34: An Soiscel
Molaise, which
influenced the design of
the missal stand

FIG. 3.36: Hand bell,
modelled on the Cashel bell

FIG. 3.37: Hinges at the
West door (detail)

FIG. 3.38: Monstrance base
detail, partially showing
enamel armorial shield and
inscription

FIG. 3.39: Altar Cross

FIG. 3.40: Three of the
altar candlesticks and
the monstrance

FIG. 3.41: Altar card
placed on altar table

THE FURNISHINGS OF THE HONAN CHAPEL

It was manufactured by J. and C. McGloughlin, the leading art-metal foundry, in Dublin.

ALTAR CARDS

In addition to the plate, the altar was also provided with elaborately illuminated altar cards in silver frames. In commissioning the cards, Sir John O'Connell was determined to banish the inferior type of altar card so commonly used in those days, 'as a rule made on the continent, badly printed, badly designed and badly framed'. He chose the artist Joseph Tierney of the Columbar Studio in Dublin, one of many illuminating artists at work throughout the country (part of the wave of Celtic Revival crafts that sprang up in the late nineteenth century).

Tierney is remembered today for two main commissions, the altar cards at the Honan Chapel and those at St Patrick's Church, San Francisco (commissioned in the 1920s and now, alas, partly disappeared). He made two sets for the Honan Chapel, each comprising three cards (two small and one large). The first set, with the Latin texts written in the Irish uncial script of the *Book of Kells*, featuring red and gold capitals and black lettering, are adorned with brightly coloured panels of modernized spiral patterns and interlacements, interspersed with figures of saints and other religions persons (FIG. 3.44). One panel, for example, shows the Holy Family in distinctively Irish mode: the Virgin is wearing a Tara Brooch, the gold cup being offered by one of the three

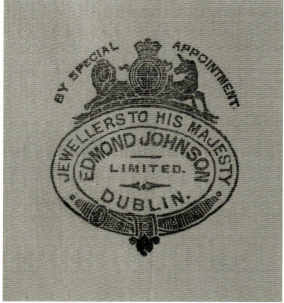

FIG. 3.42: *Boxed set of altar cards in the original maker's box*

FIG. 3.43: *Maker's mark, Edmond Johnson, Limited, Dublin, from interior of box*

FIG. 3.44:
Altar card

FIG. 3.45: *Altar card frame (detail)*
FIG. 3.46: *Altar card frame (detail)*
FIG. 3.47: *Altar card frame (detail)*

kings looks like the Ardagh Chalice, and an angel in the foreground plays a Brian Boru-style harp (FIG. 3.49, P. 80). The cards of the second set are less elaborately illuminated, and are based on the carpet pages of the early manuscripts with roundels at the corners (FIG. 3.48). The frames follow this outline with projecting squares at each mid-side featuring twelve variations on the theme of the Celtic cross (FIG. 3.46). In the case of both sets the frames are of silver with elaborate decoration, those of the first set featuring animal interlace and spirals, enriched with spots of enamel and jewels, those of the second set have chevron details and larger multicoloured enamels (FIGS. 3.45, 3.47). The cards are provided with protective leather-covered boxes lined with white satin (FIGS. 3.42, 3.43, P. 76). Like the altar plate, the frames were made by Edmond Johnson Ltd, of Dublin. Although Edmond Johnson himself had died in 1900, his firm carried on until the 1920s. He had been the last of a large family of jewellers, goldsmiths and

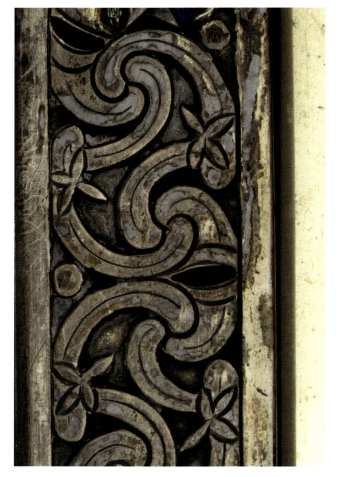

FIG. 3.48:
Altar card

Initium **Sancti Evangelii** Secundum Joannem

IN principio erat Verbum, et Verbum erat apud Deum, et Deus erat Verbum. Hoc erat in principio apud Deum. Omnia per ipsum facta sunt : et sine ipso factum est nihil, quod factum est. In ipso vita erat, et vita erat lux hominum : et lux in tenebris lucet, et tenebræ eam non comprehenderunt. Fuit homo missus a Deo, cui nomen erat Joannes. Hic venit in testimonium, ut testimonium perhiberet de lumine, ut omnes crederent per illum. Non erat ille lux, sed ut testimonium perhiberet de lumine. Erat lux vera quæ illuminat omnem hominem venientem in hunc mundum. In mundo erat, et mundus per ipsum factus est, et mundus eum non cognovit. In propria venit, et sui eum non receperunt. Quotquot autem receperunt eum, dedit eis potestatem filios Dei fieri, his qui credunt in nomine ejus : qui non ex sanguinibus, neque ex voluntate carnis, neque ex voluntate viri, sed ex Deo nati sunt *(hic genuflectitur)* ET VERBUM CARO FACTUM EST, et habitavit in nobis ; et vidimus gloriam ejus, gloriam quasi Unigeniti a Patre, plenum gratiæ et veritatis.

silversmiths active in Dublin from the latter part of the eighteenth century. He had first come to prominence in 1869 when he undertook the cleaning of the Ardagh Chalice, discovered the previous year in Co. Limerick, on behalf of its owners, the Royal Irish Academy. He wrote a detailed description of this work, pointing out that 'these necessary repairs afforded an opportunity of minutely examining the whole mode of construction of one of those marvellous specimens of early Irish workmanship'.[6] He was amazed at the metal working skills and especially the technique used in some of the enamels. Following this, Johnson became the Academy's chief restorer and technical expert. He made plaster casts of all the ancient work that came to him, and his pattern drawers overflowed with a unique collection of archaeological material. He developed a business specializing in replicas of ancient Irish objects, and by 1893 he was able to send 182 different replica items to the World's Columbian Exposition in Chicago.[7] It was from this rich repository of patterns that the Johnson firm drew in designing the altar card frames. Sadly, when the firm closed in the 1920s, all its records were burned and the unique collection of casts was discarded.[8]

BOOKS

As well as the altar cards, three elaborately bound liturgical books were provided for the altar, the bindings of which were executed by the Dublin

FIG. 3.49: *Altar card (detail)*

THE FURNISHINGS OF THE HONAN CHAPEL

FIG. 3.50:
*Frontispiece from
the Roman missal*

FIG. 3.51: *Roman missal resting on the missal stand*

FIG. 3.52: *Roman missal cover*

binder Eleanor Kelly. She had been associated for a time with the Dún Emer Guild, but also worked independently, and had come to prominence in 1911 when she bound the volume presented to Queen Mary by the women of Ireland on the occasion of the royal visit that year; her design symbolized 'the Four Winds of Erin Blowing Justice, Love, Mercy and Courage on the jewelled crown of Queen Mary'.[9] Her work was praised at the 1910 exhibition of the Arts and Crafts Society of Ireland by Oswald Reeves (founder of the Guild of Irish Artworkers), who noted that it was 'marked by a reserve in the enrichments, and the tasteful use of inlaid coloured leather and jewels'.

The largest of the books is a Roman missal (Rome 1912) in a red morocco binding with gold tooling and inlaid coloured leathers and jewels (mother of pearl, garnet, amethyst and peridot) (FIGS. 3.51–3.53). The design, front and back, consists of a central ringed cross with other subsidiary Celtic interlace motifs; the jewels appear on the front cover but not on the back and, like the leather inlays, are very subtly coloured. This is a good example of Kelly's 'ravishingly beautiful art', so called by a critic who saw her work at the Galerie Barbazanges in Paris in 1922, who went on to characterize her style as 'gentle, intimate and opulent'. Her bindings were generally supplied with a protective slip-case or box, usually covered with a hand-made paper or textile, which unfortunately in this case is now missing. Apart from the binding, this volume is notable also for its front end-paper, an illuminated heraldic panel on parchment, executed by the London art-bindery firm of Sangorski & Sutcliffe (FIG. 3.50, P. 81). In the style of the early Irish carpet pages, it depicts the arms of the Honan Hostel surrounded by those of the City of Cork, University College Cork and those of the O'Connell and Honan families. The binding was

executed in 1916, and the illuminator and binder are named on a separate leaf. Related to this volume is the rite of service, also in red morocco, bound by Eleanor Kelly with a gold-tooled cross on the front cover; this was the personal gift from Sir John O'Connell to the Chapel.

The third item is also a Roman missal (*Ordo Missae Defunctorum*), for use at the Founders' Day Mass, bound in black morocco with gold tooling and inlaid coloured leathers and jewels (amethyst and rock crystal). The elaborately key-patterned cross design on both front and back covers in based on the early Christian grave-slab of Tullylease, in north Co. Cork, and is a motif also embroidered on the black antependium and carved into the stonework of the altar. The slip-case is covered in a hand-made paper. This binding is an

FIG. 3.53: *Roman missal showing silk bookmarks*

archetypal Honan Chapel object, its design deriving not only from early Christian Ireland, but also from the province of Munster, and though simple, is rich and 'marked with splendour.'

TABERNACLE

Finally, we turn to the tabernacle on the altar, the religious focal point of the whole building. It is a carved stone structure in the form of an early Irish Christian church with two large, magnificent enamel panels on the front, one on the door, the other on the gable, made by Oswald Reeves (1870–1967), the leading enamelist in Ireland of his day (FIG. 3.54). A native of Birmingham, Reeves trained with Alexander Fisher, the man chiefly responsible for reviving the art of enamelling in Britain. He came to teach at the Metropolitan School of Art in Dublin in 1903, and was the founding father of a school of Irish metalwork and enamelling that became internationally famous. It was a group of his pupils, and others, at the 1912 International Art Congress in Dresden, who 'saved the whole credit of the UK', according to a London newspaper, 'with the really splendid exhibit of stained glass and enamels from Ireland'. Reeves is remembered today not only as a craftsman and a great teacher, but also as one of the leading lights and organizers of the Arts and Crafts movement in Ireland.

The enamelled panels in the Honan Chapel illustrate Christian themes. The upper, triangular panel, occupying the 'gable' of the tabernacle,

FIG. 3.54: *Tabernacle*
FIG. 3.55: *Tabernacle (detail showing lower enamel panel)*

FIG. 3.56: *Tabernacle (detail, showing upper enamel panel tympanum)*

shows the Blessed Trinity with the Father, Son and Holy Spirit 'in the deep blue void of Heaven', attended by two angels, carrying the sun and moon as symbols of creation (FIG. 3.56). The lower, rectangular panel attached to the bronze door depicts the Adoration of the Lamb or, as Sir John puts it, 'the Lamb of God, pouring forth His Blood for the life and nourishment of His people'. The Lamb is seen standing on a brightly coloured altar decorated with three ringed crosses, against a richly textured background of leaves and branches in silver-gilt repoussé work. Above, in the sky, the Holy Spirit, symbolized by a dove, is surrounded by flights of angels bearing the instruments of the Passion, whilst two other angels, acting as servers, kneel on the ground before the altar (FIG. 3.55, P. 85). The effect of these enamels is absolutely stunning, forming a brilliant point of luminous colour amidst the austere stonework of the Sanctuary. The Honan panels are among Reeve's finest work and may be reckoned the best on public view in Ireland.[10]

The items discussed in this article along with the textiles, windows and other artefacts in the chapel remain largely intact, a unique heritage of Irish liturgical art, each linked to each, and to the building, by an aesthetic philosophy summarized by the Chapel motto, 'Do chùm gloire De agus honora na h-Eireann' (To the glory of God and the honour of Ireland). It is vital that the collection be preserved, ideally in the chapel, in the setting for which it was designed. However, liturgical developments have rendered certain items redundant (e.g. the altar cards and the Sanctuary lamp) and they must find a new home in a museum on campus. It is to be hoped that all changes made as a result of liturgical or technical advances will be made with sensitivity and respect for Sir John O'Connell's vision of uncluttered simplicity, so that the chapel will remain both a living church and a monument to the Irish Arts and Crafts movement, of significance not only in Ireland but also on the wider European stage.

NOTES AND REFERENCES

1 Revd Sir John R. O'Connell, *The Collegiate Chapel, Cork: Some notes on the building and on the ideals which inspired it*, 2nd edn (Cork University Press, 1932). There were two subsequent publications on the chapel: Revd Prof. [Patrick] Power, *The Chapel of St. Fin Barr University College, Cork. Its history, architecture and symbolism* (Cork: Purcell & Co., no date) and Michael J. O'Kelly, *The Collegiate Chapel, Cork*, 2nd edn (Cork University Press, 1955).

2 See also J. Romilly Allen, *Celtic Art in Pagan and Christian Times* (London, 1904), the standard work on the subject; the fragment is illustrated on p. 245. The confessional grille is also based on an illustration from this book, that facing p. 258: 'Plait work on ciborium at the church of San Clemente. Rome 6th Century.'

3 For basic information on the Irish Arts and Crafts movement see Paul Larmour, *The Arts and Crafts Movement in Ireland* (Belfast: Friar's Bush Press, 1992); Nicola Gordon Bowe and Elizabeth Cumming, *The Arts and Crafts Movement in Dublin and Edinburgh 1885–1925* (Dublin: Irish Academic Press, 1998).

4 A number of items of furniture designed and made in 1986–7 by the Dublin sculptor Imogen Stuart (born Germany, 1927), were added following Vatican II. These include a massive oak altar, carved in relief with the Four Evangelists, now placed in the middle of the mosaic floor in front of the Sanctuary; a bronze ambo or reading-desk in the form of a fruiting vine; a carved oak credence table, of folding design hinged to the Sanctuary wall; an oak presider's chair adapted from the traditional three-legged cottage chair of Connemara, with a high back terminating in a Celtic cross. Other pieces were supplied to cater for the popularity of the Chapel as a wedding venue, these being a bride's chair and kneeler and a groom's chair and kneeler, the symbolism of their design being explained on labels attached beneath the seats: The Groom's Chair and Kneeler are carved in oak. They are angular-masculine in shape. The chair back is based on an evergreen tree. The tree symbolises the life in God's law. It stands for holiness, eternity and everlasting salvation. 19 IMO/GEN 87.' and 'The Bride's chair and kneeler are carved in oak. The shapes are soft and mostly carved-feminine. The chair back is based on the rainbow which stands for the covenant which God made between Him and man. The rainbow is also the symbol for peace and reconciliation. 19 IMO/GEN 87.'

Imogen Stuart also designed and made in 1997 a white marble font in the form of a pair of upturned hands, placed directly inside the west door. Also in 1997, the Co. Cork sculptor Kenneth Thompson (born Cork, 1946) made a free-standing elm candlestick to hold the altar candle, carved in relief with the words 'Lumen Christi'; and in the same year a set of twelve rectangular fumed-oak stools were made by the Co. Cork furniture-maker Eric Pearce (born 1956).

The harmonium was replaced in 1999 with a pipe organ made by Kenneth Jones & Associates of Bray, Co. Wicklow.

5 The arms commemorate the places with which the chapel is associated and the people involved with its creation (Matthew, Robert and Isabella Honan, whose bequest paid for it; Sir John O'Connell, executor of the estate and mastermind of the whole project; Sir Bertram Windle, President of the college). The arms are Munster: azure, three eastern crowns proper, or; City of Cork: or, an ancient ship between two castles in fesse gules; See of Cork: argent, a cross patée gules, charged with a crozier in pale, enfiled with a mitre-labelled or; University College Cork: per pale gules and azure, on the dexter side a lion statant gardant imperially crowned or, on the sinister side three eastern crowns proper on a chief of the third an ancient ship between two castles fesse of the first in centre chief point of achievement an open book argent garnished of the third, for motto 'Where Fin Barr taught, Let Munster learn'; Honan Hostel, Cork: vert, in the doorway of an Irish church or, the figure of St Fin Barr proper, on a chief of the second or a pale azure, between two lions passant to the dexter and the sinister respectively of the first, three antique crowns or; Honan: per pale nebuly vert and or three pheons in fesse, between two lions counter passant all counter changed; O'Connell: per fesse argent and vert, a stag trippant proper, between three quatrefoils slipped counter changed; Windle: gules, on a pile between two crosses patée in base or, three martlets of the field. (I am indebted to Maire Mac Conghail for help in identifying the arms.)

The arms of the college and the Honan Hostel are also carved in relief on the stone piers of the railings that border the chapel grounds and the college campus. The arms of the See of Cork and the hostel appear to either side of the west door. Beneath the windows depicting the Munster saints are carved the arms of the sees with which they are associated. The Honan family arms appear on the memorial tablet to the left of the chancel arch. Whoever made this tablet, which is composed of various coloured marbles embellished with mosaic, enamel and guilding, is not identified in Sir John O'Connell's book, probably because of being non-Irish. The makers of the *opus sectile* Stations of the Cross, and of the mosaic floor, are likewise not identified for the same reason. It has been suggested that Oppenheimers, a German firm with a workshop in Manchester, were responsible for the floor, and it seems likely that whoever made it also made the Stations and the memorial tablet.

6 Edward Richard Windham Wyndham-Quin, Earl of Dunraven, and Edmond Johnson, 'On an Ancient Chalice and Brooches Lately Found at Ardagh, in the County of Limerick', *Transactions of the Royal Irish Academy*, vol. 24, part III, 1874, pp. 433–54.

7 Cheryl Washer, 'The Work of Edmond Johnson: Archaeology and Commerce', in T.J. Edelstein (ed.), *Imagining an Irish Past: The Celtic Revival 1840–1940*

(Chicago: David and Alfred Smart Museum of Art, 1992). (This publication accompanied the exhibition of that name at the David and Alfred Smart Museum of Art, The University of Chicago, 5 February–16 June 1992.)

8   Douglas Bennett, personal communication.

9   'Souvenir Album presented to the Marquis and Marchioness of Aberdeen and Temair as a farewell gift by members of their staff 1905–1915' (no date, c. 1915).

10   Oswald Reeves's work has been extensively studied by both Paul Larmour and Nicola Gordon Bowe. A checklist of his works, complied by Paul Larmour, appeared in Paul Larmour, 'The works of Oswald Reeves (1870-1967), artist and craftsman: an interim catalogue', *Irish Architectural and Decorative Studies: The Journal of the Irish Georgian Society*, vol. 1, 1998, pp. 35–59.

BIBLIOGRAPHY

ALLEN, J. ROMILLY, *Celtic Art in Pagan and Christian Times* (London, 1904)

BOWE, NICOLA GORDON, AND ELIZABETH CUMMING, *The Arts and Crafts Movement in Dublin and Edinburgh 1885–1925* (Dublin: Irish Academic Press, 1998)

LARMOUR, PAUL, *The Arts and Crafts Movement in Ireland* (Belfast: Friar's Bush Press, 1992)

LARMOUR, PAUL, 'The Works of Oswald Reeves (1870–1967), Artist and Craftsman: an interim catalogue', *Irish Architectural and Decorative Studies: The journal of the Irish Georgian Society*, vol. 1, 1998, pp. 35–59

O'CONNELL, REVD SIR JOHN R., *The Collegiate Chapel, Cork: Some notes on the building and on the ideals which inspired it*, 2nd edn (Cork University Press, 1932)

O'KELLY, MICHAEL J., *The Collegiate Chapel, Cork*, 2nd edn (Cork University Press, 1955)

POWER, REVD PROF. [PATRICK], *The Chapel of St. Finnbar University College, Cork. Its history, architecture and symbolism* (Cork: Purcell & Co., no date)

WASHER, CHERYL, 'The Work of Edmond Johnson: Archaeology and Commerce' in T.J. Edelstein (ed.), *Imagining an Irish Past: The Celtic Revival 1840–1940* (Chicago: David and Alfred Smart Museum of Art, 1992)

WYNDHAM-QUIN, EDWARD RICHARD WINDHAM, EARL OF DUNRAVEN, AND EDMOND JOHNSON, 'On an Ancient Chalice and Brooches Lately Found at Ardagh, in the County of Limerick', *Transactions of the Royal Irish Academy*, vol. 24, part III, 1874, pp. 433–54

FIG. 4.1: *Replica of
the Cross of Cong*

PAUL LARMOUR

4

The Honan Chapel
The Artistic and Cultural Context

The Honan Chapel takes a very distinctive and recognizable architectural form, being designed in the Irish Romanesque style, and many of its fittings and furnishings are in close accord with that style of architecture, being in the early Irish style of art, or, as it is more popularly known, the Celtic style. Some fittings and furnishings are not in that style, but they nevertheless harmonize with the rest, sharing with them a mastery of technique and a display of superb craftsmanship. All the fittings and furnishings of the chapel, whether in Celtic style or not, were, as its creator Sir John Robert O'Connell himself put it, 'designed and fashioned for it as parts of a thought-out scheme', in an effort to make it 'an expression of the best work which can be produced in Ireland today'.[1]

What was it that determined the direction which O'Connell took in building the Honan Chapel? What accounted for the particularly Irish form of its architecture, the largely Celtic ornamentalist manner of much of its furnishings, and the overall preoccupation with unity

of artistic expression and purpose that led, in effect, to a permanent showcase of the best Irish ecclesiastical art of the day?

Culturally the most important influence on the Honan Chapel was what might be referred to as the Celtic Revival.[2] The Irish Revival of the 1830s to 1930s was part of the self-conscious attempt in the nineteenth and early twentieth century to regenerate Ireland, both spiritually and physically. It was a cultural phenomenon which was manifested in a number of ways, embracing all the arts and even extending to industry. It incorporated, at various times, the efforts of the 'language movement' which sought to reinstate the use of the native Irish language which had been widely supplanted by English; the turning to Irish subject matter in paintings, poems and plays; the adoption of traditional national symbols such as the wolf-hound, the harp and the shamrock; the growth of a 'Celtic consciousness' in the appreciation and celebration of distinctly native forms in architecture and ornamental art; and the insistence on the use of Irish materials or manufactures in building, clothing and other trades. The direct relevance of some of those things for the Honan Chapel is obvious – particularly in relation to its architectural form, ornamental detail and the deliberate use of Irish materials for most of the fabric.

The matter of architectural form and the position of the Honan Chapel in the Irish Romanesque revival is considered elsewhere; the matter of ornamental detail brings us here to what might be referred to as the Celtic Art Revival, or Celtic Revival for short.[3] The Celtic Revival came about due to the growing awareness of, and pride in, the special achievements of Irish artists of the Early Christian and Romanesque periods, combined with the general

FIG. 4.2: *The Cross of Cong (from Margaret Stokes, Early Christian Art in Ireland, 1887)*

FIG. 4.3: *Base of the High Cross, Tuam, Co. Galway, (from Margaret Stokes, Early Christian Art in Ireland, 1887)*

THE ARTISTIC AND CULTURAL CONTEXT

FIG. 4.4: *Replica of the Cross of Cong, made by Edmond Johnson for the Honan Chapel, 1916*

93

imitative or copyist tendency in nineteenth century decorative art generally. Such works as the *Book of Kells* and other early Irish illuminated manuscripts, the carved stone Irish high crosses, and the impressive heritage of early Irish precious metalwork, such as the Cross of Cong and the Ardagh Chalice, all of which were adorned with intricate interlacing patterns, were turned to for inspiration for new designs (FIGS. 4.1, P. 90; 4.2–4.4, P. 92–3). This Celtic Revival was the most dominant force in Irish applied art from the 1880s to the 1930s, although such interest had started much earlier and ended much later (if indeed it has ever ended).

The revival had started in antiquarian circles in Dublin in the 1840s, when the Irish Archaeological Society adopted initial letters from the *Book of Kells* and other manuscripts for use in its own publications of important texts, and the Celtic Society used motifs derived from the *Book of Durrow* and the Cross of Cong on its bindings (FIG. 4.5). During the 1850s the revival spread to modern jewellery, with reproductions of early Irish brooches, like the Tara Brooch, being made widely available by leading Dublin silversmiths such as Waterhouse & Co. and West & Son. By the 1860s the popularity of the revival was very evident in the rash of modern Celtic crosses which had started to appear throughout Ireland, their form and ornament being based on the original Irish high crosses of the eight to twelfth centuries, although they were usually of smaller size. An architect from Cork, William Atkins, was responsible for the

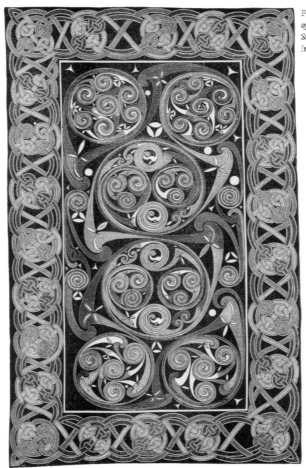

FIG. 4.5: *Page from the Book of Durrow (from Margaret Stokes, Early Christian Art in Ireland, 1887)*

design of one of the earliest and most monumental examples, the Herbert Cross of 1867 at Muckross near Killarney, Co. Kerry.

The 1870s and 1880s saw a number of modern illuminating artists become established, recreating the convoluted interlacements of early Irish art in illuminated addresses and presentation albums, while by the end of the nineteenth century Celtic ornament had been put to a number of other uses, such as wood carvings and ecclesiastical and domestic embroidery.

Cork and its artists played a significant role in this growth of interest in the revival of Celtic ornament, particularly in the period from the late nineteenth to the early twentieth century. The ascendancy of such ornament over the more traditional symbols of Ireland as a means of achieving a national identity was demonstrated at the Cork Industrial Exhibition in 1883, when the competition for the exhibition medal and certificate was won with a Celtic design, and the certificate design was also adapted for the binding of the report on the exhibition. As if to underline the point, Dr William Sullivan, President of Queen's College in Cork (now UCC), writing in the exhibition report, advocated the modern use of Celtic ornament not only for illuminations but also for stamped leather, woodwork, metal and stone work.[4] By 1902, at the Cork International Exhibition, Celtic ornament was featured not only on many of the exhibits, including a metal casket by Mary Houston, ecclesiastical embroidery by the Kenmare Convent and ceramics made of Irish clay, but also most prominently on the large panelled archway constructed within the industrial hall for the Department of Agriculture and Technical Instruction for Ireland.[5] The use of Celtic ornament was also a prominent feature in the work of the Cork School of Art in the early 1900s as seen in a

FIG. 4.6: *Silver and enamel mace made for University College Cork, 1910*

number of students' painted panels and examples of carved wooden furniture dating from that time. Teachers at the Cork School of Art were also adept at the style themselves, as evidenced by a highly ornamented enamelled metal casket designed around 1910 by James Archer who was in charge of metalwork and enamelling. James Archer, was also involved in the manufacture of a silver and enamel mace commissioned in 1910 from William Egan & Sons of Cork for University College Cork by Sir Bertram Windle, President of the college. Designed by J. Moring, it was embellished with Celtic ornamental motifs (FIG. 4.6, P. 95). The Celtic style was indeed the most popular one for decorative and applied art in Ireland by the early years of the twentieth century, and there were clearly many precedents for its use in the furnishings of the Honan Chapel.

There is, however, more to the fittings and furnishings of the Honan Chapel than mere devotion to Celtic ornamental forms for their own sake. After all, the architect and his patron could have placed an order with any number of ecclesiastical suppliers for windows, vestments and silverwork with a simple specification that the ornamental features be Irish or 'Celtic' in style. Rather than follow that well-established approach, however, they, or at least O'Connell, chose to make the chapel a celebration of the work of some of the finest artists, designers and craftworkers of the time in Ireland. Such exquisite craftsmanship as is found in their work is indicative of a third influence which is evident in the Honan Chapel, and that is the Arts and Crafts movement.[6]

The Arts and Crafts movement in Ireland was just one of a number of regional and national manifestations of a great revival of interest in handicrafts and the arts of design in the later part of the nineteenth and earlier part of the twentieth century. Internationally the movement was the most vital force in Western decorative art over that period and in Ireland, as elsewhere, its initial inspiration came from England where the movement originated. The term itself – 'arts and crafts' – was coined in 1888 at a meeting of a group of young members of the Royal Academy in London who had banded together to form an exhibition society. Their aim was to try to elevate the minor arts, which included wood-carving, embroidery, weaving, metalwork and stained glass, to the same status as painting and sculpture.

The great figurehead of the movement in England was William Morris, whose firm, founded in 1861, had been the pioneering venture in the whole business of gaining respectability for the crafts. It was under his influence that the Arts and Crafts Exhibition Society had been founded in London and very soon afterwards a number of other similar ventures started up. Their influence soon spread to America and to the rest of Europe. It also spread to Ireland where, in 1894, Lord Mayo founded the Arts and Crafts Society of Ireland. For at least thirty years the Society was to form a focus for countless men and women throughout Ireland, from enthusiastic amateurs and workers in rural art industries to fully trained professional artists and designers.

Internationally, the Arts and Crafts movement had developed essentially as a reaction to increasing industrialization and mechanization: hence the preoccupation of its leaders and advocates with things that were not only hand-made but preferably fashioned personally by the artist who had designed them (although that ideal was not always achieved). Sir John O'Connell was in accord with this 'arts and crafts' preoccupation with hand-craftsmanship and indeed in his book on the chapel praised the work of handicraftsmen over what he termed the 'machine-made church'.[7]

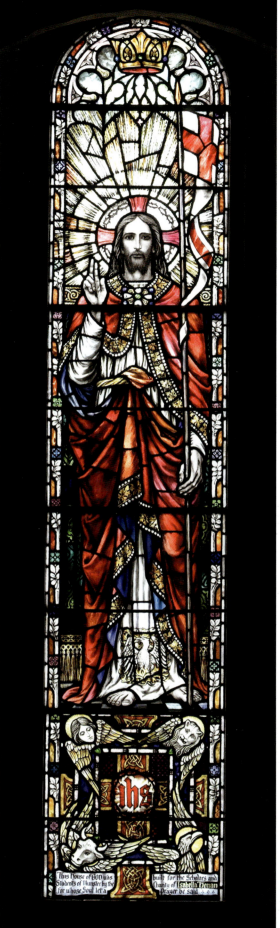

FIG. 4.7: Our Lord
window, Honan
Chapel, by Alfred Child

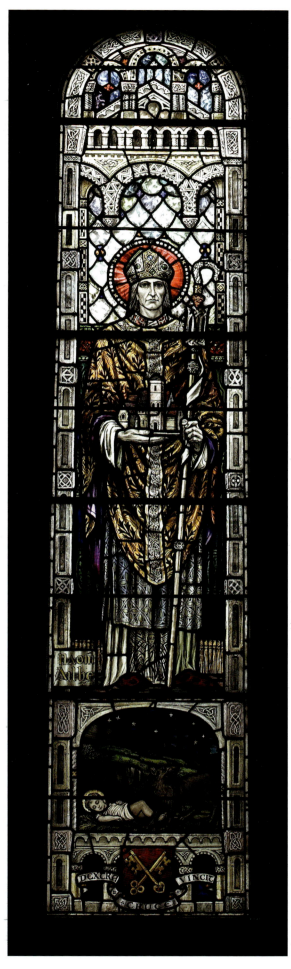

FIG. 4.8: St Ailbe
window, by Alfred Child

FIG. 4.9:
St Fachtna window,
by Alfred Child

FIG. 4.10: *St Colman*
window, by Alfred
Child

THE ARTISTIC AND CULTURAL CONTEXT

Among those whose help O'Connell enlisted when he decided to make the Honan Chapel a statement and demonstration of the best that Irish art could offer at the time were some of the leading figures in the Irish Arts and Crafts movement. There was Evelyn Gleeson, who had founded the Dún Emer Guild in 1902, a closely knit group of craftswomen skilled in embroidery and weaving, among other crafts; her firm was responsible for a number of textiles in the Honan Chapel. They had previously been involved in providing vestments and banners for Loughrea Cathedral in Co. Galway, the first important church commission of the time in which an influential patron had sought to improve the quality of church furnishings in Ireland. That patron was the wealthy Catholic landowner Edward Martyn, who had also played a part in the revival of Irish stained glass, helping persuade the well-known portrait painter Sarah Purser to set up a studio in Dublin in 1903, encouraged by the promise of a large commission for Loughrea Cathedral.

Sarah Purser was also enlisted by O'Connell, her firm, called An Túr Gloine (The Tower of Glass), being entrusted with eight of the windows at the Honan Chapel. The studio was managed for Purser by Alfred Child, who taught the craft of stained glass at the Metropolitan School of Art in Dublin. Child was responsible for the design of some of their eight windows, while others were by his studio assistants and former pupils in the School of Art, Catherine O'Brien and Ethel Rhind (FIGS. 4.7–4.15, PP. 97–102).

For the rest of the windows O'Connell turned to Harry Clarke, an emerging stained glass artist from Dublin who had been an outstanding student at the Metropolitan School of Art and was also a brilliant graphic artist and illustrator of books. Bringing in Clarke, when Sarah Purser's firm could easily have been entrusted with all of the windows, was an inspired move by O'Connell, as Clarke's personal contribution turned out to be the chief glory of the whole chapel (FIG. 4.13, P. 101).

Besides Alfred Child, two other teachers at the Dublin School of Art, also leading figures in the Irish Arts and Crafts movement, were also brought in. They were Oswald Reeves (SEE FIGS. 3.54–3.56 PP. 84–5; 3. P. 86) and Oliver Sheppard (SEE FIG. 2.5, P. 41). Reeves was a talented graphic artist and a master of enamelled metalwork, as well as being honorary secretary of the Arts and Crafts Society of Ireland and founder and first master of the Guild of Irish Art Workers; he provided the Honan Chapel with the enamelled tabernacle door and panel, later adjudged 'the finest thing of its kind in Ireland'. Sheppard was the leading sculptor in Ireland at the time, well known for his interest in Irish mythological themes; he provided the chapel with the Celtic-ornamented stone sculpture of St Finn Barr over the front entrance.

There was also William Scott, professor of architecture in the National University, not a craftsman as such but the leading 'arts and crafts' architect of the time in Ireland and an accomplished designer of Celtic Revivalist metalwork. Something of a discovery of Edward Martyn, he had previously supervised the interior furnishing and decoration of Loughrea Cathedral for which he provided a number of the designs himself. At the Honan Chapel he was responsible for designing a large wrought-iron grille for the main entrance doorway (SEE FIGS. 3.34, 3.35. P. 73)and large wrought-iron hinges for the doors themselves. (SEE FIG. 3.37, P. 74) He also designed the Sanctuary lamp and a set of altar plate.

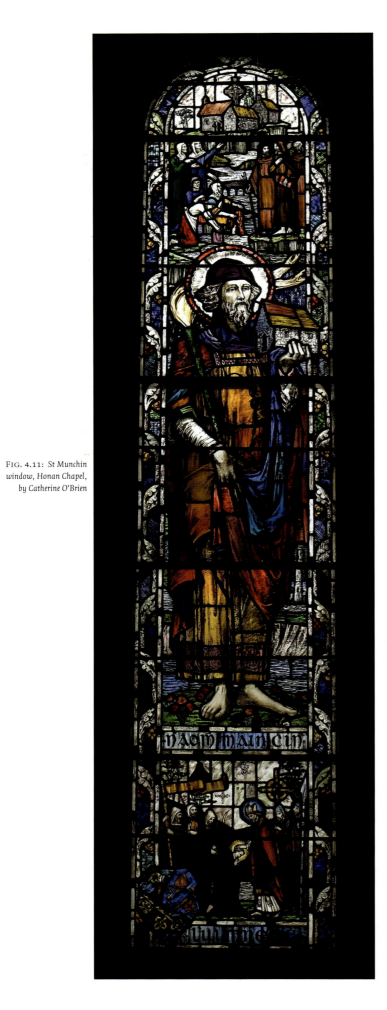

FIG. 4.11: St Munchin
window, Honan Chapel,
by Catherine O'Brien

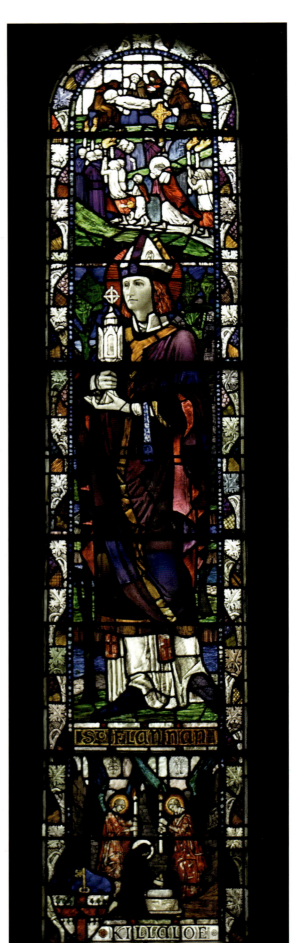

FIG. 4.12: St Flannan
window, Honan Chapel,
by Catherine O'Brien

THE ARTISTIC AND CULTURAL CONTEXT

FIG. 4.13:
*St Gobnait window
(detail), Honan
Chapel, by
Harry Clarke*

Normally the work of these artists and designers was only seen together at the periodic exhibitions organized by the Arts and Crafts Society of Ireland, shown for a short period and then dispersed. One important thing that Sir John O'Connell did in Cork was to provide a permanent showcase for the best of these artists, and so, apart from all else it represents, the Honan Chapel stands today as an unparalleled shrine to the Irish Arts and Crafts movement. Not only was O'Connell clearly influenced by the movement but, as if to underline his active contribu-

tion to it at the Honan Chapel, he was brought into the council of the Arts and Crafts Society by 1917 and became the chairman of the executive committee.

The various artistic and cultural influences on the Honan Chapel – the Irish Revival, the Celtic Art Revival and the Arts and Crafts movement – show that it was clearly not an isolated phenomenon but, far from diminishing its impact, the realization of its integral position in Irish art and life of the time gives extra value and meaning to its achievement.

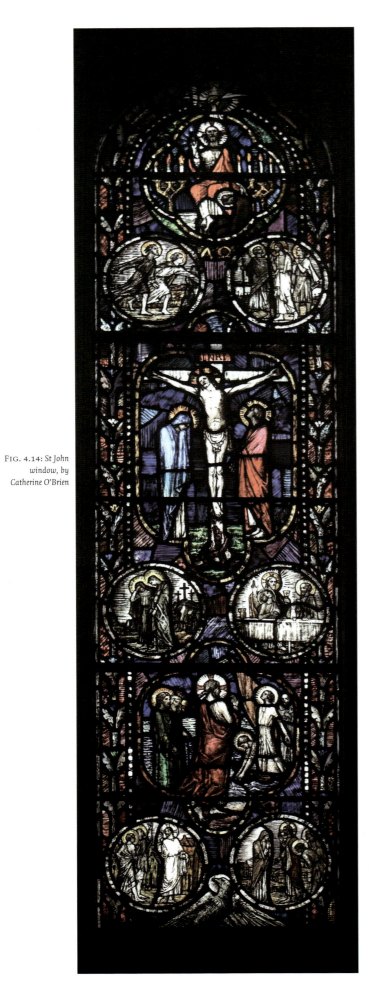

FIG. 4.14: *St John window, by Catherine O'Brien*

FIG. 4.15: *St Carthage window, by Ethel Rhind, An Túr Gloine*

Notes and References

1   Revd Sir John R. O'Connell, *The Collegiate Chapel, Cork*, 2nd edn (Cork University Press, 1932), p. 58.

2   See Paul Larmour, 'Irish Revival', in B. de Breffny (ed.), *Ireland: A Cultural Encyclopaedia* (London: Thames & Hudson, 1983), p. 117.

3   See P. Larmour, *Celtic Ornament, Irish Heritage Series: 33* (Dublin: Eason & Son Ltd, 1981);and P. Larmour, 'Celtic Revival', in de Breffny, op. cit., pp. 58–9.

4   See *Cork Industrial Exhibition 1883: Report of Executive Committee, Awards of Jurors, and Statement of Accounts* (Cork: Purcell & Co., 1886), pp. 263–4.

5   Illustrated in *The Irish Rosary*, vol. vi, no. 10, October 1902, p. 744.

6   See P. Larmour, *The Arts and Crafts Movement in Ireland* (Belfast: Friar's Bush Press,1992); and P. Larmour, 'Arts and Crafts Movement', in de Breffny, op. cit., p. 36.

7   O'Connell, op. cit., pp. 17–18.

Bibliography

Cork Industrial Exhibition 1883: Report of Executive Committee, Awards of Jurors, and Statement of Accounts (Cork: Purcell & Co., 1886)

O'Connell, Revd Sir John R., *The Collegiate Chapel, Cork*, 2nd edn (Cork University Press, 1932)

Larmour, Paul, *Celtic Ornament, Irish Heritage Series: 33* (Dublin: Eason & Son Ltd, 1981)

Larmour, Paul, 'Celtic Revival', in B. de Breffny (ed.), *Ireland: A Cultural Encyclopaedia* (London: Thames & Hudson, 1983), pp. 58–9

Larmour, Paul, 'Irish Revival', in B. de Breffny (ed.), *Ireland: A Cultural Encyclopaedia* (London: Thames & Hudson, 1983), p. 117

Larmour, Paul, 'Arts and Crafts Movement', in B. de Breffny (ed.), *Ireland: A Cultural Encyclopaedia* (London: Thames & Hudson, 1983), p. 36

Larmour, Paul, *The Arts and Crafts Movement in Ireland* (Belfast: Friar's Bush Press, 1992)

5

The Honan Chapel
An Iconographic Excursus[1]

The Honan Chapel is commonly, and rightly, considered to be one of the highlights of the so-called 'Celtic Revival' of early-twentieth-century Ireland, displaying as it does motifs both decorative and structural that are recognizably derivative of the art and architecture that flourished in Ireland and Britain between the seventh and twelfth centuries (e.g. O'Kelly 1955, p. 1; Rynne 1972, pp. 33–4; Sheehy 1980, pp. 163–4; Larmour 1992, p. 133; Teehan & Heckett 1995, p. viii; Teehan 1996, p. 13).

The four elements meeting to form a cross-shape as the central motif of a zoomorphic knotwork design featured in the floor mosaics at the west end of the chapel, for instance, is a detail found in manuscripts such as the late-seventh-century Lindisfarne Gospel Book (London, British Library, MS Cotton Nero D.IV, f. 26v: Alexander 1978a, fig. 38), the eighth-century Lichfield Gospels (Lichfield, Cathedral Library, Gospel Book, p. 220: Alexander 1978a, fig. 77) and, of course, the Book of Kells, dated to AD 800 (Dublin, Trinity

FIG. 5.1A: *Mosaic floor (aerial view), showing zoomorphic interlace flanking the sunburst, located at the west end of Honan Chapel*

FIG. 5.1B:
Book of Kells (detail)

College Library, MS 58, f. 114r: Meehan 1994; (SEE FIGS. 5.1A/B).

Likewise, the beast-head with the river flowing from its mouth featured in the floor mosaics at the west end of the central aisle recalls the decoration of artefacts as diverse as early Christian psalters where the beast-head formed part of the initial letter 'B' of *Beatus*, the opening word of the first psalm (e.g. the tenth-century *Harley Psalter*, London, British Library, MS Harley 2904, f. 4: Alexander 1978b, p. 15), and the twelfth-century Cross of Cong (FIG. 5.3B) that was reproduced as the altar cross of the Honan Chapel itself (SEE FIG. 3.39, P. 74). And of course, structurally, the design of the chapel incorporates the façade of the twelfth-century Romanesque chapel of St Cronan at

Roscrea, Co. Tipperary and the interior of Cormac's Chapel at Cashel, Co. Tipperary, with its repeated barrel vaulting and the use of chevroned pilasters and decorated cushion capitals in the blind arcading of the nave and chancel (FIGS. 5.2A/B; 5.4A/B, PP. 108–9).

A ROMANESQUE ICONOGRAPHY OF SPACE

It is not simply the motifs and structural features that are reminiscent of this earlier art and architecture, however. The manner in which they are employed in the chapel is also consistent with the design of earlier ecclesiastical buildings. Treatises of the twelfth and thirteenth centuries describe how churches of the time were

FIG. 5.2A: *Western façade of St Cronan's, Roscrea, Co. Tipperary*

AN ICONOGRAPHIC EXCURSUS

FIG. 5.3A: *River mouth floor mosaics at the west end of the central aisle, Honan Chapel*

FIG. 5.3B: *Cross of Cong (detail of beast head)*

FIG. 5.2B: *Western façade of the Honan Chapel*

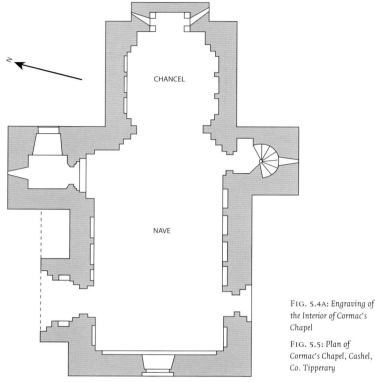

FIG. 5.4A: *Engraving of the Interior of Cormac's Chapel*

FIG. 5.5: *Plan of Cormac's Chapel, Cashel, Co. Tipperary*

intended, in their layout and the organization of their decoration, to situate the individual and the Church (as a structure, institution and Christian community) within the wider, universal context of the Divine and the created world through the image of the Crucifixion (e.g. Mâle 1949; Panofsky 1957; Duby 1981; Snyder 1989, pp. 255–401).[2]

Consideration of the design and decoration of Cormac's Chapel provides some insight into how these concerns could be expressed.[3] As in other churches of the period, the chancel, which was the ritual and symbolic focus of the building (being the site of the altar and thus the area occupied by the priest during the celebration of the sacraments), represented the head of Christ. The nave, the area occupied by the congregation, the 'Body of the Church', represented the body of Christ, and the transepts (at Cormac's Chapel formed by the twin towers at the crossing of the nave and chancel) were intended to represent the arms of Christ on the cross, outstretched to embrace all four corners of the world (north,

south, east and west). Such symbolic constructs explain why, in some cases, the chancel could be set at a slight angle to the nave (as is the case at Cormac's Chapel), in order to replicate the hanging head of Christ on the cross, and why a prominent feature could be set in the north side of the nave – to represent the wound made in Christ's side by Longinus the Spear-bearer. At Cormac's Chapel it is perhaps not accidental that an elaborate tomb is set in the exterior north wall of the nave in just this situation (FIG 5.5).

Within churches designed in this manner the decoration was intended to lead the individual entering the building on a metaphorical journey that would, at one level, lead the Christian from this life to the next. Thus, the entrance to the church, usually quite elaborate, was regarded as marking the transition between the two worlds; the body of the church (the nave) was the means by which the journey was made; and the east end, usually the most elaborate part of the church, symbolized heaven established on earth at the end of time. Even at Cashel, where most of

FIG. 5.4B: *Interior of Honan Chapel (looking east)*

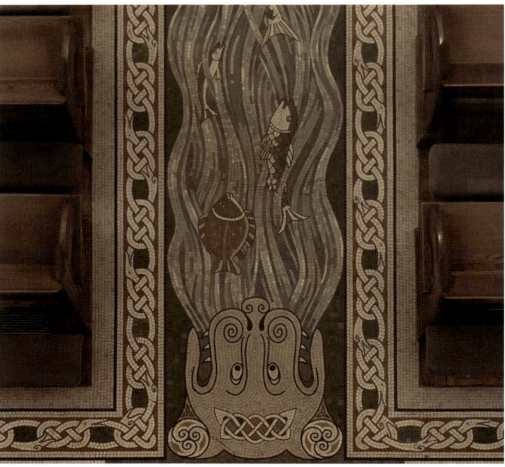

FIG. 5.6: Floor mosaic representing
the sunburst (detail), west end of
Honan Chapel

FIG. 5.7: Floor mosaic showing
beast head and start of river
(detail), centre aisle, Honan Chapel

the original applied decoration has disappeared, it is possible to see that the focus of the building was at the east end. Here, brightly coloured frescoes are still visible on the walls and roof of the chancel, while the windows are angled in such a way that the sunlight would have hit the altar from both sides (Crotty 1988; McGrath 1987; Perry 1995).

THE ICONOGRAPHIC SPACE OF THE HONAN CHAPEL: TRAVERSING THE FLOOR

Against such a background it is possible that the early Christian art and architecture of Ireland and Britain inspired not only the structural features and motifs used to decorate the Honan Chapel but also the manner in which that decoration was arranged. It may be that the mosaics, carvings, stained glass windows and furniture of the building were organized in order to exploit themes similar to those celebrated symbolically in the design of the earlier churches.

Indeed, on entering the Honan Chapel, the individual is led up the nave to the chancel at the east end by the mosaics covering the floor. These are arranged in four stages:

1 Those at the threshold of the west end, which illustrate a sunburst and stars surrounded by signs of the zodiac and flanked by zoomorphic interlace (FIG. 5.6).

2 Those in the central aisle of the nave, which form a river filled with fish flowing from the beast-head (FIG. 5.7).

FIG. 5.8: *Mosaics north side of sea-creature (aerial overview)*

FIG. 5.9: Floor
mosaics representing
sea-creature (detail),
east end of chapel nave

FIG. 5.10: Floor
mosaics north side of
sea-creature (detail)

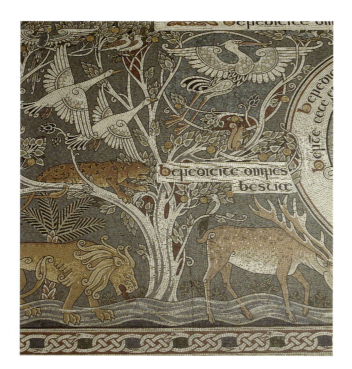

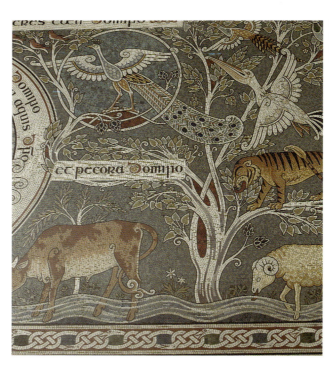

FIG. 5.11: Floor
mosaics on south
side of sea
creature (detail)

AN ICONOGRAPHIC EXCURSUS

3 Those at the east end of the nave at the chancel step, which feature a fantastical sea-creature flanked by a number of animals drinking from the river, and trees, filled with birds, growing from its waters (FIGS. 5.8, P. 111; 5.9–11; 5.14, P. 115).

4 Those set in the chancel before the altar, which illustrate the world surrounded by symbols of creation: the plants and animals of the earth, the planets of the heavens, and all the forces of nature (FIG. 5.15, P. 117).

Much has been written on the striking appearance of these mosaics and the manner in which they celebrate the created world in all its infinite variety (O'Connell 1932, pp. 34–6; O'Kelly

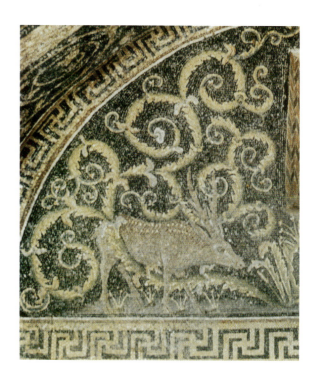

FIG. 5.12A: *Illustration showing floor mosaics, stags drinking from the River Life, Mausoleum of Galla Placidia, Ravenna, Italy, c. 425*

FIG. 5.12B: *Floor mosaics (detail of stag)*

1955, p. 7; Larmour 1992, pp. 133–4). Nevertheless, the Latin verses that accompany them demonstrate that the floor mosaics do more than simply illustrate or even celebrate such subjects. Rather, they point, quite literally, to the symbolic significance of the space to be traversed through the chapel, for they record passages from the Old Testament book of Daniel (3:56–7, 78–81): verses that mark the opening and closing of the Canticle of the Three Hebrews (the *Benedicite*), which was sung during the Office of Lauds on Sundays and Feast Days (see p. 126).[4] Furthermore, in this Office the Canticle was followed by the last three psalms of the psalter: Psalms 148–50. A verse from the first of these is preserved in the mosaics at the point where the western end of the nave meets the central aisle. Together these passages give a clear indication that the decoration of the chapel, and the manner in which it has been organized, can be understood within the framework of the celebration of Lauds.

In the early Christian Church this Office was celebrated at cock-crow so that it ended just before the break of day. In theological terms it was understood to stress that the first gleam of dawn should bring to the mind of the faithful Christian the notion that it was at dawn that Christ rose from the dead, conquering night and death. It thus celebrates the coming day, the Resurrection of Christ and the spiritual light that he made to shine on earth (Cabrol 1910). Historically, the Office of Lauds is deemed to be one of the most ancient of the

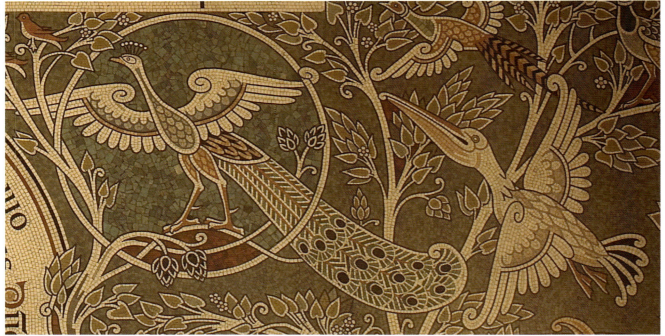

FIG. 5.13:
*Floor mosaics
(details of
pelican and
peacock)*

FIG. 5.14: *Aerial
overview of floor mosaics
at the east end of the nave*

Divine Offices and some of the earliest documentary evidence for its celebration in the form it was to take in the Western Church is found in an Irish manuscript of the seventh century: the *Antiphonary of Bangor* (Milan, Biblioteca Ambrosiano, MS C.5.inf.). In the order of the Office set out in this manuscript, the *Benedicite* is followed by the three psalms (148–150), then by a Gospel reading of the Resurrection, a hymn celebrating the Resurrection, and finally, by a hymn to the martyrs of the Church (Warren 1893; cf. Curran 1984).

THE THRESHOLD

Turning to the pictorial decoration of the floor of the chapel, it is not hard to see how the mosaics of the nave celebrate the notions of light and life that are integral to the themes of Lauds and lead the onlooker to an understanding of the Resurrection. At the threshold, the sun functions as more than a vague hint at such notions, dispelling as it does, in size and brilliance, the stars of night that flicker between its beams. In this setting the signs of the zodiac surrounding the central motif of the sun function iconographically to signify Christ's dominion over time, as they do in Christian art of the early twelfth century: while the moon wanes and the seasons change, the sun continues to shine forth.[5]

THE NAVE

The next stage of mosaic decoration begins with the beast head from which the river flows up the length of the nave. It may not be irrelevant to note here that this head incorporates a series of tripartite motifs: three spirals, trefoil knots and a band of interlace that forms three saltire crosses (FIGS. 5.3A,

P. 107; 5.7, P. 110). While such apparently Christological and Trinitarian references may be coincidental, they would not be out of place in the art of early Christian (Insular) manuscripts, such as the seventh-century *Book of Durrow* (Dublin, Trinity College Library MS 57, ff. 85v, 124v: Meehan 1996, figs. on pp. 48, 58; cf. Hawkes 1997). Certainly the river flowing from this beast head is one filled with life: its waters teem with fish (FIG. 5.7, P. 110). This aspect, perhaps accentuated by the potential Christological and Trinitarian symbols, indicates that this is a 'river of life' which in medieval iconographic terms incorporates both the rivers of Paradise (which are the rivers of eternal life) and the Christian community receiving sustenance from the Church, the institution that, through its sacraments, provides the means of achieving everlasting life.

FIG. 5.15: *Floor mosaics in the Chancel (overview)*

THE EAST END OF THE NAVE

By traversing these waters the individual approaches that area of the chapel which marks the transition between the nave and the chancel: the area that is filled with trees, animals and birds surrounding the fantastic beast floating on the waves of the river. The presence of this creature (FIG. 5.9, P. 112) has been anticipated by the verse of Psalm 148 at the west end of the chapel that invokes the praise of 'dragons and all the depths' (*dracones et omnes abyssi*); it is confirmed by the inscription accompanying the beast itself that invokes the blessing of 'whales and all that move in the waters' (*cete et omnia quae moventur in aquis*). Visually it is a creature that combines both dragon and whale.

In biblical literature and medieval exegesis such a creature functions as a very potent image

benedicite omnia opera domini domino laudate et superexaltate eum in saecula

of death. In part this was due to the story of Jonah, swallowed and regurgitated by a whale, which in art was represented as a fantastical sea-beast (e.g. an early fifth-century sarcophagus in the Lateran Museum, Rome: Grabar 1961. Even in the bible this event was understood to fore-shadow the Resurrection. Christ himself is cred-ited with invoking Jonah to explain his own forthcoming death and resurrection (Matthew 12:38–45; Luke 11:29–32): as Jonah was cast up by the whale after three days, so Christ rose from the dead after three days, during which he de-scended into hell.[6] With such associations the sea-creature in the floor mosaics of the Honan Chapel, which is both whale and dragon, can be understood to represent death overcome by the Resurrection and life everlasting: the icono-graphic significance of the creatures and flower-ing trees that flank and surround it.

The trees growing from the waters of the river are a common image in Christian art of the Tree of Life that both grows in Paradise and is Christ (FIGS. 5.10, 5.11, P. 112; 5.14, P. 115). By extension, the creatures sheltering in the branches of such a tree can be understood to represent the Christian community sustained by Christ and sheltered by the Church founded on him (Greenhill 1954, pp. 338–49). It is not only these notions, however, that are figured by the mosaics at this point. The linking of Paradise, Christ, the Church and Christian community with the waters of the river also invokes the re-lated themes of baptism and resurrection, in that the ritual of baptism was understood to mir-ror the events of death and rebirth: by descend-ing into and emerging from the waters of bap-tism, the catechumen symbolically leaves be-hind the sins of the world to be reborn into the life of the Church (Underwood 1950).

Such associations are indicated in the selec-tion of animals and birds illustrated. The stag drinking from the water at the foot of the tree, for instance (FIG.5.12A, P. 113), is an image with a long history in Christian art, appearing as early as the fifth century in the mosaics of the 'Mausoleum' of Galla Placidia in Ravenna (Grabar 1966, fig. 25; cf. Underwood 1950; FIG. 5.12B, P. 113). In such contexts, it was under-stood to symbolize the faithful Christian over-coming the snares of the devil after baptism by continuing to receive spiritual sustenance from the words of Christ and the sacraments of the Church. Likewise, the lion, also shown drinking from the waters of the river in the floor mosaics (FIG. 5.10, P. 112), functioned in Christian art as a symbol of the resurrection because, according to medieval animal lore, the female of the species was believed to suffocate her young at birth, but discovering her mistake after three days, was able to breathe life back into them (Charbonneau-Lassay 1992, pp. 10–11; Hicks 1993, p. 108).

The pelican, featured in the branches of the tree on the south side of the nave floor (FIG. 5.13, P. 114), had a similar symbolic val-ue. Following the death of his young after an at-tack on the nest by a serpent, the father was be-lieved to resuscitate his young with his own blood, produced by piercing his breast with his beak, a demonstration of grief that resulted in his death (Curley 1979, p. 9; Charbonneau-Lassay 1992, pp. 258-66). In Christian art the pelican was thus a common image symbolizing Christ sustaining the faithful Christian with his life-giving blood. The peacock, also featured in the branches of the tree on the south side (FIG. 5.13, P. 114), was a similarly well-established symbol. This creature, it was believed, had flesh that did not decay: three days after death and burial it could be exhumed and its flesh eaten with impunity. Thus, from an early date (e.g. the fourth-century doors of Santa Sabina, Rome: Volbach 1961, fig. 102) the image of this bird

FIG. 5.16: *Interior views of the chancel and Sanctuary, Honan Chapel*

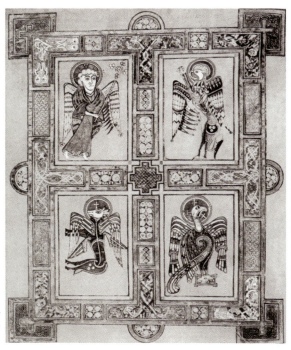

FIG. 5.17: *The Book of Kells, four Evangelist symbols, vol. 27*

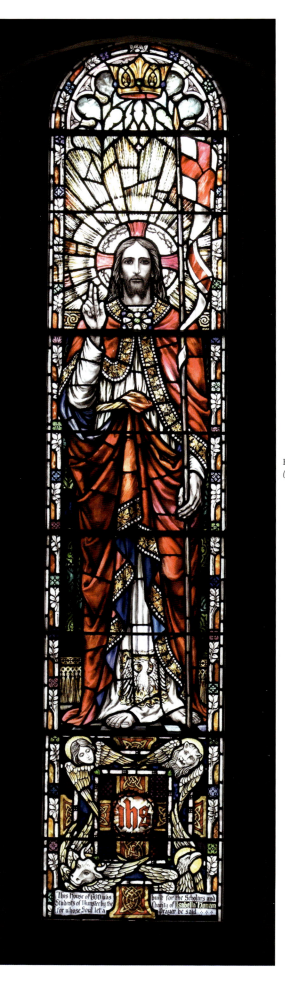

FIG. 5.18: *East window (Christ in Majesty)*

was used in Christian art to symbolize the sacrament of the Eucharist and the everlasting life available through the bread – the body of Christ (Underwood 1950, n. 186; Hawkes forthcoming).

By incorporating such well-established iconographic reference points, the floor mosaics at the east end of the nave provide a concerted presentation of life and resurrection into eternal life through repeated allusions to Christ, the sacraments of his Church, and the general resurrection at the end of time when, it was understood, heaven would be re-established on earth.[7]

THE CHANCEL

It is in the chancel itself that this eventuality is pictured in the mosaics, almost understated in their restrained presentation of a perfectly created world. Here, the mountains, rivers, trees and animals of the central medallion present a world that is both the paradise of the *Book of Genesis* and the eternal paradise that will be restored at the end of time. Around this world

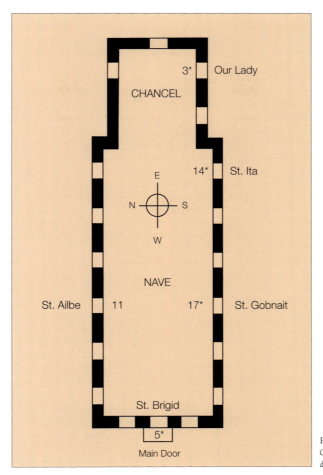

FIG. 5.19: *Plan of Honan Chapel showing the windows dedicated to female saints*

are images of the seasons, the elements, the forces of nature and, on the horizontal axis, two of the most potent symbols of resurrection already illustrated at the foot of the chancel steps: the lion and the peacock. Overall, the chancel mosaics summarize all the subjects (of life, death and resurrection as figured in heaven and earth) that have preceded them in the nave and, moreover, they present these subjects within the cycle of Christian history that begins with the earthly paradise of creation and ends with the heavenly paradise re-established at the end of time (FIG. 5.15, P. 117).

VIEWING THE SACRED SPACE

Having traversed the length of the chapel, with each step of the metaphorical journey having been laid out in the inscriptions and pictorial decoration of the floor, the individual is finally confronted by the setting of the chancel mosaics, and it is here that their comparative restraint becomes most apparent. For not only are the subdued colours and geometric presentation of the chancel mosaics in direct contrast to the overflowing abundance of the trees and animal life at the east end of the nave, they also lie in a setting in which the decoration of all media functions as an elaborate and brightly coloured iconographic statement of Christ Resurrected: Christ as he will appear at the end of time (FIG. 5.16, P. 119).

The east window, for instance, features Christ clothed in the red and white of majesty looking out over and commanding the entire space of the chapel (FIG. 5.17). This is not a representation of Christ Crucified, or Christ Incarnate, a subject often illustrated in the east window,[8] but rather, Christ as he will appear at the time of the Second Coming when he returns to rule in eternity.

On the bright red hanging below this window (the dossal), which acts as the backdrop to the altar, are the brilliantly coloured figures of four winged creatures inspired by the

Book of Kells (SEE FIGS. 6.27, P. 150; 5.18). In Christian art these creatures commonly symbolized the writers of the four Gospels, but they were also the four beasts of the Apocalypse that in the Book of Revelation are described as circling the throne of heaven (Revelation 4:8). As such they refer both to the unified message of salvation preserved in the Gospels and to the point of that message: the Second Coming of Christ that is the time of the general resurrection.

Set midway between these symbols, on the altar itself, is the tabernacle, on which is depicted, in glowing enamels, both the Trinity (in the form of the Father, Son and Holy Spirit) and the *Agnus Dei*, the Lamb of God (see Lamb, pp. 84–6 in this volume; (FIGS. 3.54, 3.55, 3.56). This creature represents both the sacrificial Lamb of the Crucifixion set on his altar with the chalice and flanked by angels carrying the tools of the Passion, and the Lamb of the Resurrection, enthroned and flanked by the angelic attendants of the heavenly throne.

Lastly, embroidered on the gold-coloured altar frontal is the image of Christ enthroned in Majesty, surrounded by a halo of glory and flanked by the saints of the early Irish Church: Ita, Columcille, Patrick, Brigid, Fin barr and Colman (SEE FIGS. 6.23–6.26, PP. 149–50). Together, these four sets of images that fill the east end of the chapel form a systematic and sustained presentation and celebration of Christ Resurrected and ruling in majesty throughout eternity. Recognizing this, it becomes clear that the chapel through which the individual has journeyed has, in fact, been (symbolically) surveyed by Christ the King, not only from the east window, but also from the altar in all his multiple representations. From this perspective, the journey made by the individual through time and space has

occurred in the presence of, and watched over by, the Divine.

It has, moreover, been undertaken in the company of the saints that flank the body of the church in the windows: twelve of them in the north and south windows of the nave. Indeed, it would seem that, watched over by Christ and his saints, the individual making the journey through the chapel has been (iconographically) subsumed into that august body of martyrs celebrated at the close of the Office of Lauds in the *Antiphonary of Bangor* (Warren 1893, ff. 12v–13r; Curran 1984, pp. 184–9). In this hymn God is exalted as the king of heaven, a remote figure clothed in glory (stanzas 2, 8 and 9) and surrounded by a choir of saints for whom his death, resurrection and ascension into eternal life are a triumph which has strengthened them in their faith, enabling them to obtain their crowns of immortality and reign with him in heaven (stanza 7: Curran 1984, p. 79). It is a panegyric that provides a very fitting summary of the setting in which the iconographic journey through the chapel has been made.

THE ANTIQUARIAN CONTEXT

This, at least, is one way of reading the decoration of the Honan Chapel. But it is perhaps worth examining the extent to which this hypothetical iconographic excursus might have been relevant in the context of an early-twentieth-century Celtic Revival ecclesiastical structure. It is, perhaps, worth turning to consider the extent to which such a programme might have been intended by those responsible for the design of the Honan Chapel.

Certainly O'Connell's official history of the Honan Chapel (see Chapter 1) makes it clear that he had read the works of the nineteenth-century antiquarians whose

FIGS. 5.20: *Details of the floor mosaics at the east end of the nave (aerial overview)*

studies have formed the basis of all subsequent scholarship on the art, material and literary cultures of the early Christian Church in Ireland and Britain. One of these was Margaret Stokes's book on *Early Christian Art in Ireland* (published in 1887; cf. Stokes 1878). In discussing the decorative and structural sources for the chapel (St Cronan's at Roscrea, and Cormac's Chapel at Cashel), O'Connell not only refers to the buildings and artefacts identified by Stokes as those which she and her contemporaries deemed to be definitive of the material culture of early Christian Ireland (Sheehy 1980), he also reproduces a number of her illustrations: namely, those of Cormac's Chapel.[9] Stokes's book (a second-hand copy of which was received by the College library in November 1914 when the Honan Chapel was in its early stages of construction) clearly played an important part in the design of the building.

It did not simply function as a source of inspiration for the specific features selected to construct and decorate the chapel, however. It also provided information about the iconographic significance of these features. In discussing the art of early Christian Ireland, Stokes makes it clear that not only could that art be understood to have had a symbolic value, she also describes how certain literary works were fundamental to understanding that symbolism. Among these she lists *The Bestiary*, that medieval source of animal lore, which she cites with the example of the lion as a symbol of the Resurrection. She goes on to say that in the early Christian art of Ireland:

a system of such symbols was developed, expressive of the salient points in religion. [These] came into use, not necessarily for doctrinal purposes, but as expressive of religious faith. By adhering to the plan laid down in such works . . . the walls and cupolas as well as pavements of the churches were intended to picture forth the Divine plan for man's salvation, to be the mirror of God's work in Creation (Stokes 1887, p. 127).

FIGS. 5.20A, : *Details of the floor mosaics at the east end of the nave (aerial overview)*

Such a statement could well describe the iconographic significance of the Honan Chapel. It certainly illustrates the nature of the scholarship that is likely to have informed those responsible for its design.

As is evident in Stokes's work, this was a scholarship that embraced the visual and the iconographic, but it also involved the liturgical. The *Antiphonary of Bangor*, that early Irish manuscript that preserves one of the earliest articulations of the *Benedicite* and the Office of Lauds with its closing hymn to the martyrs of heaven, was published in 1893 and a facsimile of it was acquired by the College library in October 1915. It is perhaps not irrelevant to note here that, in addition to any influence the closing hymn may have had on the overall setting of the chapel, the verse of the *Benedicite* in the *Antiphonary* that corresponds to the sentence set round the sea-creature at the east end of the nave, does not refer specifically to 'whales' (*cete*) as the mosaics do. Given the way in which the other creatures figured in the floor mosaics are all portrayed in

an apparently accurate manner, the zoologically inaccurate nature of the so-called 'whale' is rather startling, particularly as it is accompanied by the identifying inscription. However, in the *Antiphonary*, the word used to refer to the sea-creature is *belvae*, a Latin term denoting a specifically monstrous beast – the very thing that is depicted by the mosaics (Warren 1906, f. 9v, lines 3–4; see p. 126).

Another text that would have been familiar to the patrons of the Honan Chapel and may have played a part in its iconographic design is the Old Irish treatise on the Mass preserved in the eighth-century *Stowe Missal* (Dublin, Royal Irish Academy, MS D.II.3). This manuscript was transcribed by Charles O'Conor in the early nineteenth century and subsequently translated by Margaret Stokes's brother, the philologist Whitley Stokes, in 1903 after its return to Ireland in 1883 (Warren 1915, p. ix). The relevance of this particular treatise lies in its observation that the priest, facing the altar with his back to the congregation for the celebration of

AN ICONOGRAPHIC EXCURSUS

mass (as was still the case in the rituals of the early twentieth century), represents Longinus in relation to Christ on the cross. For, it says, 'westwards was Christ's face on the cross . . . and eastwards was the face of Longinus; what to him was the left, to Christ was the right' (Warren 1915, p. 41; p. 38 for Old Irish version in Warren 1906, f. 66).

Apart from the fact that this is the point of view of Christ figured at the east end of the Honan Chapel, the relevance of this text lies in its potential to explain the almost unique disposition of the saints in the chapel windows which set the female saints, except St. Brigid, along the south side of the building (FIG. 5.19, P. 121). Elsewhere, where images of women are systematically arranged in relation to one side

of a church, it is always the north side – the left, sinister side (from the point of view of the priest facing east). In the Honan Chapel, however, the female saints stand uniquely on the left from Christ's point of view, facing west. Such an unusual arrangement is perhaps best understood in the light of a text like that of the Old Irish treatise on the Mass preserved in the *Stowe Missal*, which clearly articulates the symbolic value of Christ's perspective, facing west on the cross which is, after all, the symbolic space of the church itself.[10]

CONCLUSION

Overall, it does seem probable that those responsible for the design of the Honan Chapel

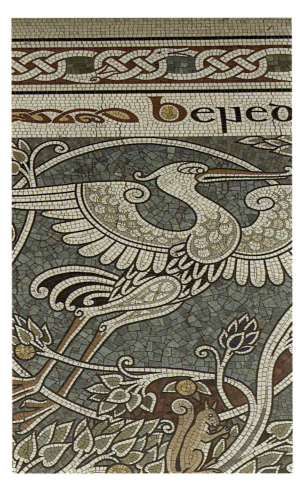

FIGS. 5.20B, 5.20C:
Details of the floor mosaics at the east end of the nave (aerial overview)

were as learned in their understanding of early Christian spirituality and its iconographic expression as their early medieval counterparts. The details of the decoration were selected not simply to recall motifs deemed typical of what was understood to be the 'Celtic Church', they were also selected with an overall iconographic programme in mind. It was a programme that articulated, in a complex, multivalent and integrated fashion, the position of the individual and 'the Church' within the wider, universal context of the Divine and, in the words of Margaret Stokes, 'his plan for man's salvation'. It is an iconography that would have been relevant in the early Christian world, and one that was not irrelevant to the Church of the early twentieth century in Cork. Where Finbarr taught, learning was indeed well established.

Appendix

THE FLOOR MOSAIC INSCRIPTIONS

Each inscription is transcribed in the Latin, followed by an English translation taken from the Douay Bible, with references to the relevant biblical passages and corresponding sections in the *Antiphonary of Bangor* (AB: Warren 1893).

THRESHOLD
Inscription round sunburst:
BENEDICTUS ES DOMINE IN FIRMAMENTO COELI / ET LAUDABILIS ET GLORIOSUS ET SUPEREXALTATUS IN SAECULA
Blessed is the Lord in the firmament of heaven/ and above all to be praised and glorified for ever (Daniel 3:56; AB f. 8v, line 16).

Inscription by river mouth:
LAUDATE DOMINUM DE TERRA / DRACONES ET OMNES ABYSSI
Praise the Lord from the earth / ye dragons and all ye depths (Psalm 148:7; AB f. 9r, line 14).

EAST END OF THE NAVE
Outer inscription round sea-creature:
BENEDICITE MARIA ET FLUMINA DOMINO
Bless the Lord all ye seas and rivers (Daniel 3:78; AB f. 9v, line 1).

Inner inscription round sea-creature:
BEN[EDICI]TE CETE ET OMNIA QUAE MOVENTUR IN AQUIS D[OMI]NO
Bless the Lord ye whales and all that move in the waters (Daniel 3:79a; AB f. 9v, line 3–4, where 'belvae' is used instead of 'cete').

Inscription at chancel step:
BENEDICITE OMNES / VOLUCRES COELI DOMINO
Bless the Lord all ye fowls of the air (Daniel 3:80a; AB f. 9v, line 5).

Inscription flanking sea-creature:
BENEDICITE OMNES BESTIAE / ET PECORA DOMINO
Bless the Lord all ye beasts and cattle (Daniel 3:81; AB f. 9v, line 6)

CHANCEL
Inscription round central medallion:
BENEDICITE OMNIA OPERA DOMINI DOMINO / LAUDATE ET SUPEREXALTATE EUM IN SECULA
Bless the Lord all ye works of the Lord / Praise and exalt him above all for ever (Daniel 3:57; AB f. 8v, line 14).

Notes and References

1   The author would like to thank Nyree Finlay and Éamonn Ó Carragáin for their advice and encouragement during the preparation of this paper.

2   For treatises, see e.g. Abbot Suger (1081–1151), *Sugerii Abbatis Sancti Dionysii Liber: De Rebus in Administratione sua Gestis* (Panofsky-Soergel 1979) and William Durandus, *Rationale Divinorum Officiorum*, 1286 (Webb 1906). Stokes (1900, p. 271), whose work was known by those responsible for the design of the Honan Chapel cites Durandus in her discussion of the symbolic value of early Christian art in Ireland.

3   This foundation, with its royal patronage and cruciform shape, could well have been intended (in the context of prestigious twelfth-century churches) to reflect the ideas expressed in treatises of the time. For general discussions of the history and archaeology of Cormac's Chapel, see e.g. De Paor 1967; Stalley 1981; Hodkinson 1994; O'Keeffe 1994.

4   It should be noted that all the creatures and elements featured in the floor mosaics (although lacking specific identifying inscriptions) are also referred to in the Canticle. At the west end of the chapel are the heavens and waters (v. 60) and the sun and stars (vv. 62–3). At the east end of the nave are the beasts and cattle (v. 81) and the fowls of the air (v. 80). In the chancel are the showers (v. 64), fire and heat (v. 66), cold, frost and ice (vv. 67–70), night and day, and light and dark (vv. 71–2), lightening and clouds (v. 70), the earth, mountains and hills (vv. 74–5), all plants (v. 76) and seas and rivers (v. 78). O'Connell (1932, p. 34) notes that the inscriptions were inspired not simply by the verses of Daniel 3 but also by an 'old Gaelic poem' (cf. Larmour 1992, p. 134). The mosaic verses are, nevertheless, in Latin rather than Old Irish, and O'Connell himself (1932, p. 35) cites the verses of the Canticle when describing the details of the floor decoration (cf. O'Kelly 1955, p. 7). Although he does not identify the 'old Gaelic poem', he may have had in mind the 'Litany of Creation' (Plummer 1924, pp. 102–7), a poem modelled on other Old Irish litanies, which is distinguished by having all its petitions based on appeals to natural objects (Plummer 1924, pp. xxiii–xxiv). It is preserved in a sixteenth-century manuscript (Dublin, Royal Irish Academy, MS 23.N.10, p. 92) in the collection of the early nineteenth-century antiquarian Sir William Betham, who was a central figure in the construction of a perceived early medieval Irish 'Celtic' culture and civilization through his publications on Irish Antiquarian Researches (1826–7).

5   Signs of the zodiac are a common feature of the entrances of Romanesque churches (e.g. Vézelay, France, 1120–32: Snyder 1989, fig. 352) and they occur in medieval Irish manuscripts (Stokes 1900, p. 275). Furthermore, at the time the Honan Chapel was built it was believed that the signs of the zodiac were

included in the decoration of the so-called 'Cross of Muiredach' at Monasterboice, Co. Louth (Stokes 1900, pp. 278–83.

6   The depiction of the whale as a fantastical creature in early Christian images of Jonah is the result of this Christ–Jonah association and the concomitant association of the whale with Leviathan (Job 41:1; cf. Psalms 74:14; 104:26 and Isaiah 27:1), which in both biblical and exegetical texts was regarded as a figure of death overcome by Christ.

7   For discussion of the Christian significance of the other creatures featured in the branches of the trees and drinking from the river in the floor mosaics, see particularly Curley 1979 and Charbonneau-Lassay 1992.

8   For examples of Christ Incarnate figured in the east window see St Alphonsus (RC), Barntown, Co. Wexford (designed by A.W.N. Pugin in 1848); the parish church (CoI) at Crosshaven, Co. Cork (designed by William Burges in the 1860s); Castletownshend (CoI), Co. Cork (where the east window was designed by Harry Clarke in 1918).

9   Compare O'Connell, 1932, figs. facing pp. 23 and 27 with Stokes 1887, figs. 101–2. Stokes's work also demonstrates how the art of seventh- to ninth-century Ireland and Britain came to be associated in the minds of the late-nineteenth-and early-twentieth-century Celtic Revivalists (such as O'Connell) with the architecture and stone-carving of twelfth-century Hiberno-Romanesque structures: 'As regards England, it is true that the architecture of the Norman style of the eleventh and twelfth centuries . . . was of foreign origin [but], in Ireland the decoration of the Romanesque doorway of the twelfth century is but a repetition in stone of the illuminated pages of the scribe of the seventh century who, in his turn, repeats the graceful and varied designs of the pre-Christian worker in bronze and gold [relics of the late Celtic period].' (Stokes 1878, pp. 4–5; cf. p. 11. See above, notes 2, 5).

10 The tendency to set the saints of the early Irish Church in the windows of the nave of Roman Catholic churches seems to have developed in Ireland during the course of the medieval revival of the nineteenth century. A.W.N. Pugin's cathedral at Killarney (begun in the 1830s and finished in the 1870s) provides one example, while that of his son, E.W. Pugin, at Cobh, Co. Cork (begun in 1868), where the saints are set in the clerestory windows of the nave, provides another. (Church of Ireland medieval revival buildings of the same period, while sometimes including early Irish saints in the nave windows, do not do so systematically in such a way as to translate the nave visually, in symbolic form, into the 'Body of the Church' peopled by the (Irish) saints of heaven. The church at Castletownshend, for instance, sets St George and the Virtues, Faith and Charity, alongside St Patrick.) More comparable with the Honan Chapel is the oratory at Gougane Barra, Co. Cork (c. 1902) where the windows display only the early Irish saints in the nave of the building (Gobnet, Colman,

Eitin, Ita, Fachnan, Brendan); St Fin Barr and the Virgin Mary (as patron of the Church in Ireland) are figured in the lights of the east window. Here, in stark contrast to the Honan Chapel, the two female saints (Ita and Gobnet) are set in the north and south sides of the nave while the Virgin is set in the north light of the east window.

BIBLIOGRAPHY

ALEXANDER, J.J.G., *Insular Manuscripts 6th to the 9th Century* (London: Harvey Miller, 1978a)

CABROL, F., 'Lauds', *The Catholic Encyclopaedia*, vol. 9 (London: Encyclopaedia Press, 1910)

CHARBONNEAU-LASSAY, L., *The Bestiary of Christ*, translated by D. M. Dooling (New York: Arkana Books, 1992)

CROTTY, G., 'A Romanesque Fresco in Cormac's Chapel', *Tipperary Historical Journal*, 1988, pp. 155–8

CURLEY, M.J. (trans.), *Physiologus* (Austin: University of Texas Press, 1979)

CURRAN, M., *The Antiphonary of Bangor and the Early Irish Monastic Liturgy* (Dublin: Irish Academic Press, 1984)

DE PAOR, L., 'Cormac's Chapel: The Beginnings of the Irish Romanesque', in E. Rynne (ed.), *North Munster Studies* (Limerick: Thomond Archaeological Society, 1967)

DUBY, G., *The Age of Cathedrals: Art and Society 980–1420* (Chicago University Press, 1981)

GRABAR, A., *Christian Iconography: A Study of Its Origins* (Princeton University Press, 1961)

GRABAR, A., *L'Âge d'or de Justinien* (Paris: Librairie Gallimard, 1966)

GREENHILL, E.S., 'The Child in the Tree: A Study of the Cosmological Tree in Christian Tradition', *Traditio*, vol. 10, 1954, pp. 323–71

HAWKES, J., 'Symbolic Lives: The Visual Evidence', in J. Hines (ed.), *The Anglo-Saxons From the Migration Period to the Eighth Century: An Ethnographic Perspective* (Woodbridge, Suffolk: The Boydell Press, 1997)

HAWKES, J., 'Church and Sculpture in Anglo-Saxon England: The Case of the Masham Column', in H. Gittos (ed.), *Ritual and Belief: The Rites of the Anglo-Saxon Church* (London: Henry Bradshaw Society, forthcoming)

HICKS, C., *Animals in Early Medieval Art* (Edinburgh University Press, 1993)

HODKINSON, B., 'Excavations at Cormac's Chapel, Cashel, 1992 and 1993: A Preliminary Statement', *Tipperary Historical Journal*, 1994, pp. 167–74

LARMOUR, P., *The Arts and Crafts Movement in Ireland* (Belfast: Friar's Bush Press, 1992)

MÂLE, E., *Religious Art from the Twelfth to the Eighteenth Century* (Princeton University Press, 1949)

MCGRATH, M., 'The Materials and Techniques of Irish Medieval Wall Paintings',
    Journal of the Royal Society of Antiquaries of Ireland, vol. 117, 1987, pp. 96–124

MEEHAN, B., *The Book of Kells* (London: Thames & Hudson, 1994)

MEEHAN, B., *The Book of Durrow: A Medieval Masterpiece at Trinity College Dublin*
    (Dublin: Town House, 1996)

O'CONNELL, J. R., *The Collegiate Chapel, Cork: Some notes on the building and on the ideals
    which inspired it*, 2nd edn (Cork University Press, 1932)

O'KEEFFE, T., 'Lismore and Cashel: Reflections on the Beginning of Romanesque
    Architecture in Munster', *Journal of the Royal Society of Antiquaries of Ireland*, vol. 124,
    1994, pp. 118–52

O'KELLY, M. J., *The Collegiate Chapel, Cork*, 2nd edn (Cork University Press, 1955)

PANOFSKY, E., *Gothic Architecture and Scholasticism* (New York: Meridian Books, 1957)

PANOFSKY-SOERGEL, G. (ed.), *Abbot Suger on the Abbey Church of St Denis and Its Art
    Treasures*, 2nd edn (Princeton University Press, 1979)

PERRY, M., 'The Romanesque Frescoes in Cormac's Chapel, Cashel', *Ireland of the
    Welcomes*, vol. 44.2, 1995, pp. 17–19

PLUMMER, C. (ed.), *Irish Litanies* (London: Henry Bradshaw Society, 1924)

RYNNE, E., 'The Revival of Irish Art in the late 19th and early 20th Century',
    Topic: A Journal of the Liberal Arts, vol. 24, 1972, pp. 29–36

SHEEHY, J., *The Rediscovery of Ireland's Past: The Celtic Revival 1830–1930*
    (London: Thames & Hudson, 1980)

SNYDER, J., *Medieval Art: Paintings, Sculpture, Architecture, 4th–14th Century*
    (New York: Harry N. Abrams Inc., 1989)

STALLEY, R., 'Three Irish Churches with West Country Origins', *Medieval Art and
    Architecture at Wells and Glastonbury* (London: British Archaeological
    Association, 1981)

STOKES, M., *Early Christian Architecture in Ireland* (London: Chapman & Hall, 1878)

STOKES, M., *Early Christian Art in Ireland* (London: Chapman & Hall, 1887)

STOKES, M., 'Christian Iconography in Ireland', *The Archaeological Journal*, vol. 57,
    1900, pp. 270–86

UNDERWOOD, P.A., 'The Fountain of Life in Manuscripts of the Gospels',
    Dumbarton Oaks Papers, vol. 5, 1950, pp. 41–138

VOLBACH, W.F., *Early Christian Art* (London: Thames & Hudson, 1961)

WARREN, F.E., *The Antiphonary of Bangor* (London: The Henry Bradshaw Society, 1893)

WARREN, F.E., *The Stowe Missal*, vol. 1: Facsimile
    (London: Henry Bradshaw Society, 1906)

WARREN, F.E., *The Stowe Missal*, vol. 2: Printed Text
    (London: Henry Bradshaw Society, 1915)

WEBB, B., *The Symbolism of Churches and Church Ornaments: a translation of the 'Rationale
    Divinorum Officiorum' written by William Durandus*, 3rd edn (London: Gibbings, 1906)

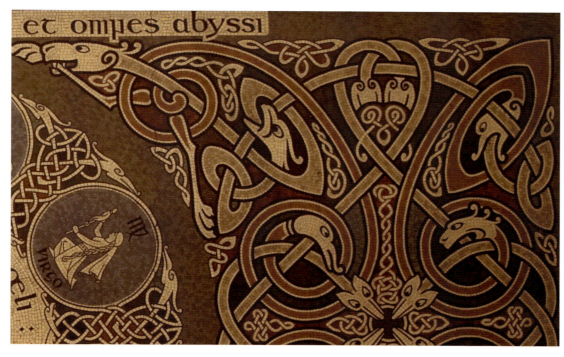

FIG 5.21: *Detail of floor mosaics at west end of nave*
FIG. 5.22: *Detail of floor mosaics at west end of nave*

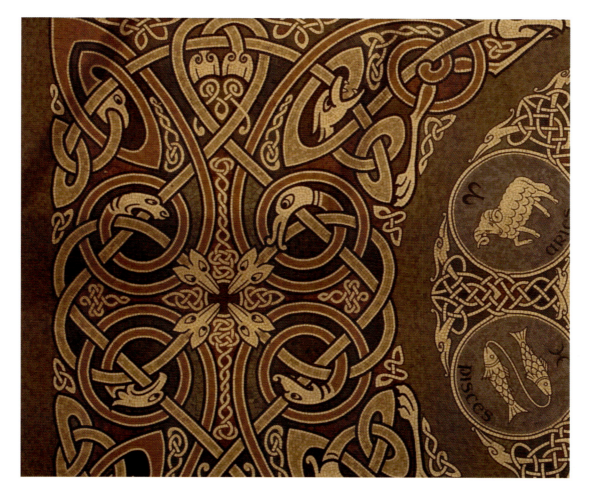

AN ICONOGRAPHIC EXCURSUS

The Embroidered Cloths of Heaven
The Textiles

Had I the heavens' embroidered cloths,
Enwrought with golden and silver light,
The blue and the dim and the dark cloths
Of night and light and the half-light,
I would spread the cloths under your feet;
But I, being poor, have only my dreams,
I have spread my dreams under your feet,
Tread softly because you tread on my dreams.

W.B. Yeats, He Wishes for the Cloths of Heaven.[†]

The textiles commissioned for the Honan Chapel included all the articles necessary for the church's life of worship. They may be divided into two parts: the first, the vestments and accessories associated with the celebration of the sacraments, and the second, those items which furnish the altar and chancel. Most of these items are linked with the vestments since they make up sets specific to the seasons of the Church's year. For example, there are altar frontals (antependia) and the hangings behind the altar (dossals) to match each set of chasub-les, copes and dalmatics for festivals, penitential and ordinary seasons. The vestments were made by William Egan & Sons, Cork, and the altar furnishings by the Dún Emer Guild, Dublin. Presently there is a known total of about ninety pieces and these are mainly listed in the inventory compiled in 1989.[1] Most are no longer in use since the reforms initiated by the Second Vatican Council in 1962.

VESTMENTS

In the first group there are sets and part sets of gold, white, red, violet, black and green vestments and Eucharistic accessories, each designated to be used at different times during the year. In general terms, the gold and white are for festivals; the red for Whitsuntide and feast days of martyrs; green was used between Epiphany and Lent, and between Trinity and Advent; violet for Advent and Lent; and black for funerals and Masses for the dead. The sets to be used for High Mass would consist of

133

chasuble, cope, two dalmatics, stoles, maniples, humeral veil, chalice veil and chalice burse.[2] The chasuble had undergone changes in cut and form since it was first worn as a garment proper to the celebration of Mass in the late fourth century AD. It had originally been a semi-circle of cloth which, if sewn together at the front, would create a 'little house' or casula around the wearer.[3] As the centuries passed the chasuble was cut more slimly so it was more practical in use but the Honan Chapel chasubles differ in design from others of the early twentieth century. The vestments were cut to what was believed, from contemporary sculptures, to be an early Irish pattern.[4] Chasubles and copes were certainly worn in the early medieval period in Ireland but, as there are no

examples surviving, the pattern was deduced perhaps from representations of bishops on high crosses, like that at Moone, Co. Carlow or the wooden carving of St Molaise now in the National Museum of Ireland.[5,6]

The embroideries on the vestments are all of the Early Irish style drawing their inspiration from the *Book of Durrow* and the *Book of Kells* (FIGS. 6.1, P. 124; 6.2–6.4; 6.11, P. 141). They are worked on Irish poplin, which is a cloth of plain (tabby) weave made with a silk warp and a wool weft; often the wool was a fine merino from Australia.[7] The cloth needs to be light and relatively cool as vestments were worn over other clothing. The typically ribbed effect of poplin is created by using a fine, dense warp and a thicker cylindrical

FIG. 6.2: *Green chasuble*

THE EMBROIDERED CLOTHS OF HEAVEN

FIG. 6.3: *Red chasuble*
FIG. 6.4: *Black chasuble*

THE EMBROIDERED CLOTHS OF HEAVEN

135

FIG. 6.5, 6.6: Gold
chasuble (details, symbolic
representation of the four
Evangelists as influenced by
the Book of Kells)

FIG. 6.7: Inscription
from the gold chasuble,
sewn onto the reverse of
the front of the garment

weft system. When the weft picks are woven in, the silk warp ends completely cover them but the 'ribs' stand out.

The exception is the gold set, worn at festivals which is made from cloth of gold. This weave incorporates gold metal thread in its weft system, which gives the fabric a rich and glowing impression (FIGS. 6.6, 6.7; 6.8–6.10, PP. 138–40). Several firms in Dublin were then still weaving poplin and cloth of gold; they include Richard Atkinson Ltd, Thomas Elliott & Sons, Pyms, and Frys, all well established in their manufacture.[8] The cloths that constitute the vestments and altar furnishings, both poplin and cloth of gold, are now precious survivals since sadly they are no longer being made in Dublin. Indeed the Honan Chapel textiles constitute a sizable archive of these fabrics that have been so closely associated with Ireland.

Thomas Elliott & Sons' last premises in Clonakilty, Co. Cork closed in 1979 but poplin is still woven in Belfast by Richard Atkinson Ltd.

Their sample books from the nineteenth- and twentieth-centuries include poplins seemingly very similar to the Honan textiles.[9] Linen surplices based on an antique pattern were also made up; unlike many contemporary examples they have no lace edgings or decorations.

The vestments, except the cloth of gold set, were all designed by John Lees of Cork, and the sewing and embroidery of all sets were carried out in the workshops of William Egan & Sons, Cork. The firm was long established with a strong tradition for excellence, having been founded in 1823.[10] A group of about thirty girls completed the work, over an eighteen-month period with Barry Michael Egan in charge. The cloth of gold set was designed by Ethel Josephine Scally, who died in 1915, before she could see her work completed. The chasuble in this set displays Celtic-style embroideries, although at some time in the past they have been cut from the original cloth and remounted, presumably due to deterioration. Most regrettably the cope in this set has not survived

Of your Charity

Pray for the souls of Matthew, Robert and Isabella Honan,
the founders of this Chapel and Hostel.
Pray for the welfare here and hereafter of the Warden and
Students of the Honan Hostel.
Pray for the welfare here and hereafter of Sir John O'Connell
who built this chapel and of his wife Dame Mary O'Connell.
Pray for the soul of Ethel Josephine Scally (who died on the
28th July, 1915.) who designed this Chasuble. and for the welfare
here and hereafter of Barry Michael Egan who made it and
for all who worked on it namely

M. Barrett.	N. Ahearne.
N. Harte.	M. Countie.
A. Calnan.	K. Cramer.
K. Allman.	G. Good.
M. Dermond.	M. E. Jenkins.
M. Twomey.	N. Barry.

The making of this Chasuble was ended in the workshop
of Barry Michael Egan in Patrick Street in the City of Cork
on the 25th day of September, 1916.

well, but the quality of the cloth can still be seen in part. It also seems that some sets of vestments are now incomplete.

Unfortunately the records that would give us information on the commissioning and making of the vestments do not seem to exist. Only a little information on Egan's business has survived; a newspaper article and letters from Barry Egan give some information, showing that the textiles workshops were in the main building.[11] Paul Larmour, in his book on the Irish Arts and Crafts movement, quotes a letter of Sir John O'Connell he found in a book in a Belfast library which gave the information on the length of time taken to finish the work, and the number of workers involved.[12] However, one of the pleasing aspects of the textiles is the more intimate knowledge of the women who made and embroidered the vestments afforded by the inscription sewn into the interior of the chasuble. This gives all their names including that of Ethel Scally the designer, and a prayer for the repose of her soul. The inscription also shows that the work was under the direction of Barry Michael Egan and that it took place in Egans' premises at 32 Patrick Street, Cork (FIG. 6.7, P. 137). It is clear that this dedication was cut away from an original lining and transferred to a new one.

There seem to be several reasons why conditions in Cork were right at the time for this flowering of talent and skill. A very immediate one is that Barry Egan, as a young man, spent several years of apprenticeship in silver-

FIG. 6.8: *Gold chasuble*
FIG. 6.9: *Gold chasuble (detail)*

THE EMBROIDERED CLOTHS OF HEAVEN

smithing and vestment-making, in both Belgium and France. In 1900 he went to Paris where he spent time with Biais Frères, one of the most important manufacturers of these items whose premises were in la place Saint Sulpice.[13] It was on his return that Barry Egan set up an embroidery and vestment workshop above the existing shop in Patrick Street. He would have been in sympathy with Sir John O'Connell's ideals, exemplified in the Honan Chapel, as he was a fervent nationalist; later, during the time of the Black and Tans terrorism in Cork City, he suffered the burning of his premises for his beliefs.[14]

There had also been a movement in Cork from the middle of the nineteenth-century to promote female employment and skills.

Numerous groups were set up by convents, benevolent ladies of all denominations, and by the Church of Ireland, all of whom trained and sometimes employed girls in crochet-work, silk hairnet-making, knitting, making shirt fronts, general needlework and embroidery. The girls in turn trained and employed others on a sub-contracting basis. There were schemes connected with large commercial textile establishments who ran industrial schools-cum-factories with mainly young women employees who thus developed sewing skills.[15] The founding of the Cork School of Art and of a Cork School of Needlework in the 1880s, and the general development of interest in decorative textiles, led to a climate sympathetic to the ideals of the Arts and Crafts

FIG. 6.10: *Gold chasuble (detail, depicting the Honan Chapel crest)*

FIG. 6.11: *Black chasuble (detail)*

THE EMBROIDERED CLOTHS OF HEAVEN

Movement.[16] By 1900 the Irish Arts and Crafts
Society had a Munster Committee, chaired by
Ludlow Beamish with Walter Mulligan ARIA as
secretary and Michael MacNamara of the Cork
School of Art as a member.[17]

Another development was that of the
Irish lace industry; it was at this time that
Cork, Youghal, Limerick, Carrickmacross and
other lace flourished. It has been noted by
Earnshaw that

*Drawn work, flowering, sewed muslin and cut linen
were established in Ireland well before the potato
famines of the 1840s but it was the famines that
stimulated the development of the Female Industrial
Movement in the counties of the south and west, and led
to the formation of the Cork Embroidery School and the
growth and progress of superbly rendered openwork
embroideries. One of the 25 Glasgow firms already
employed in the 'muslin trade' sent an agent, teachers
and all the materials needed for the industry to begin. . .
much excellent work was done at the Presentation
Convent itself.*

The impetus towards the development of this
type of work later fell away.[18]

On the design side, the lace industry
encouraged both men and women in this field.
For example, Michael Holland trained at the
Cork School of Art, and in about 1910 worked at
Dwyer & Co., where he directed production of
superb crochet pieces.[19] The period of expansion
enjoyed by the Cork woollen industry from the
mid-nineteenth century to the 1920s also encouraged and developed textile skills generally.[20]

ALTAR FURNISHINGS

The second group of textiles includes the altar
frontals and dossals all made by Evelyn Gleeson
and the Dún Emer Guild in Dublin. They are of
course used in conjunction with the appropriate
vestments at the different seasons.

The black set is used for the annual
Founders' Day Mass, which takes place in the
third week of October, and is traditionally the
ceremonial memorial for the Honan family

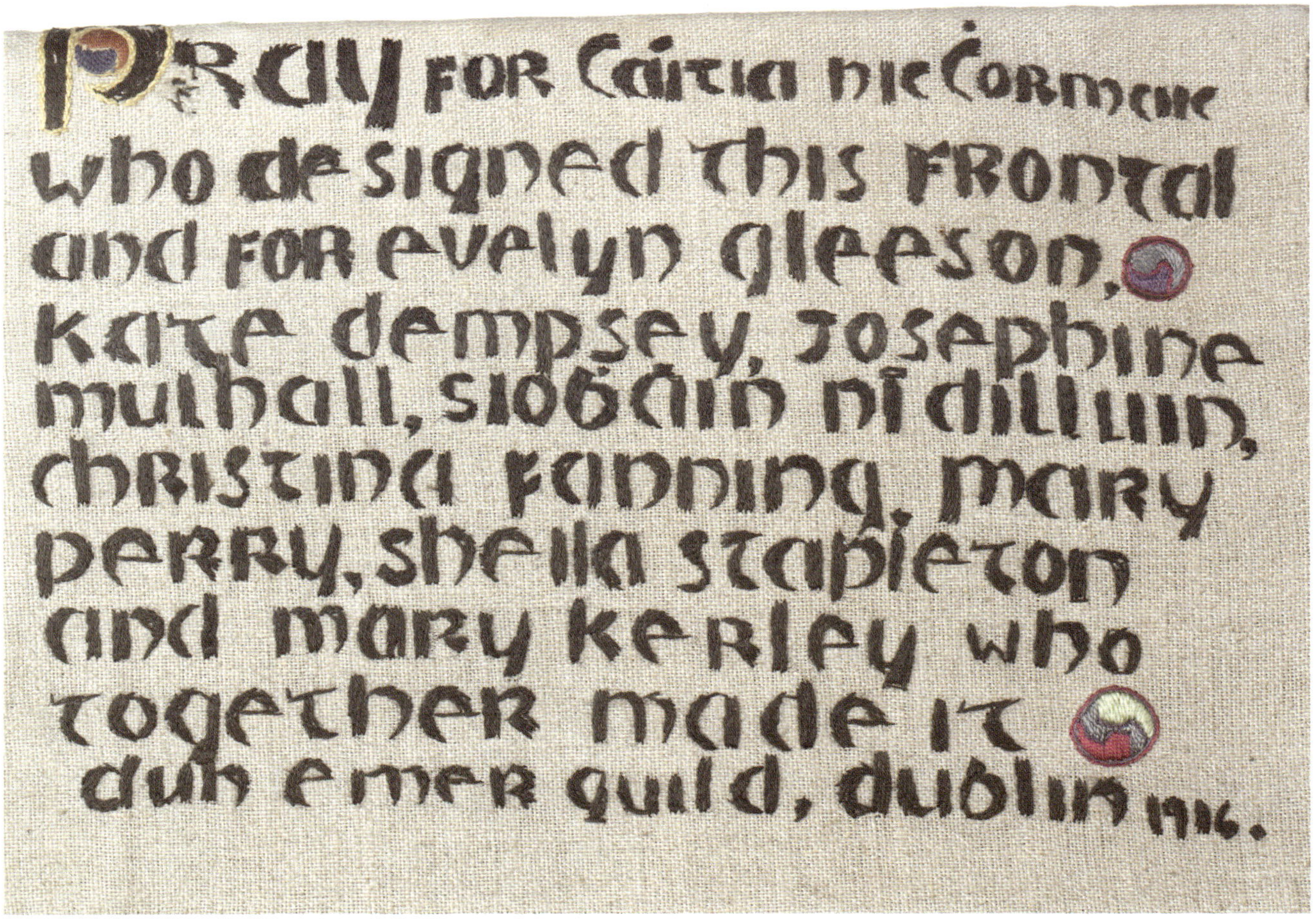

PRAY FOR Cáitin nic Cormaic
who designed this frontal
and for evelyn gleeson,
kate dempsey, josephine
mulhall, siobáin ní dilluin,
christina fanning, mary
perry, sheila stapleton
and mary kerley who
together made it
dún emer guild, dublin 1916.

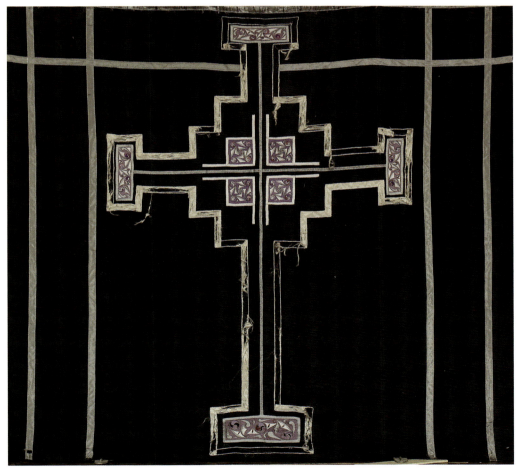

FIG.6.13: *Inscription on the black frontal from the Dún Emer Guild*

FIG. 6.14: *Black dossal (detail)*

THE EMBROIDERED CLOTHS OF HEAVEN

(FIGS. 6.12, 6.15, P. 144). On the linen backing of both frontal and dossal are inscriptions painted (frontal) and embroidered (dossal) in black giving the names of the women who designed and worked on them, and the date and place of manufacture (FIGS. 6.13, 6.32, P. 155). The violet set is embroidered with Celtic interlace patterns and motifs based on the iconography of the Crucifixion (FIGS. 6.15, 6.16).

There is a white antependium with panels marked out with blue appliqued silk ribbon and embroideries that show it was made for the Feast Days of the Blessed Virgin Mary (FIG. 6.17). Here are scenes from the life of Mary which embody a delicacy and charm totally suitable to their subject. First in the top left-hand panel there is the Annunciation (*Mater dolorosa*, the

FIG. 6.15: *Violet antependium (detail)*
FIG. 6.16: *Violet dossal (detail)*

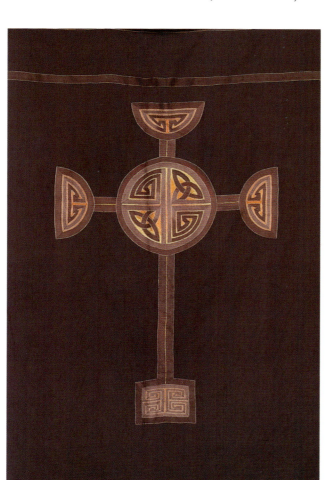

Sorrowing Mother) (FIG. 6.33, P. 157), then the Assumption (*Regina coeli*, the Queen of Heaven) in the top centre, and finally the Nativity (*Mater Dei*, the Mother of God) on the right (FIGS. 6.18, 6.19). Delightful red-headed Irish angels pay their respects to Mary and her babe, and assist in the other panels. An interlace-filled roundel is placed in the main centre panel and two further embroideries were executed for the two side main panels (FIG. 6.20, P. 146). There is also a matching dossal. In these pieces a different spirit is at work and the embroideries show another source of inspiration from the Egan vestments.

Three other fine textiles made by the Guild are two embroideries, the banner of St Finn Barr, and the altar frontal of Christ with Irish saints, and the third a wool tapestry dossal. The banner shows St Fin Barr in the vestments suited to a bishop, but wearing only one glove. Behind the gloved hand a small tree is bursting into flower and on the other side of the saint a lamb is standing. The saint's gloved hand refers to the legend attributed to him that Christ touched his hand

FIG. 6.17: *White antependium*

FIG. 6.18: *White antependium (detail, Mater Dei)*

FIG. 6.19: *White antependium (detail, Regina coeli)*

whilst he was praying, leaving his hand glowing and he then, out of humility, wore a glove to disguise the fact. The small tree is a hazel bush Fin Barr caused to break into flower in the winter-time.[21] The entire surface of the banner is embroidered in a variety of stitches, including variations of laid and cord work, and satin and split stitch (FIG. 6.21).

The frontal is also made with a linen ground completely covered with embroidery in silk floss thread of fine quality in a similar variety of stitches (FIG. 6.22, P. 148). It is designed in three panels, the central one being larger than the two side sections. In the central roundel, or mandorla, is a seated figure of Christ in Majesty holding the Book of the Gospels and flanked by the four traditional

mystical symbols of the Evangelists. In these Matthew is represented by a man, Mark by a lion, Luke an ox, and John an eagle. On the gold background of the frontal there are small self-coloured discs scattered randomly across the embroidered cloth. They enclose cross, triskel and triangular motifs and are perhaps reminiscent of discs found in the *Book of Kells* (for example on the leg of the winged calf on folio 27v).[22] From the left of the frontal the other figures are St Ita in the left-hand panel, (FIG. 6.23, P. 149) in the centre panel St Columcille and St Patrick (FIG. 6.24, P. 149) to the left of Christ, St Brigid and St Fin Barr to his right, and St Colman in the right-hand panel (FIG. 6.25, P. 149). The figure of St. Fin Barr is clearly worked from the same design as that used for the banner.

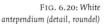
FIG. 6.20: *White antependium (detail, roundel)*

THE EMBROIDERED CLOTHS OF HEAVEN

FIG. 6.21: *Banner of St Fin Barr*

naom ᛭ barra

FIG. 6.22: *Antependium (detail, Christ in Majesty, surrounded by the mystical symbols of the Evangelists)*

The choice of Christ in Majesty as the central figure of the frontal reinforces the interpretation that the whole scene is drawn from the description of the Second Coming in the *Revelation of St John the Divine*. The red colours of his robes share the same depth and intensity as those used by Sarah Purser for the Christ in Majesty in the stained glass windows immediately above the altar. Although the representation of Christ is not drawn from the *Book of Kells*, is seems that the design for the chair on which he sits comes from the chair of St John the Evangelist in folio 291v.[23]

There is an interesting comparison of the figures to be drawn with an altar frontal, made at the Glasgow School of Art by the then head of embroidery there, Ann MacBeth. This frontal was made for the Cathedral Church of St Mary the Virgin, Glasgow with central figures of Mary and a female figure robed as a bishop, perhaps representing the Church, and two flanking angels. These are all worked in coloured silk floss threads on a cream silk ground. The work is lighter in spirit and execution than the Honan frontal but the stance of the robed figure and the style of the Virgin suggest a relationship between the two. The Glasgow piece was made in 1909–10, some years earlier than the Dún Emer embroidery.[24] There were many links between Ireland and Scotland at the time. For example, the Irish-born Phoebe Traquair, resident in Edinburgh, showed some of her work in 1904 in the Irish Arts and Crafts Society exhibition in Dublin. At that time Evelyn Gleeson was on the IACS committee and wrote enthusiastically in the IACS journal of the artistic merit and essential Irishness of Traquair's work.[25] The work of the embroidery department of the Glasgow School of Art was regularly discussed in the journal *The Studio*, as happened in 1916 (vol. LVII). Also in the same journal in 1916 two sets of the Honan Chapel vestments were featured, so it seems likely that Evelyn Gleeson might well have been familiar with Ann McBeth's work.[26]

FIG. 6.24:
Antependium (detail,
St Columcille and
St Patrick)

FIG. 6.23: Antependium
(detail, St Ita)

FIG. 6.25: Antependium
(detail, St Brigid,
St Fin Barr and St Colman)

FIG. 6.26: *Wool tapestry dossal (detail, symbols of the Evangelists)*

FIG. 6.27: *Green altar frontlet (detail)*

THE EMBROIDERED CLOTHS OF HEAVEN

FIG. 6.28: *Carpet (for the altar steps, detail)*

The wool tapestry dossal is a work of great visual richness set on a deep red ground (FIG. 6.26, P. 150). The tapestry is divided into four panels containing the symbols of the Evangelists, closely based on folio 27v of the *Book of Kells* where the four figures are grouped together on the same page. In this folio the symbols are set into rectangular panels which are further enclosed in rectangular borders inside which are varied interlaced, circular, squared and stepped decorative motifs. In the Dún Emer dossal the symbols are not boxed in but are enclosed in a golden circle. The rectangular panels are here released from the constriction of the manuscript page and outline the four segments of the tapestry. The squared and stepped motifs with a little interlacing are lightly reused and reinterpreted together.[27] There are many echoes of the geometric elements used in the *Book of Durrow* in, for example, folios IV, 2r, 125v and 248r (FIG. 6.12, P. 142).[28]

The design and weaving of carpets were particularly dear to Evelyn Gleeson's heart since she had trained in this speciality in London.[29] The Guild made a set of three carpets for the chancel, altar foreground and altar steps in rich greens, reds and blues (FIG. 6.28). The chancel carpet has a central stepped geometric pattern, the other two have narrow side-panels of similar decoration. Dún Emer always used Irish wool, which was spun and dyed to order.[30]

It is clear that Evelyn Gleeson was completely in tune with Sir John O'Connell's conviction that the chapel and its contents should be simple, beautiful and Irish. In a transcript of her article on 'Irish Handknotted Carpets' she writes

My aim in designing Dún Emer carpets is to make them Irish, to bring into them the old Irish colour as described in The Making of Ireland. *Blue and green and variegated and purple of fine brilliance to embody the blue of our skies, the sapphire of our lakes, the purple of our mountains and the variegated beauty of the bog-land flowers combined with the flowing curves dear to the Celtic scribes, the sharp relief of the fret and the intriguing charm of interlacing.*[31]

There is also a single round cushion, with St John's eagle; perhaps there were three others originally to make up a set of the Four Evangelists. The design is very close to that of the eagle on the dossal.

The three elements around the altar, the dossal, altar frontal and carpets, and indeed the banner, were clearly designed together. The green in the mandorlas of the Evangelists' symbols in the tapestry is echoed both in the main background colour of the carpets and in the mandorla behind the Christ in Majesty on the altar frontal. The carpet patterns pick up the panels of decoration along the sides and top of the dossal and on the narrow bands dividing the panels on the altar frontal. The gold of the frontal matches that of the banner of St Finn Barr and the vivid red dossal complements the decorative elements of the carpets. Geometric banding and interlace in all these pieces provide an integrity to the whole, while each element of decoration retains its own interpretation of the chosen motif.

The embroideries on both the vestments and altar furnishings made a large contribution to the unity of vision achieved in the original master design of John O'Connell. They are an integral part of the breathtaking visual unity of the chapel together with the saints in the stained glass windows, the Stations of the Cross and the mosaics (FIGS. 6.27, P. 150; 6.30–6.32, PP. 153–5). Indeed the glowing colours of the vestments and their rich embroideries when worn by the cele-

FIG. 6.29: *Antependium (detail)*

THE EMBROIDERED CLOTHS OF HEAVEN

FIG. 6.30:
*Gold altar
frontlet (detail)*

brants of the Mass would have brought to life and movement the static elements of the chapel. In that restricted space the robed figures must have added an immediacy and warm vitality to the liturgy. In the context of early twentieth-century church furnishings, the simplicity of design and materials would have been in sharp contrast to that seen elsewhere in Irish churches, where generally there was a strong influence from France, Italy and Belgium.

DÚN EMER GUILD

The Dún Emer Guild was started in 1902 by Evelyn Gleeson and Susan (Lily) and Elizabeth (Lolly) Yeats, sisters of William Butler and Jack Yeats, who had all met earlier when living in London.[32] The high quality output of the Guild was an important part of the Celtic Revival, and the Arts and Crafts movement in which it was active for many years; it finally closed in around 1964 after a long decline. In its heyday it was very productive and successful, with tapestries, carpets, vestments and embroideries pre-eminent. There was also a printing and publishing press, and later enamel work was undertaken.[33] Evelyn Gleeson was so determined to weave tapestries authentically that she borrowed an old loom from the National Museum.[34]

After 1908 the Yeats sisters were no longer connected with the Guild, leaving to set up their own enterprise, Cuala. Later Evelyn Gleeson's niece, Katherine or Kitty Mac-Cormack, having been brought up at Dún Emer, began to work as a designer and part of the group. May Kerley, a niece of Augustine Henry the eminent scholar, was also an important member of the group. Both these names appear on the inscriptions on the black altar frontal and black dossal described earlier.

We can learn something of the background to the Guild's part in executing the commissions for the chapel since among the papers left by Evelyn Gleeson are some that make clear her commitment to the project. The transcript of an article describes her difficulties in carrying on an expanding business at the start of the Great War of 1914–18

Then came the war with high prices scarcity of materials and all sorts of minor difficulties. It was then that the building of the Honan Chapel in Cork called on the workers to put forth all their efforts to make a Tapestry and carpets worthy of the exquisite setting afforded by the beautiful little Celtic church. The Trustee of the Honan Bequest gave the Guild workers a great opportunity and it may be truly said that down to the smallest and youngest it was appreciated.[35]

Here it is appropriate to underline the interesting role played by women artists and craftworkers in the Irish Arts and Crafts movement. As was also true in Scotland and England, young women eagerly took advantage of the opening and development of art colleges in both Dublin and Cork. Alternatively, like the Yeats sisters, they taught themselves the skills they needed to thrive outside the home. From the names quoted here, it can be seen that the Honan treasures stem from the talents of Sarah Purser, Eleanor Kelly, Evelyn Gleeson and the women named on the textiles, just as much as from the gifted men involved (FIG. 6.32). It was an exciting time for women as they enthusiastically became engaged with the wider world.

The coincidence of the consecration of the chapel taking place in the fateful year of 1916

FIG. 6.31: *Gold altar frontlet (detail)*

underscores the fact that the creative influences and motivations behind the artworks there must come from the immediately pre-revolution years of the colonial experience. Those inspirations were different for each of the people responsible for the Honan textiles. John O'Connell, lawyer, priest and instigator of the project, drew on the historical and spiritual strengths of the early Irish experience, with a strong emphasis on devotional practice.[36] Little is known of the creative influences on John Lees, designer of the majority of the vestments. However, the choice of motifs from early Christian illuminated manuscripts used with Irish poplin cloth identify clearly known symbols of nationality. Barry Michael Egan, the executor of the vestments has, as we have

seen, a highly professional and seasoned businessman imbued with the nationalist patriotism of his native Cork. From his continental and general experience he would have recognized how ground-breaking in European terms the vestments were in design and materials.

Evelyn Gleeson came from that strain of Irishness that in the late imperial period could move easily between the two cultures. Her years in London gave her an insight into the tenets of the Arts and Crafts movement. The combination of the South Kensington years and the evenings at such gatherings as the Irish Literary Society with the Yeats sisters gave a new direction to her energies, and provided a perfect synthesis for her talents. The return to

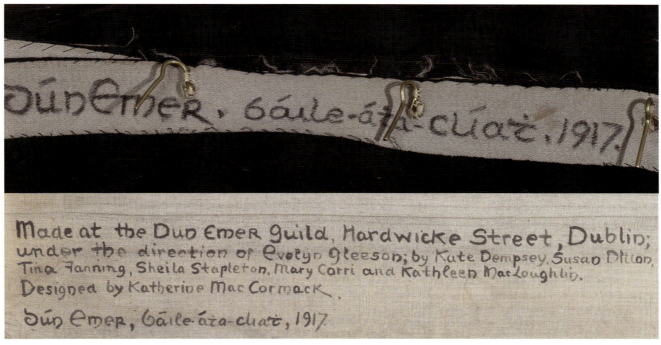

FIG. 6.32: *Black antependium (detail, showing inscription)*

Dublin in 1903, born of a desire to be where such fundamental changes were taking place, led to the execution of many works which brilliantly illustrated the forces at work in society.

It is interesting that these protagonists were employing several different constructs of Irishness from different time periods. The use of Celtic designs drawn from the *Book of Kells* and *The Book of Durrow* is masterfully executed but has clear antecedents in the last years of the nineteenth and the first years of the twentieth century in, for example, the work of the Donegal Industrial Fund and Kenmare Convent, Co. Kerry.[37] The choice of poplin cannot be associated with the early Christian period, having been introduced by the Huguenots in the seventeenth-century, but it was certainly a product closely identified with Ireland. It had been so successful that it was chosen by Queen Victoria for her wedding dress.[38] Equally, the looms used by Gleeson were 'old' but only in so far as they were of the *haute lisse* type, suitable for tapestry-weaving. Since it seems that tapestry-weaving was introduced into Ireland in the early sixteenth-century but that no identifiable Irish examples still exist from that period, the 'oldness' is a limited concept.[39] Figures in the gold altar frontal and banner seem drawn from nineteenth-century interpretations of possible 'Celtic' dress unrelated to what is seen, for example, in the *Book of Kells*.

CONCLUSION

Finally, why choose W.B. Yeats' poem to precede this chapter, leaving aside that it is loved by so many people?[40] It came to mind in thinking over the background to the Honan textiles. Although the poem was written before 1899, it certainly seems likely that Yeats had a clear idea of how 'heavens' embroidered cloths' might

have looked. Living in London, he had become a friend of William Morris; between 1886 and 1894 his sister Lily had worked with Morris's daughter May in that family's embroidery workshop in Hammersmith. Lily learnt to embroider and sometimes design textiles there.[41]

Textiles were central to the vision of the Arts and Crafts movement, not marginalized, as they sometimes are nowadays. Later, both William and Jack were very supportive of their sisters' involvement in the Dún Emer Guild, giving advice and specific designs for different projects. Just as every part of the Chapel and its contents has its own integrity and value, so all the arts and crafts of the Celtic renaissance were held in high esteem. William Yeats' imagery, imbued with the sense of the power of cloth, seems an appropriate, though unwitting description of the dazzling textiles made for the Honan Chapel. They hold their own among the other beautiful objects that were made for the encouragement of true spirituality in the worship of the Honan congregation.

FIG. 6.33: *White antependium (detail, Mater Dolorosa)*

ACKNOWLEDGMENTS

I would like to thank Dr Patrick Kelly and Dr Bernard Meehan, Keeper of Manuscripts at Trinity College, Dublin for access to the Evelyn Gleeson Archive. I would also thank Ms Patricia McCarthy, City Archivist, for her help in finding papers relating to Barry Michael Egan in the Cork City Archives, Peter Lamb for sharing information with me and Liz Arthur for discussing the work of Ann McBeth. I appreciated the time and attention given to my research by Mr David Nicholson of Richard Atkinson Ltd, Belfast.

Mater ✠ Dolorosa

NOTES AND REFERENCES

† Reproduced courtesy of A.P. Watt Ltd., London.

1 Elizabeth Wincott Heckett and Virginia Teehan *The Honan Chapel Collection, University College Cork – an Inventory* (Unpublished, 1991)

2 Raymund James, *The Origin and Development of Roman Liturgical Vestments* (Exeter: Catholic Records Press, 1934), pp. 3-12

3 ibid., p. 4

4 M.J. O'Kelly, *The Collegiate Chapel, Cork*, 3rd edn (Cork University Press, 1966), p. 15

5 Peter Harbison, *Guide to the National Monuments in Ireland* (Dublin: Gill & Macmillan, 1975), p. 17

6 Fergus O'Farrell, 'The Inishmurray Statue of St. Molaise: a re-assessment' in Etienne Rynne (ed.), *Figures from the Past – Studies on Figurative Art in Christian Ireland in Honour of Helen M. Roe* (Dún Laoghaire: Glendale Press for the Royal Society of Antiquaries of Ireland, 1987), pp. 205–8

7 Mary Campion, 'An old Dublin industry – poplin' (from the old Dublin Society, 28 November 1962) *Dublin Historical Record* 1963, vol. 18, pp. 1–14

8 ibid., pp. 12–13

9 I am grateful to Mr David Nicholson of Richard Atkinson Ltd. for being kind enough to show me the sample books and to give generously of his time in guiding me through the whole process of making poplin.

10 *The Cork Examiner*, 28 November 1979, p. 8

11 ibid., and unpublished letters of Barry Egan in the Cork Archives Institute

12 Paul Larmour, *The Arts and Crafts Movement in Ireland* (Belfast: Friar's Bush Press, 1992), p. 134

13 Eoin O'Mahony 'Our notable men' *The Chrystal, Cork*, July 1927, p. 200

14 Unpublished letter of Barry Egan in the Cork Archives Institute

15 Maura Cronin 'Work and Workers in Cork city and county 1800–1900' in Patrick O'Flanagan and Cornelius G. Buttimer (eds.), *Cork History and Society* (Dublin: Geography Publications, 1993), p. 738

16 Peter Murray 'Art institutions in nineteenth-century Cork' in Patrick O'Flanagan and Cornelius G. Buttimer (eds.), op. cit., pp. 813–72, 841, 856–69

17 Paul Larmour, 1992, p. 78

18 Pat Earnshaw, *Youghal and other Irish Laces* (Guildford: Gorse Publications, 1988), p. 33

19 ibid., p. 31

20 Andy Bielenberg, 'British Competition and the Vicissitudes of the Irish Woollen Industry: 1785–1923' *Textile History*, vol. 31, no. 2, November 2000, pp. 202–21, pp. 215–7

21 M.J. O'Kelly, op. cit., p. 14

22   Bernard Meehan, *The Book of Kells: an Illustrated Introduction to the Manuscript in Trinity College, Dublin*, 2nd edn, (London: Thames & Hudson, 1997), plate 5, folio 27v, the symbols of the Four Evangelists

23   ibid., plate 37, folio 291v

24   Liz Arthur, 'Ann McBeth (1875–1948)' in Jude Burkhauser (ed.) *'Glasgow Girls' – Women in Art and Design 1880–1920*, (Edinburgh: Canongate, 1997), pp. 153–7. The altar frontal, now in the Glasgow Museums and Art Galleries is illustrated on pp. 156-7

25   Paul Larmour, op. cit., pp. 74, 76

26   Liz Arthur in Burkhauser, op. cit., p. 154 and Paul Larmour, op. cit., p. 134

27   Evelyn Gleeson wrote the following to an unidentified newspaper editor on the subject of interpreting early Irish designs and the Arts and Crafts movement:

The examples that survive of our country's art are so intricate and so ancient the task of carrying on the style is peculiarly hard. It needs much study, much sifting much knowledge of the ornament of other countries and of the standards of modern taste, before it can find success. Many people think mere copying is sufficient. On the contrary, what is needed is to grasp faithfully the combined boldness and finish, the severe convention and the delightful fancy revealed in Irish decorative art to make one's own the generous spirit that grudged no labour and no time and the mastery of detail that yet does not obscure grace of form.

Evelyn Gleeson Archive, Manuscript Library, Trinity College, Dublin (10676/18/18)

28   Bernard Meehan, *The Book of Durrow: a Medieval Masterpiece at Trinity College Dublin* (Dublin: Town House, 1996), pp. 10, 15, 58, 79

29   In a letter from Evelyn Gleeson to a Mr Gwynn in relation to a proposed article on Irish carpets she writes

As I had years before while I was an art student in London made some carpet designs to the order of Mr. Alexander Millar a great friend of mine and the chief carpet designer in successor to Wm. Morris who told me I had an exceptional colour sense and boldness and originality in the work I did for him I thought I would try to produce some Irish carpets as there were none as far as I know.

Evelyn Gleeson Archive, Manuscripts Library, Trinity College, Dublin (10676/18/11)

30   Kitty MacCormack, niece of Miss Gleeson in an interview with Irene French Eagar on the Women's Magazine Radio Éireann programme (June 13, no year given) stated that in the process of carpet-making all the wool used was Irish, and was specially spun and dyed. Evelyn Gleeson Archive, Manuscripts Library, Trinity College, Dublin. (10676/5/6)

31   This transcript is in the Evelyn Gleeson Archive in the Manuscripts Library, Trinity College, Dublin. (10676/5/7)

32   Joan Hardwick, The Yeats sisters: a biography of Susan and Elizabeth Yeats (London: Pandora, 1996), pp. 117–21

33   Paul Larmour, op. cit., pp. 151–61

34   Mairead Dunlevy, 'The Honan Chapel – a visionary monument' in this volume, pp. 1–16, in this volume.

35   This transcript of 1917 is in the Evelyn Gleeson Archive in the Manuscripts Library of Trinity College, Dublin (10676/5/3)

36   Revd Sir John O'Connell, The Collegiate Chapel, Cork, 2nd edn (Cork University Press, 1932), Chapters 1 and 2 'Some thoughts on Church building' and 'The Hiberno-Romanesque: its origin and development.'

37   Paul Larmour, op. cit., pp. 15–26

38   Mary Campion, op. cit., pp. 1–14. A piece of the poplin produced for Queen Victoria's wedding dress is still in the possession of Richard Atkinson Ltd.

39   In about 1525 AD Piers Butler and his wife Margaret Fitzgerald, later Earl and Countess of Ormond, are said to have brought over to Kilkenny Flemish craftsmen to introduce the weaving of tapestries, Turkey carpets, diapers and cushions. The Reports of the Royal Commission on Historical Manuscripts 1870, appendix to second Report, pp. 224–5 (MSS. of O'Conor Don).

40   W.B. Yeats, 'He wishes for the cloths of heaven' from The Wind among the Reeds, 1899 in W.B. Yeats: selected poetry (London: Pan Books/Macmillan, 1975) p. 35

41   Linda Parry, William Morris Textiles (London: Weidenfeld & Nicolson, 1983), p. 31

BIBLIOGRAPHY

ARTHUR, LIZ, 'ANN MCBETH (1875–1948)' in Jude Burkhauser (ed.) 'Glasgow Girls' – Women in Art and Design 1880–1920, (Edinburgh: Canongate, 1997), pp. 153–7

BIELENBERG, ANDY, 'British Competition and the Vicissitudes of the Irish Woollen Industry: 1785-1923' Textile History, vol. 31, no. 2, November 2000, pp. 202–21

CAMPION, MARY, 'An old Dublin industry – poplin' (from the old Dublin Society, 28 November 1962) Dublin Historical Record 1963, vol. 18, pp. 1–14

CRONIN, MAURA, 'Work and Workers in Cork city and county 1800-1900' in Patrick O'Flanagan and Cornelius G. Buttimer (eds.), Cork History and Society (Dublin: Geography Publications, 1993).

EARNSHAW, PAT, Youghal and other Irish Laces (Guildford: Gorse Publications, 1988)

HARBISON, PETER, Guide to the National Monuments in Ireland (Dublin: Gill & Macmillan, 1975)

HARDWICK, JOAN, The Yeats sisters: a Biography of Susan and Elizabeth Yeats (London: Pandora, 1996)

HECKETT, ELIZABETH WINCOTT, AND VIRGINIA TEEHAN The Honan Chapel Collection, University College Cork – an Inventory (Unpublished, 1991)

JAMES, RAYMUND, *The Origin and Development of Roman Liturgical Vestments*
   (Exeter: Catholic Records Press, 1934)

LARMOUR, PAUL, *The Arts and Crafts Movement in Ireland.* (Belfast: Friar's Bush Press,
   1992)

MEEHAN, BERNARD, *The Book of Durrow: a Medieval Masterpiece at Trinity College Dublin*
   (Dublin: Town House, 1996)

MEEHAN, BERNARD, *The Book of Kells: an Illustrated Introduction to the Manuscript in
   Trinity College, Dublin*, 2nd edn (London: Thames & Hudson, 1997)

MURRAY, PETER, 'Art institutions in nineteenth-century Cork' in Patrick O'Flanagan
   and Cornelius G. Buttimer (eds.), *Cork History and Society* (Dublin: Geography
   Publications, 1993).

O'FARRELL, FERGUS, 'The Inishmurray Statue of St. Molaise: a re-assessment' in
   Etienne Rynne (ed.), *Figures From the Past – Studies on Figurative Art in Christian Ireland
   in Honour of Helen M. Roe* (Dún Laoghaire: Glendale Press for the Royal Society of
   Antiquaries of Ireland, 1987), pp. 205–8

O'KELLY, M.J., *The Collegiate Chapel, Cork*, 3rd edn (Cork University Press, 1966)

O'MAHONY, EOIN, 'Our notable men' *The Chrystal*, Cork, July 1927, p. 200

O'CONNELL, REV SIR JOHN, *The Collegiate Chapel, Cork*, 2nd edn (Cork University
   Press, 1932)

PARRY, LINDA, William Morris Textiles (London: Weidenfeld & Nicolson, 1983)

YEATS, W.B., *W.B. Yeats: Selected Poetry* (London: Pan Books/Macmillan, 1975)

NICOLA GORDON BOWE

A New Byzantium
The Stained Glass Windows by Harry Clarke

There are seventeen stained glass windows in the Honan Chapel, eleven of which were designed and made by Harry Clarke when he had barely left the Dublin Metropolitan School of Art. They are jewelled masterpieces which impressed visitors as much when they were installed as they do now, and established Clarke's reputation before his twenty-eighth birthday.[1]

His older colleague in the Arts and Crafts Society of Ireland, the master enamellist and metalwork teacher at the Dublin Art School, P.O. Reeves, who had wrought the tabernacle and other altar furniture in the chapel, wrote a rapturous and perceptive review in The Studio magazine:

These windows reveal a conception of stained glass that stands quite alone. The remarkable power of expressing the subject is not greater than that shown in solving the problems of design and application to a window, not greater than the extraordinary command of all the technical resources of the art. There has never been before such mastery of technique, nor such application of it to

the ends of exceeding beauty, significance and wondrousness. No one has ever before shown the great beauty that can be obtained by the leads alone, nor the mysterious beauty and 'liveness' that each piece of glass receives at the hands of this artist, nor the jewelled gorgeousness of 'pattern' that may be given to a window that teems with subject, interest and meaning. These windows accept their 'architectural place' to a fine degree, with an ease and certainty . . . The light as it passes through them is marvellously transformed, not alone by the colour . . . but by ingenuity of individual craftsmanship, and it is this transformed, glorified and vitalized light in all its varied and 'live' qualities, that holds the surpassing beauty and significance.[2]

Thomas Bodkin, barrister, collector, critic and subsequently the first director of the National Gallery of Ireland, wrote that 'nothing like Mr Clarke's windows in the Honan Chapel had been made or seen before in Ireland. Their sustained magnificence of colour, their beautiful and most intricate drawing, their lavish and mysterious symbolism, combine to produce an

163

effect of splendour which is overpowering' (FIG. 7.1).[3]   Others declared that the gap had been bridged between the middle ages and the twentieth century. Patrick Abercrombie, who had come to Ireland to work on his new town plan for Dublin, wrote: 'these windows are amazing, the best modern glass I have ever seen. They knock the William Morris and Burne-Jones windows hollow.'[4] Clarke's influential school magazine, published by the Jesuit Belvedere College, referred to the 'considerable attention' his windows had attracted when exhibited in his Dublin studio – even before their installation:

It is difficult to know what to admire most in Mr. Clarke's windows, whether the colour scheme, the marvellous use of symbolism or the entire originality of treatment. There is a complete departure from the common unattractive window so often erected at a fixed price per foot. Mr. Clarke has given us real works of art. His windows are to most others in this country what the oil painting from the brush of a great artist is to the common oleograph.[5]

It was the Belevederian old boy network which was to prove crucial in securing this commission for Clarke. He had attended the Dublin college in the eighteenth-century heart of the city, just round the corner from the Georgian house at 33 North Frederick Street where his family lived above their church-decorating and stained glass studios, although he had left, aged fourteen, to gain experience in the business. By 1907, he had become a stained glass apprentice in his father's studio, while studying at night at the Dublin Metropolitan School of Art under A.E. Child, trained in the London studio workshop of the English Arts and Crafts master artist-craftsman, Christopher Whall.[6] It was Child and his father's principal Dublin glass

FIG. 7.2: *Harry Clarke, self-portrait (1914), reproduced in his illustrated Hans Andersen's Fairy Tales (1916)*

painter, William Nagle RHA, who would provide Clarke with the rudiments of stained glass, as would his reading of Ruskin (windows should be 'serene, intense, brilliant like flaming jewellery', their colours 'deep, mysterious and subdued'[7]) and Christopher Whall's seminal book, *Stained Glass Work: A Text-book for Students and Workers in Glass* (London, 1905) with its insistence on the relationship between architecture, light and stained glass, on the artist as designer and craftsman and on the thorough knowledge of materials as the basis for style. Between 1910 and 1913, on a stained glass scholarship at the School of Art, Clarke's designs, cartoons and worked-up panels caused a sensation by winning a gold medal for three years running at the National Competition held annually in London. It was the dramatic intensity, symbolic treatment, the colour, 'rich, sombre and of great beauty', and the 'very ingenious and beautiful arrangement of the leading'[8] of his long, narrow *Judas* panel of 1913, with its central figure and tiny

A NEW BYZANTIUM

FIG. 7.3: *Margaret Crilley, Portrait of Clarke shortly before their marriage, 1914*

FIG. 7.4: *Sean Keating, 'Thinking out Gobnet' (1917) a portrait of Harry Clarke on the Aran Islands*

interwoven attendant figures, inspired but by no means dependent on medieval glass, which gives the first indication of his unique treatment in the forthcoming Honan Chapel commission (SEE FIG. 7.22, P. 177).[9]

From the summer of 1912, the Rt. Hon. Laurence Ambrose Waldron, J.P., P.C., stock-broker, connoisseur, bibliophile and a governor of Belvedere College, had begun to take a particular interest in the career of the shy but witty and cultured ex-Belvederian art student whose stained glass and book illustrations were winning so many prizes. His first and lifelong patron, Waldron, began to commission work from Clarke and to invite him to his epicurean gatherings at Marino, the house overlooking Killiney Bay that his cousin, L.A. McDonnell, had rebuilt for him in an Arts and Crafts style in 1909. Here, Clarke would meet most of his future Irish patrons, including the ex-Belvederian Bodkin, Sir John O'Connell, the Honan legal trustee, and Sir Bertram Windle, President of University College Cork. Waldron,

Bodkin, O'Connell and Windle all served with Clarke, as well as William Alphonsus Scott,[10] Oswald Reeves, Austin Molloy and Evelyn Gleeson of the Dún Emer Guild, on the council of the revised Arts and Crafts Society of Ireland, while O'Connell chaired its executive committee, on which Clarke and Scott both served; Windle chaired the Munster sub-committee on which the chapel's architect, James McMullen, served. In November 1913, Waldron was instrumental in securing a government travel scholarship for Clarke, now that he had left the School of Art, so that he could study medieval glass in England and France, while supplementing his grant with a prestigious commission he had been given in December by the London publishers George Harrap to illustrate *Hans Andersen's Fairy Tales* (FIG. 7.2). He made valuable visits and contacts in London and in Paris, where the medieval glass collections in the Cathedral of Notre Dame, in Cluny, in the old Trocadéro museum and, further afield, in Chartres, Amiens and Rouen Cathedrals deeply affected him, and provided rich sources of inspiration for the Honan Chapel windows.[11]

He returned to Ireland shortly before the First World War was declared, setting off for Inishere in August with his art school friend Austin Molloy, as they had done since 1909, accompanied by another fellow student, Sean Keating, on his first Aran Island visit. Sketches by all three men would be reflected in the Honan commission: for example, in a painting by Keating, *Thinking about Gobnet*, which depicts Clarke pensively slumped amongst sceno-graphic stone relics in an Aran Islanders' Sunday-best báinín-cloth suit and cowhide pampooties (FIG. 7.4, P. 165).[12]

On 19 October 1914, Clarke met Sir John O'Connell, the Dublin solicitor, governor (and

old boy) of Belvedere College and Killiney neighbour of Waldron, to whom the Honan family of Cork had bequeathed funds in 1913 for a new collegiate chapel within the grounds of the University. Work had already started in December on a deliberately restrained Hiberno-Romanesque building dedicated to St Finn Barr, on the approximate site of whose school and monastery it was being built; simple decoration and skilled craftsmanship were to be integral to its spirit and structure.[13] As Ireland had no extant medieval glass to emulate, the blind windows in an evocative engraving by P. Skelton of the interior of Cormac's Chapel in Cashel were offered as possible inspiration, while Robert Elliott's warnings against 'sham medievalism' were heeded: 'a

FIG. 7.5: *Engraving of interior of Cormac's Chapel, Cashel from a drawing by Margaret Stokes*

A NEW BYZANTIUM

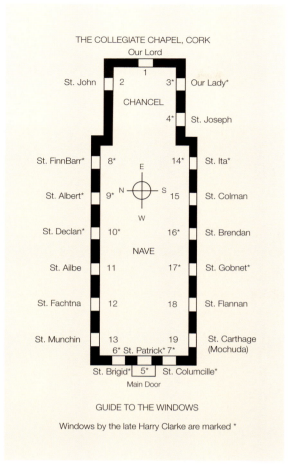

THE COLLEGIATE CHAPEL, CORK
Our Lord

| | 1 | |
| St. John | 2 | 3* | Our Lady* |

CHANCEL

4* St. Joseph

St. FinnBarr*	8*	14*	St. Ita*
St. Albert*	9*	15	St. Colman
St. Declan*	10*	16*	St. Brendan

NAVE

St. Ailbe	11	17*	St. Gobnet*
St. Fachtna	12	18	St. Flannan
St. Munchin	13	19	St. Carthage (Mochuda)

6* St. Patrick* 7*

St. Brigid* 5* St. Columcille*

Main Door

GUIDE TO THE WINDOWS

Windows by the late Harry Clarke are marked *

FIG. 7.6: *Plan of the windows in Honan Chapel. Clarke's windows are marked with a * (from Sir J.R. O'Connell's The Collegiate Chapel, Cork)*

FIG. 7.7: *St Patrick window (detail, illustrating the open missal at the foot of St Patrick)*

stained glass window should not be . . . an imitation chromo-lithograph of a mediaeval panelled saint, which has none of the reproductive utility of a lithograph, and none of the translucent charm of pre-reformation glass' (FIG. 7.5).[14] More bluntly, Whall had instructed, 'keep your pictures for the walls and your windows for the holes in them'.[15] Sir John was determined to ensure that the windows represent the finest design and execution 'by Irish artists and craftsmen working in Ireland',[16] adhering to the credo adopted by An Túr Gloine (The Tower of Glass), the Dublin co-operative stained glass studio set up by the painter Sarah Purser in 1903 for graduates of A.E. Child's classes at the School of Art: 'each window should be in all its artistic parts the work of one individual artist, the glass chosen and painted by the same mind and hand that made the design and drew the cartoon'.[17]

Since 1901, A.E. Child had been supervising the design and execution of the stained glass in Loughrea Cathedral, Co. Galway, a shrine to Irish craftsmen and women of the Celtic Revival, for which An Túr Gloine artists would provide stained glass between 1903–1940. Sarah Purser therefore presumed that all the Honan Chapel windows, which were to depict Our Lady, St Joseph, and St John in the chancel, the *Trias Thaumaturga* (Saints Patrick, Columcille and Brigid, the three wonder-working saints of Ireland) over the west end entrance and 'the patron saints of the dioceses of the province of Munster and other saints closely bound up with Cork' in the nave, would automatically go to An Túr Gloine (FIG. 7.6)[18] She had apparently been promised eight before Clarke was approached. However, she had not bargained with Waldron's intervention. Shortly before Clarke was summoned by Sir John, Waldron went to stay with his old friend Sir Bertram Windle, who was instrumental in the erection of the chapel.[19] The result was that Clarke was invited to prepare a design for *St Brigid*, and then for *Saints Patrick, Columcille, Gobnait* and *Ita*. The formal commission to

FIG. 7.8: St Patrick, St Brigid and St Columcille windows, which are situated over the entrance at the Honan Chapel

make these five windows came the following January, with an invitation to compete for further windows. Sarah Purser was not pleased. In the end, all An Túr's windows were made between April and August 1916.[20] They were divided between Child, who did five (*Our Lord risen and triumphant, St Ailbe, St Colman, St Fachtna, Scenes from the life of Our Lord according to the Gospel of St John*), Catherine O'Brien, who did two (*St Flannan* and *St Munchin*), and Ethel Rhind, who did one (*St Carthage*). None is especially remarkable, although beguiling narrative details are threaded through O'Brien's and her bright colours harmonize more successfully with Clarke's than the tonally subdued range used by Child and Rhind. Clarke eventually made six windows in 1915, in the following

order: *Saints Patrick, Brigid and Columcille, St Finn Barr, St Ita, St Albert*; three in 1916, *St Gobnait, St Declan* and *St Brendan*; and the two chancel windows, *Our Lady* and *St Joseph* in 1917, after the chapel had been consecrated the previous November.

On the strength of this and his major commission to illustrate *Hans Andersen's Fairy Tales* in black and white and colour, Harry Clarke married Margaret Crilley, a painter and former fellow student, at the end of October 1914. They moved into a new flat above the Clarke studios and he proceeded to work on the five minutely detailed, coloured small-scale Cork designs, while ordering sheets of 'antique' pot metal glass in shades of deep blue and green for *St Patrick* from Hetley's, the studios' main stained

FIG. 7.9: *The miraculous consecration of St Fin Barr and Maccuirp, (R.H.), St Fin Barr window (detail), Honan Chapel*

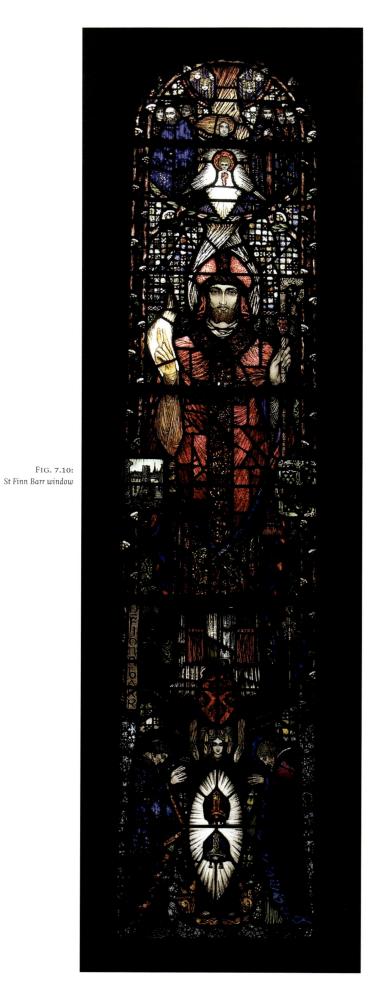

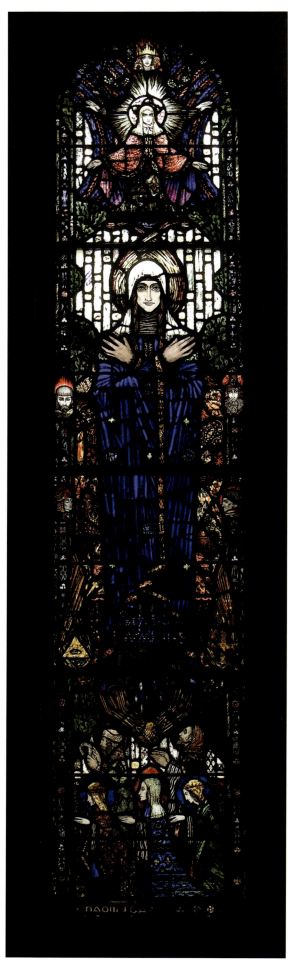

FIG. 7.12: *Cartoon for St Declan window*

FIG. 7.13: *St Declan window*

FIG. 7.14: *Cartoon
for St Albert window*

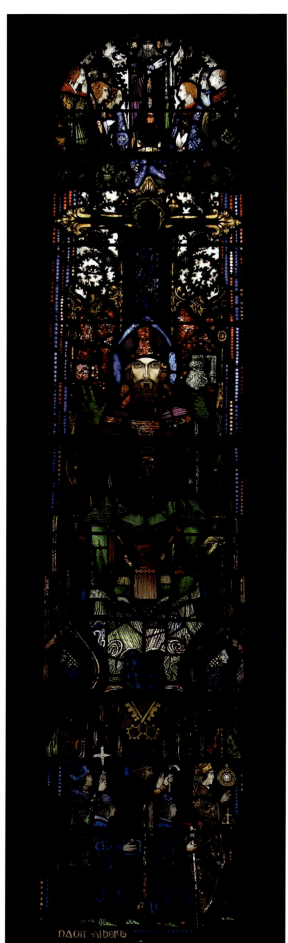

FIG. 7.15: *St Albert window*

A New Byzantium

FIG. 7.16: *Photograph of the Clarkes' house in Mount Merrion, Dublin, taken c. 1975*

glass suppliers in London, and further pots to be specially made at Chance's in Birmingham.

In mid-March, the day after his twenty-sixth birthday, he began two months concentrated work on St *Patrick*, the largest of all the Honan Chapel windows (11'6" x 2'10"). After cartooning it up to size, so that it resembled a completely revised, monochrome replica of the final window, he selected, cut and waxed up each piece of glass on to a cutline, before painting, aciding and staining, and finally leading up the whole structure. He paid his father's studios 25 shillings per foot for supplies (including coal for the kiln), glazing and fixing, and was assisted, particularly while he was in England getting glass, by his friend Austin Molloy, whose name appears on the window.[21] When he had made St *Brigid* and St *Columcille*, smaller flanking lights of great beauty in deep ruby and blue, the three-light window was exhibited in the Clarke studios, a custom he adopted henceforth. Once the cartoon for his first nave window, St *Finn Barr*, was completed, Harry and

Margaret Clarke spent a belated honeymoon in the Aran Islands in August (FIGS. 7.7–7.10, PP. 167–170).

Each window demanded considerable research before the colour scheme, overall composition and decorative and symbolic details relating to each saint's life, personality, character and mythology could be designed. Clarke consulted a range of antiquarian and contemporary sources, popular, traditional, erudite and historical, which he ingeniously wove into the rich tapestry around each seemingly entranced, resplendent figure. Some, like St *Ita*, necessitated several revisions until he was satisfied with them, and the war affected the sending of supplies from England. St *Albert* followed St *Finn Barr* and St *Ita*, over whose troublesome predella panel Bodkin had advised him. The well-reviewed exhibition of all five windows in the studios led to a commission for six further windows, leaving An Túr Gloine with their original eight (FIGS. 7.11–7.15, PP. 170-72).

In the summer of 1916, after the upheavals of
the Republican Insurrection, the Clarkes
moved out of the centre of Dublin into a cottage
in Mount Merrion Avenue in Blackrock,
in whose north-facing mews he set up a studio
for drawing and cartooning (FIG. 7.16,
P. 173). Under considerable pressure for special brown glass flashed on blue for *Brendan*, extra wide-grooved lead for *Gobnait's* thick
blue slabs,[22] and particular flesh tones, he
managed to meet his October deadline and
complete the sumptuous *St Gobnait*, *St Brendan*
and *St Declan* windows for the nave in time for
the Chapel's consecration on 5 November
(FIGS. 7.17–7.19; 7.20, 7.21, P. 176).[23] At the
same time, his Hans Andersen illustrations
were published in England and America, to
enthusiastic reviews. Sir Bertram Windle
thought his windows were 'quite wonderful
beyond all'[24] and Sir John O'Connell dedicated
a copy of his account of the chapel: 'To Harry
Clarke – A slight memorial of the Author's
admiration for his imagination in designing
and his skill in executing the windows in
the Honan Chapel – November 1916' (FIG.
7.23, P. 178).[25]

On 28 April 1917, Clarke showed *Our Lady*
and *St Joseph*, his last two Honan Chapel windows, privately in the studios before they were
sent down to Cork. On the same day, *The Irish
Builder and Engineer* ran a detailed account of all
the stained glass in the chapel, welcoming it as
devoid of the 'foreign abominations' too read-
ily imported, and setting it in its full Revivalist
context. In previous issues, it had praised the
Ruskinian integrity of purpose in the conception and the realization of a unique achievement in Irish craftsmanship.[26] Shortly after,
Sir John O'Connell would articulate the deep
national hope for independent, imaginative
expression and confidence, which the current

FIG. 7.17:
St Gobnait window

A New Byzantium

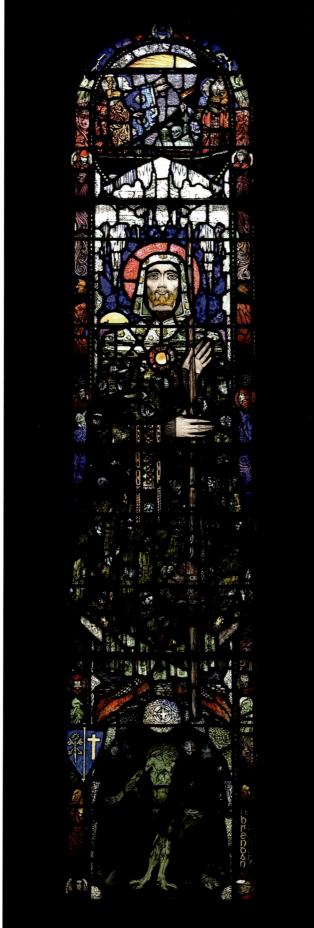

FIG. 7.20:
St Brendan window

revival in artistic native craftwork offered, in FIG. 7.21: St Brendan
window, (detail) his foreword to the Arts and Crafts Society of Ireland's fifth exhibition catalogue (designed and illustrated by Clarke).[27]

Throughout the Honan Chapel commission, Harry Clarke had taken great pains to seek out the exact materials he needed: for the last two windows, he wanted particularly limpid flashed blues made by the English glassmakers Millar & Beale, and other full-bodied tones from Hartley Woods in Sunderland, rather than the studios' usual stock from Chance's, which did not stain sufficiently well (FIG. 7.24, P. 178). Lead was becoming scarce because of the war and no company would undertake to ship over from Sheffield the fluoric acid he needed for his exacting etching work; eventually, the studios' book-keeper, Miss Sullivan, went over and illicitly smuggled it back in a small leather case. The very limitations of this demanding craft served only as a challenge for Clarke's perfectionism. Each window is filled with hundreds of often tiny pieces of glass, varying greatly

A NEW BYZANTIUM

in thickness, many of them made of a layer of colour which is flashed on the surface of either clear or another coloured glass when moulten; when thus coated, the top layer may be acid-etched as many times as there is a body of colour in the glass, and stained on the reverse with silver nitrate, giving a range of yellows, from pale lemon to deep burnished orange (see the details of the honey-robber and Gobnait's handmaiden in St Gobnait) (FIGS. 7.18, 7.19, P. 175). Only then did painting and firing the glass begin, before the appropriate widths of lead were milled to enclose each, often very thick, piece of glass (particularly blue and ruby).[28]

Clarke began by visualizing a dominant colour key for each window: red for the divinely radiant sixth-century Finn Barr the Red-headed and for Joseph, father of Jesus; blue (traditionally) for ethereal, otherworldly Brigid of Kildare and for Our Lady of Sorrows, also for the sixth-century ascetic Ita the Wise of Ballyvourney (the Brigid of Munster), born Deirdre, the daughter of a chieftain of the Decies, and for the miracle-making abbess Gobnait of Ballyvourney; yellow, symbolizing brightness, goodness and faith, for compassionate Columcille of Derry and Iona, known as 'The Dove of the Churches', and for seafaring Declan of Ardmore of the Decii and his companion Ruanus; green for Patrick of Tara as bishop of learning, dignity, justice and faith, for the eighth-century missionary devotee of the Cross, Albert of Cashel and Ratisbon in Bavaria, and for Brendan the Navigator of Kerry and

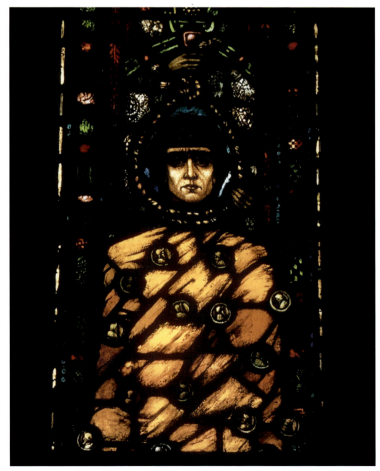

FIG. 7.22: Judas
1913, detail of the
stained glass section

Clonfert. Each jewelled tapestry can be seen in abstract terms as a symbolic orchestration of colour by light. This conforms to traditional medieval iconography and, conceptually, relates to Wassily Kandinsky's treatise, *Über das Geistige in der Kunst* of 1911, translated into English as *The Art of Spiritual Harmony* in 1914, which discusses the departure of art from the objective world, exploring colour as 'the power which directly influences the soul', to reach man's internal world. Kandinsky considers Goethe's theory that every colour has a spiritual association, and corresponding musical vibration, so that blue (a colour Clarke especially loved and used to great effect in his stained glass and book illustrations) may be transcendental, beyond the body, intense and boundless:

The power of profound meaning is found in blue, and first in its physical movements 1) of retreat from the spectator, 2) of turning in upon its own centre. The inclination of blue to depth is so strong that its inner appeal is stronger when its shade is deeper. Blue is the typical heavenly colour. The ultimate feeling it creates is one of [supernatural] rest . . . In music a light blue is like a flute, a darker blue a cello; a thunderous double bass; and the darkest blue of all – an organ (FIG. 5.17, P. 174).[29]

Clarke's use of a deep, rich, royal blue, so thick that it seems to pulsate and throb in the honeycomb-lozenged robe of Gobnait and the jewelled mantle of Ita, is powerful, even when overpainted with a miniature mitred bishop or a tiny gravestone marked with his own initials. His dramatic and intricate juxtaposition of ruby and

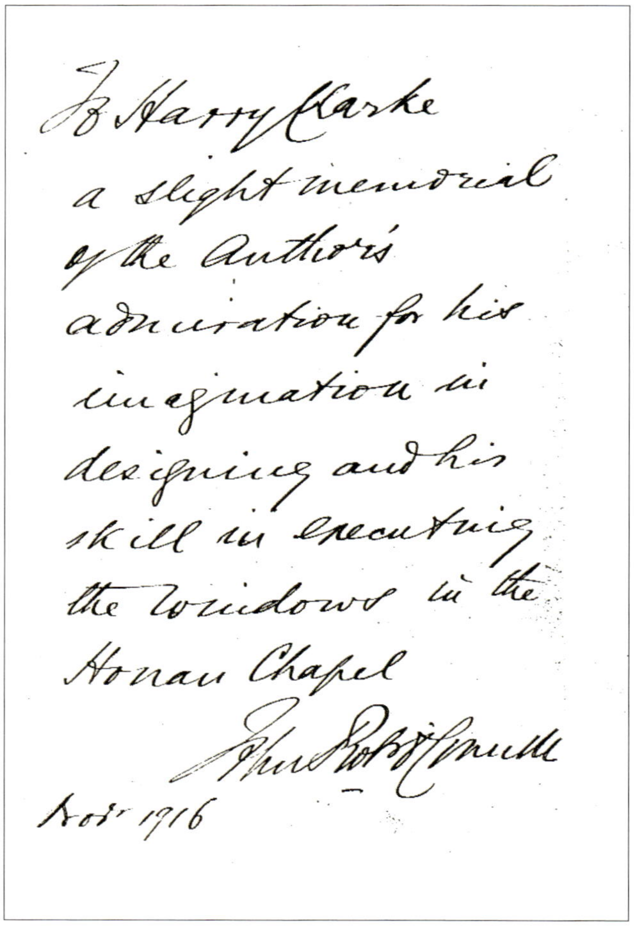

FIG. 7.23: *Sir John O'Connell's dedication to Clarke in his book The Collegiate Chapel, Cork (1916)*

FIG. 7.24: *Jar of blue Norman slab glass owned by Clarke*

To Harry Clarke
a slight memorial
of the Author's
admiration for his
imagination in
designing and his
skill in executing
the windows in the
Honan Chapel
John Robert O'Connell
Nov 1916

FIG. 7.25:
St Brigid window

FIG. 7.26:
St Brigid window
(enlarged detail of
tiny beading in
the borders)

FIG. 7.27: St Gobnait window
(detail of honeycomb lozenged shaped
glass forming her robe)

FIG. 7.28: Leon Bakst's costume
design for 'The Martyrdom of St
Sebastian', 1911

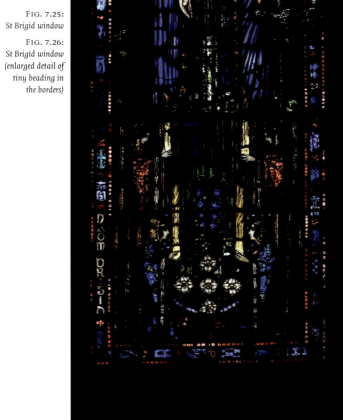

FIG. 7.29:
*St Gobnait window
(detail of St
Gobnait's profile)*

A NEW BYZANTIUM

FIG. 7.30: *Alesso Baldovinetti Portrait of a Lady in Yellow*

FIG. 7.31: *St Gobnait window (detail)*

blue (often in tiny beaded borders) in both these and the kaleidoscopically sumptuous *Brigid* window, (FIGS. 7.25, 7.26, P. 179) refers back to his seminal studies of early medieval stained glass in England and in the Île de France, giving the strong harmonic effect of which Kandinsky writes.[30]

Each window is filled with a synthetic wealth of art historical allusions, often unexpected, and too legion to document fully in this short chapter. For example, the appropriately honeycombed mantle Gobnait wears, in her principal and subsidiary miracle-working images as patron saint of bee-keeping, is taken directly from the Ballets Russes costume Léon Bakst designed for Ida Rubinstein in *The Martyrdom of St Sebastian* in 1911, while her dramatically highbrowed profiled head is directly derived from Alesso Baldovinetti's fifteenth-century *Portrait of a Lady in Yellow* (National Gallery, London), and her deathly pale skin, burnished red hair and tapering fingers adapted from Marcus Gheerhaerts the Younger's sixteenth-century Ditchley Portrait

of Elizabeth I, (National Portrait Gallery, London) (FIGS. 7.27, 7.28, P. 179; 7.29–7.31).[31] One of Brigid's angels (lower right-hand) is taken from Ambrogio de' Predis' bonneted *Portrait of a Lady* (National Gallery, London), while Ita's hieratic features refer to those of the Empress Theodora in the Byzantine mosaic interior of the Church of San Vitale in Ravenna. The principal figure of Brendan, steadfastly gazing out to sea in a carbuncle-encrusted leather hooded cloak, is based on Gustav Klimt's commanding figure of Hygieia from his 1901 *Medicine* frieze (destroyed in 1945 in Vienna), while the tiny border angels with windswept hair accompanying Declan's pre-Patrician companion saints derive from another unexpected Vienna Secession source, Berthold Löffler's Kunstshau poster of 1908 (FIGS. 7.32, 7.33, P. 182). The luxuriantly bearded, slippered and green-silk-gloved Albert, majestically enthroned, is based on two twelfth-century stained glass figures: Chartres Cathedral's *Notre-Dame de la Belle Verrière* and Canterbury Cathedral's *Ozias* (FIGS. 7.34, 7.35,

FIG. 7.32: *St Declan window (detail of angel from the border)*

FIG. 7.33: *Berthold Löffler Kunstschau Wien, 1908, poster design*

P. 183), while the tortured, emaciated spectre of Judas encountered by Brendan and his terror-struck companions is inspired by the pitted fiends in the seven-light medieval *Last Judgment* window in the Church of St Mary the Virgin at Fairford, Gloucestershire, which Clarke had specially visited in 1914 (FIGS. 7.36, 7.37, P. 184).[32] Similarly, Joseph is based on the fourteenth-century figure of the Prophet Zephaniah, removed from Winchester College Chapel to the Victoria & Albert Museum in about 1855 (FIG. 7.38, P. 185). At the foot of the melancholy Byzantinized *Virgin Mary as Mother of Sorrows*, St Cronan of Roscrea, with his *Cronan na Magdine* parchment sheet of musical notation and forlorn company of early Christian emblem-bearing martyrs, is flanked by four tiny Japonist seals; these refer to Japanese seal designs and to stained glass quarries designed by Henry Payne's Birmingham School of Art students, reproduced in Whall's *Stained Glass Work*. Such references greatly appealed to his art-loving, connoisseur patrons (FIG. 7.39, P. 185).

However abundant his sources, a study in themselves, Clarke is brilliantly able to weave an extraordinary wealth of fascinating, carefully researched, narrative and symbolic detail into the challengingly long, narrow compositions around his beautifully apparelled, saintly figures.[33] Portrayed in heavenly ecstasy, they gaze with the dignity and repose Sir John O'Connell sought, episodes from their earthly travails picturesquely recorded with a miniaturist's unerring brush in vignettes above and below them. Nonetheless, the woefully metamorphosized fallen angels from the Paradise of Birds island which adorn the borders of the *Brendan* window, St Brendan's sore-tried contemporaries, St Ita the Wise, St Brigid, Erc, Jarlath, Finian, the blind Addagh and 'the poor monk with the Iron in his Head', and the awesome encounter of the saint and his terrified disciples with ravaged Judas Iscariot made some visitors uneasy, even though such details reveal Clarke's essentially medieval love of the macabre and the sublime.

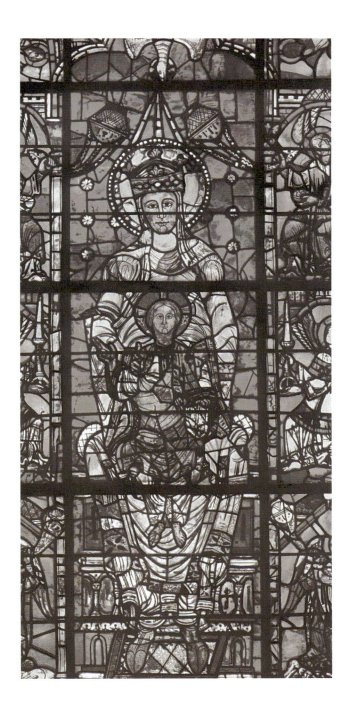

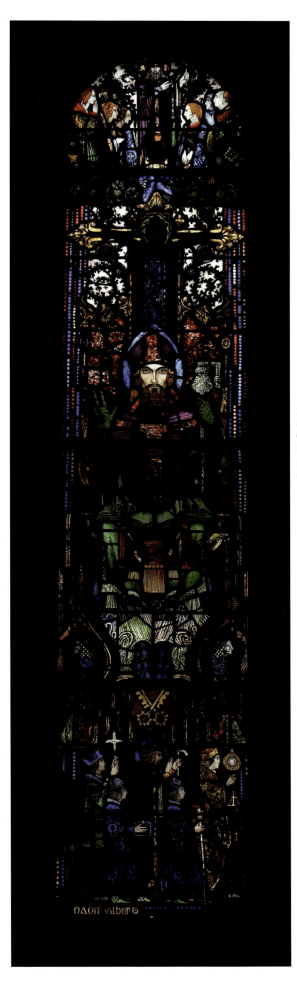

FIG. 7.34: *Notre-Dame de la Belle Verrière, Chartres Cathedral, (detail)*

FIG. 7.35: *St Albert window, Honan Chapel*

Sir Bertram Windle's cousin, the writer Edith Oenone Somerville, who would commission Clarke's next church window, a *Nativity* (1918) for St Barrahane's, Castletownshend, Co. Cork, thought them 'supremely lovely' 'very beautiful, mostly & very diabolic'

very wonderful in colour . . . I preferred the western three-light window & I almost disliked the blue one [Ita], & the Aubrey Beardsley female face [Gobnait] thought horrible; so modern & conventionally unconventional . . . The actual glass has a quality of burning & furious brilliance that I have never seen anywhere else. The blue robe, for instance, hits your eyes like a living flame or a blast of wind. Perfectly amazing, but not quite pleasant . . . His windows have a kind of hellish splendour – In a chapel

dedicated to the Infernal Deities they would be exactly right, gorgeous & sinful.[34]

Another eminent contemporary Irish writer and painter, the visionary and critic, George 'AE' Russell, wrote nearly ten years later:

Looking at [his] windows, I imagine that if one scraped a little the subconscious mind of the artist, you would let in a flood of rich colour out of some inner luminous aether, where the fire is more brilliant than the eye can see, and the only way he could recreate that colour for us was by the art he practises. There is not a square inch in the windows which is not invented . . . The limitations of the technique only seem to inspire Clarke, and from jewelled crowns to shoe buckles, there is endless invention.[35]

FIG. 7.36: *Last Judgement window, Church of St Mary the Virgin, Fairford, Gloucestershire (detail)*

FIG. 7.37: *Judas, from St Brendan window, Honan Chapel (detail)*

A NEW BYZANTIUM

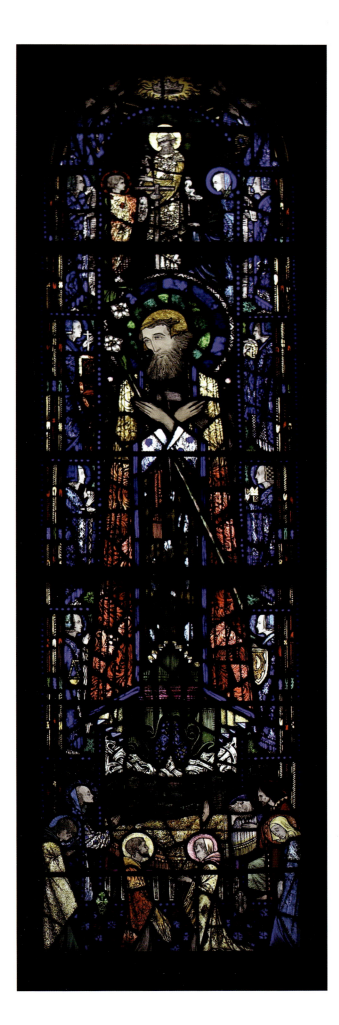

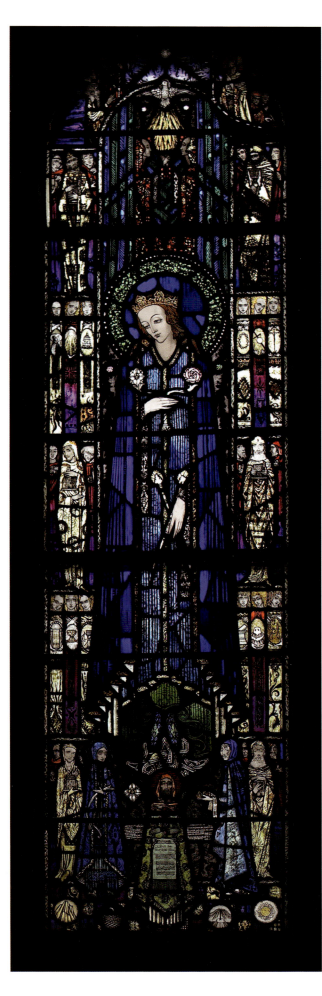

FIG. 7.38: *St Joseph window*

FIG. 7.39: *Virgin Mary as Mother of Sorrows window, Honan Chapel*

NOTES AND REFERENCES

1   Remarkably, although Clarke's windows were documented (along with its eight neighbours by fellow artists of An Túr Gloine stained glass co-operative) in the Revd Sir John O'Connell's book, *The Collegiate Chapel, Cork: Some Notes on the Building and on the Ideals Which Inspired It*, 2nd edn (Cork University Press, 1932) and mentioned in contemporary features on Clarke, and in James White and Michael Wynne's *Irish Stained Glass: a Catalogue of Stained Glass Windows by Irish Artists of the 20th Century* (Dublin: Furrow Trust; Gill & Son, 1963), they received little critical or contextual attention until 1979. Then, for *Harry Clarke*, the major exhibition mounted by the Douglas Hyde Gallery, Trinity College, Dublin, the *St Gobnait* window was shown, along with her design and cartoon and those for most of the other windows, and documented in the context of Clarke's achievement as a major Symbolist and Arts and Crafts figure. Thus, the author's accompanying catalogue, an article, ' "A Host of Shining Saints": Harry Clarke's Stained Glass in Cork' (*Country Life*, July 12, 1979, pp. 114–117) and Jeanne Sheehy's pioneering book, *The Rediscovery of Ireland's Past: the Celtic Revival 1830–1930* (London: Thames & Hudson, 1980) led the way to Bowe, *The Life and Work of Harry Clarke* (Dublin: Irish Academic Press, 1989), where the windows are examined individually and within a national and international framework.

2   P.O. Reeves, 'Irish Arts and Crafts', *The Studio*, vol. 72, no. 295, October 1917, pp. 21–2. Reeves' love of the stained glass at Chartres and his insistence on a 'genuine Celtic character', devoid of 'slavish reversion to ancient forms', were well known to his students, who were Clarke's contemporaries at the Dublin Metropolitan School of Art.

3   Thomas Bodkin, 'The Art of Mr Harry Clarke', *The Studio*, vol. 79, no. 320, November 1919, p. 46. This long article, probably prompted by E.A. Taylor, the Glasgow designer and Paris correspondent of *The Studio* in Paris, where Clarke had met him with his wife Jessie M. King, was the first to appraise Clarke's versatile and prolific output in an international Arts and Crafts context.

4   Unsourced but quoted in White and Wynne, op.cit., p. 13, the first publication to chronicle and catalogue twentieth-century windows in Ireland.

5   'News of Our Past', *The Belvederian*, vol. 4, no. 3, Summer 1917, pp. 36–8.

6   See Nicola Gordon Bowe, David Caron and Michael Wynne, *A Gazetteer of Irish Stained Glass: the Works of Harry Clarke and the Artists of An Túr Gloine*, (The Tower of Glass) 1903–1963 (Dublin: Irish Academic Press, 1988), Introduction and biography of Child; also Nicola Gordon Bowe and Elizabeth Cumming, *The Arts and Crafts Movements in Dublin and Edinburgh 1885–1925* (Dublin: Irish Academic Press, 1998), catalogue entry under Child. For Whall, see [Peter Cormack], *Christopher Whall, 1849–1924, Arts & Crafts Stained Glass Worker*: [catalogue of an

exhibition held at the] William Morris Gallery, London Borough of Waltham Forest, 17th November 1979-3rd February 1980 (London: Libraries and Arts Department, London Borough of Waltham Forest, 1979) and the revised edition of Whall's *Stained Glass Work: a Text-Book for Students and Workers in Glass* (Bristol: Morris & Juliet Venables, 1999) with an introduction by Peter Cormack.

7   John Ruskin, *The Stones of Venice*, 11, Appendix 12, 3rd edn (London: George Allen, 1898). Whall preached Ruskin's *Aratra Pentelici* (1872) in his inspirational book, which was the basic text used by Child in his teaching. Similarly, Ruskin's gospel 'Design in beauty and build in truth' was to guide James McMullen in his Cork chapel. In 1913, through an English designer his father employed, Clarke would meet Karl Parsons, a distinguished pupil of Whall, who subsequently became one of Clarke's closest friends.

8   Quoted by the judges, Walter Crane, Selwyn Image and Byam Shaw in the *Board of Education, National Competition, 1914: List of Successful Competitors and Reports of the Examiners with Illustrations* (London: s.l., 1915).

9   For this *Judas* panel, see Nicola Gordon Bowe *Harry Clarke: a Monograph and Catalogue*, published to coincide with the exhibition 'Harry Clarke', 12 November to 8 December 1979, at the Douglas Hyde Gallery (Dublin: Douglas Hyde Gallery, 1979), p. 97 and *The Life and Work of Harry Clarke* (Dublin: Irish Academic Press, 1989), pp. 23–5 and colour plate 2. The panel is currently on loan to the Hugh Lane Gallery of Modern Art, Dublin.

10   Professor of Architecture at the National University of Ireland and designer of much of the Honan Chapel metalwork. See Bowe and Cumming, op.cit., 1998, catalogue entry 182 under Scott, p. 189.

11   His prize-winning stained glass panel, *The Baptism of St. Patrick* (1912), was on display in the Palais du Louvre as part of the prestigious Exposition des Arts Décoratifs de Grande Bretagne et d'Irlande.

12   Inscribed in Irish and dated 29 August 1917. Clarke would draw a caricature of himself wearing pampooties with Molloy in 1909, and make these distinctive slippers a feature of his Honan Chapel St. *Brendan the Navigator*.

13   The spelling adopted by O'Connell in his book was 'Finn Barr', although Clarke uses an Irish form, 'Fionnbarr', which is inscribed vertically as though on parchment in the left-hand border. The nave saints' names are inscribed in Gaelic script, and mostly in an Irish form; many of the tiny incidental figures' names are written in minuscule script, often on their haloes.

14   Robert Elliott, 'On Stained Glass', *The Irish Rosary*, February 1903, reproduced in Robert Elliott, *Art and Ireland* (Dublin: Sealy, Bryers & Walker, [1906], p. 201

15   Christopher W. Whall, *Stained Glass Work* (London: John Hogg, 1905) , p. 84

16   John R. O'Connell, 'The Painted Windows', op. cit., 1932, p. 41.

17   Printed in the co-operative's 25th anniversary booklet, *An Túr Gloine, Twenty-Fifth Anniversary Celebration* (Dublin: 1928), p. 24.

18   O'Connell, op.cit., 1932, p. 41.

19   Miss Honan had stipulated that the chapel could only be built if Sir Bertram remain as President of the University. Should he leave, the funds would be diverted to another charitable endeavour. Sir Bertram, who appointed O'Connell, was as frequent a visitor to Waldron's Killiney house as Waldron was to his at Cork University.

20   See An Túr Gloine *Work Journal no. 1*, p. 186, order no. 402 (National Gallery of Ireland). I am grateful to Dr David Caron for this reference.

21   The words, 'Pray for poor Harry Clarke / who made this window / And for Austin Molloy, / who helped him June 1915' are inscribed in the open pages of a golden missal in the centre of the border at the base of the window. Molloy had won a silver medal at the 1914 National Competition for a *St Michael and the Dragon* window.

22   Clarke had special square-sided jars of thick, deep blue Norman slab glass made for his *St Ita* and *St Gobnait* windows by Chance's of Oldbury, Birmingham, which he ordered through the Studios' main stockist, Hetley's of Soho Square in London. These jars, whose sides were diamond-cut to give five lumpy slabs of glass, thicker in each centre and therefore ideal for trapping light and colour, were a hallmark of English Arts and Crafts glass, and as fundamental to it as the mid-nineteenth-century rediscovery of 'antique' pot metal was to Victorian glass. It was first made in 1889 under the direction of the architect E.S. Prior.

23   Although St. Declan was not fixed properly until January 1917.

24   Quoted in Sister Monica J. Taylor, S.N.D., *Sir Bertram Windle: Bertram Coghill Alan Windle: a Memoir* (London: Longmans, Green & Co., 1932), p. 254.

25   I am grateful to Cal Hyland to drawing my attention to this presentation copy.

26   Mysteriously, only the mosaic floor and the *opus sectile* are not Irish-made, even though An Túr Gloine had been producing good *opus sectile* since 1906.

27   Held in Dublin, at the Metropolitan School of Art in June and July, in Belfast in October, and in Cork in November 1917, it included Clarke's cartoons for the *St Brigid*, *St Gobnett* [sic] and *Our Lady* windows, each for sale. Sir John's aspirations should also be seen in the context of the contemporary World War, in which thousands of young Irish lives were sacrificed, and in the aftermath of the inflammatory political situation in Ireland.

28   Clarke described his exacting technique, fundamentally based on the medieval glass he so admired, in a letter to Bodkin on 26 July 1919 (Bodkin MSS, T.C.D.) and in an article, 'Some Notes on Stained Glass', *Illustrated Country Review*, vol. 5, no. 8, November 1925; see Bowe, op. cit., 1989, Appendix 1.

29   Wassily Kandinsky, *The Art of Spiritual Harmony*, translated by M.T.H. Sadler as *Concerning the spiritual in art* (New York: Dover, 1977), p. 38.

30   Kandinsky had emulated this a few years earlier in his tempera canvases and

reverse paintings on glass with painted frames, based on his ethnographic studies of primitive religious art; see Peg Weiss, *Kandinsky and Old Russia: The Artist as Ethnographer and Shaman* (New Haven: Yale University Press, 1995).

31 For Waldron, Clarke would synthesize the profiled image of Gobnait with Donatello's fifteenth-century *Virgin and Child* terracotta and gilt relief panel in the Victoria & Albert Museum into a small stained glass roundel of *The Madonna and Child* in 1915 and, in 1917, adapt a number of the tiny attendant figures into a processional frieze of nine panels illustrating J.M. Synge's poem, 'Queens'. For the latter, on which Clarke was working towards the end of the Honan Chapel commission, see Bowe, op. cit., 1989, pp. 72-80 and Liam Miller and Bowe, *Synge's Queens*, printed by the Dolmen Press and published privately.

32 Clarke's fascination with the Judas legend, which he knew from Matthew Arnold's poem 'Saint Brandan' and the medieval *Navigatio Sancti Brendani Abbatis*, dates from his 1911 student panel, *St. Brendan and the Unhappy Judas.*

33 See Bowe, op. cit., 1989, Ch. 3.

34 Diary entries for 14 January and 27 March 1917 and letter 23 March 1917 to her cousin, Cameron, quoted by Otto Rauchbauer, *The Edith Œnone Somerville Archive in Drishane: a Catalogue and an Evaluative Essay* (Dublin: Irish Manuscripts Commission, 1995) (© Christopher Somerville, Drishane Archive).

35 G.W. Russell (Æ), 'The Work of Harry Clarke', *Irish Statesman*, 8 August 1925, p. 692.

BIBLIOGRAPHY

'News of Our Past', *The Belvederian*, vol. 4, no. 3, Summer 1917, pp. 36–8

An Túr Gloine Work Journal no. 1, p. 186

An Túr Gloine, Twenty-fifth Anniversary Celebration (Dublin: 1928)

Board of Education, National Competition, 1914: List of Successful Competitors and Reports of the Examiners with Illustrations (London, 1915)

BODKIN, THOMAS, 'The art of Mr Harry Clarke', *The Studio*, vol. 79, no. 320, November 1919, p. 46

BOWE, NICOLA GORDON, ' "A Host of Shining Saints": Harry Clarke's Stained Glass in Cork', *Country Life*, 12 July, 1979, pp. 114–117

BOWE, NICOLA GORDON, *Harry Clarke: a Monograph and Catalogue, Published to Coincide with the Exhibition 'Harry Clarke', 12 November to 8 December 1979, at the Douglas Hyde Gallery* (Dublin: Douglas Hyde Gallery, 1979)

BOWE, NICOLA GORDON, David Caron and Michael Wynne, *A Gazetteer of Irish Stained Glass: the Works of Harry Clarke and the Artists of An Túr Gloine, (The Tower of Glass) 1903–1963* (Dublin: Irish Academic Press, 1988)

BOWE, NICOLA GORDON, *The Life and Work of Harry Clarke* (Dublin: Irish Academic Press, 1989)

BOWE, NICOLA GORDON, AND ELIZABETH CUMMING, *The Arts and Crafts Movements in Dublin and Edinburgh 1885–1925* (Dublin: Irish Academic Press, 1998)

Clarke, Harry, 'Some Notes on Stained Glass', *Illustrated Country Review*, vol. 5, no. 8, November 1925

[CORMACK, PETER], *Christopher Whall, 1849–1924, Arts & Crafts Stained Glass Worker: [catalogue of an exhibition held at the] William Morris Gallery, London Borough of Waltham Forest, 17th November 1979–3rd February 1980* (London: Libraries and Arts Department, London Borough of Waltham Forest, 1979)

ELLIOTT, ROBERT, 'On Stained Glass', *The Irish Rosary*, February 1903

ELLIOTT, ROBERT, *Art and Ireland* (Dublin: Sealy, Bryers & Walker, [1906])

KANDINSKY, WASSILY, *The Art of Spiritual Harmony*, translated by M.T.H. Sadler as *Concerning the Spiritual in Art* (New York: Dover, 1977)

MILLER, LIAM, AND NICOLA GORDON BOWE, *Synge's Queens* (Dolmen Press: published privately)

O'CONNELL, REV SIR JOHN, *The Collegiate Chapel, Cork: some notes on the building and on the Ideals which Inspired It*, 2nd edn (Cork University Press, 1932)

RAUCHBAUER, OTTO, *The Edith Œnone Somerville Archive in Drishane: a catalogue and an evaluative essay* (Dublin: Irish Manuscripts Commission, 1995)

REEVES, P.O., 'Irish Arts and Crafts', *The Studio*, vol. 72, no. 295, October 1917, pp. 21–2

RUSKIN, JOHN, *The Stones of Venice*, II, Appendix 12, 3rd edn (London: George Allen, 1898)

RUSSELL, G.W., (Æ), 'The Work of Harry Clarke', *Irish Statesman*, 8 August 1925, p. 692

SHEEHY, JEANNE, *The Rediscovery of Ireland's Past: the Celtic Revival 1830–1930* (London: Thames & Hudson, 1980)

TAYLOR, SISTER MONICA J., S.N.D., *Sir Bertram Windle: Bertram Coghill Alan Windle: a Memoir* (London: Longmans, Green & Co., 1932)

WEISS, PEG, *Kandinsky and Old Russia: The artist as ethnographer and shaman* (New Haven: Yale University Press, 1995)

WHALL, CHRISTOPHER W., *Stained Glass Work* (London: John Hogg, 1905)

WHALL, CHRISTOPHER, *Stained Glass Work: a Text-Book for Students and Workers in Glass* (Bristol: Morris & Juliet Venables, 1999) with an introduction by Peter Cormack

WHITE, JAMES, AND MICHAEL WYNNE *Irish Stained Glass: a Catalogue of Stained Glass Windows by Irish Artists of the 20th Century* (Dublin: Furrow Trust; Gill & Son, 1963)

The Re-Ordering of The Honan Chapel

In order to understand the re-ordering of the Honan Chapel that took place in the mid-eighties it is helpful to understand the story of the liturgy. Liturgy is the whole range of public worship of the Church – from the Anglo-Saxon word 'wortchipe', giving worth to God. Recognizing that everything good comes from God, you ascribe worth par excellence to God. Essentially it is connected to other people – even when we pray by ourselves, at least when we are Christians we pray as the body of Christ.

Some people think there was never any change in the way Mass was celebrated, pretty well from the Last Supper to the present day. The Mass began as something very simple, which became more and more elaborate and complex; all sorts of court ceremonial which didn't have any direct bearing on Christianity was incorporated. I would say that since Vatican II we have been re-discovering something of the simplicity and the flexibility of the past – that is the overall pattern.

To look at one or two things in detail, all the liturgical forms, all the types of worship – they all go back to a Jewish original. And when this rather simple Jewish original was used by a community which no longer spoke Aramaic or some other semitic dialect, things happened. But it still remained fairly simple for the first four centuries, in spite of the change of language, which obviously did make for a number of alterations and adaptations. A big change certainly took place towards the early part of the fourth century when the Emperor Constantine became a Christian. For Christianity, from having been a persecuted religion, became a sort of state religion. It would be fair to say that the fourth century was a great creative period in the liturgy, both East and West. We could think, for example, of the great liturgical compositions: eucharistic prayers of this time. There were less happy innovations too, e.g.

bishops and priests taking on some of the court trappings of governors and other state dignitaries.

From the fourth to the sixth centuries in Rome, the liturgy was still popular in the sense of being understood by the people and of their participating in it. But the clericalization of the liturgy had begun and the people were beginning to be marginalized.

Another sort of watershed seems to have been round about the eighth century when, particularly, the great Emperor Charlemagne was very concerned with the pattern of worship in his dominions, where the liturgy was quite different from that in Rome. In stark contrast to Roman simplicity, it favoured allegory, the sense of mystery, elaborate ceremonial. This suited the temperament of those northern people. Charlemagne sought uniformity on a Roman model. But this was never really achieved. No sooner had the Roman sacramentaries been introduced to Gaul than they underwent a change. Liturgists like Alcuin saw to it that much of the Gallican tradition would be maintained. Inculturation went hand in hand with Romanization. And then a strange thing happened in the tenth century. This Gallicanized liturgy found its way back to Rome and began to feature in the official liturgical books. We are heirs to this amalgam of liturgical reforms. Thus what was considered to be the 'pure' Roman liturgy, representing an unbroken tradition, is in fact a fusion or confluence of prayer – forms and rites.

I think one has to accept that a certain amount of superstition or superstitious practices did get involved and one might say that in this period, from about the seventh or eighth century onwards, the active part taken by people became drastically reduced – they couldn't understand the language, Latin, in which it was prayed; they often couldn't see very much because the erection of things like rood screens, so they became more and more passive and the liturgy became more and more clerical in the way it was celebrated. And then, thinking about it, people mistakenly came to regard the liturgy as being primarily or solely the affair of the clergy and the priests.

Around about the ninth century, communion in the hand seems to have gone. How often were people going to communion in the ninth century? The answer is perhaps once a year, whereas in the earlier centuries they were going daily. In the ninth century, not only were priests in the habit of celebrating Mass every day, but sometimes several times a day – seven times a day, some document mentions even twenty times.

So, there was an enormous contrast between the priests, some of them saying Mass very, very often and the laity only going to communion once a year. As far as the clergy was concerned, the Mass was something that they did as often as possible in order to gain as much grace for themselves or sometimes to gain grace for other people who had asked them and sometimes paid money so that Mass should be said for their intentions; whereas in the early Church the attitude would have been much more: 'this is something which we as a community are doing, but we do it through the priest'.

In the ninth century the layman didn't go to communion out of a notion of his unworthiness (which was strongly inculcated in him by other people who thought he was unworthy). It was, of course, a very rough age, but there is quite an alarming shift in emphasis from the first three centuries as we know it and the eight, ninth and tenth centuries.

There was a great emphasis on the externals of worship. The connection between the internal and external is tremendously important – Our Lord hit out very strongly against the Pharisees; earlier still you have the Prophets hitting out against an approach to worship which concentrates almost exclusively on the externals and ignores the interior attitude which must express itself in, for example, social justice, one of the things the Prophets are very concerned with.

In the Middle Ages, because the ordinary people couldn't understand Latin, there was almost inevitably an emphasis on the visual, just as there was somewhat later, about the twelfth century, because they weren't encouraged to go to communion regularly. And because there was a great love of the person of Our Lord, (you think of St Francis and people like that) also, a great belief in His presence in the Eucharist (this is His body and blood), they put all those together. He is there, but we are not allowed to receive Him. Well, maybe at least we can see Him, look at Him in the host. And it is about that time you get first of all the introduction of the elevation and later on the introduction of the Feast of Corpus Christi and processions and benediction. Now this very admirable emphasis on adoration, I think one has to see it as secondary compared with the actual purpose of the Eucharist.

The next big watershed was the Council of Trent. The medieval persisted until then. There must have been something wrong, otherwise there wouldn't have been a reformation. The complaints made by the early reformers nearly always started with the liturgy. So something was wrong with the liturgy. The Council of Trent wished to do two things: to clean up the worst abuses – and it certainly had a long inventory of abuses: it mentions avarice, ignorance, superstition. Its other aim was to get back to the early liturgy of the Fathers of the Church. The difficulty in that respect was that at that time the question hadn't been studied – you might say scientifically – so there wasn't the information available that was available to the people who devised the new rites or revised our rites by the mandate of the fathers of Vatican II. At Trent they didn't have the information so they stuck to a medieval liturgy, often with many of its faults. And they standardized the liturgy.

The reforms of Vatican II represent a return to the older and more authentic tradition: frequent communion, restoration of the chalice to the laity, communion in the hand, the exchange of peace, etc. The communal nature of the liturgy is again emphasized. We worship not as disparate individuals, but as the Body of Christ. The reform of Vatican II was not a drastic one. Eamonn Duffy, author of *The Stripping of the Altars*, is critical of some of the post-conciliar liturgical reforms and of the 'iconoclasm' that followed. One would have to agree that the implementation of the liturgical constitution *Sacrosanctum Concilium* has not always been characterized by sensitivity.

The key statement in *Sacrosanctum Concilium* is: 'in the restoration and promotion of the sacred liturgy, the full and active participation of all the people is the aim to be considered before all else, for it is the primary and indispensable source from which the faithful are to derive the true Christian spirit.'

When Sir John Robert O'Connell, with the support of Sir Bertram Windle, F.R.S., set out to build the Honan Chapel, it was to provide a liturgical space for the old rite. There is the great divide between the nave and the chancel – divided by a great arch and the altar is at the back of the chancel – and this style is that of ninth and twelfth-century Romanesque. It clearly separated clergy and people. The priest was facing the back wall.

There were murmurings of the contemporary in Romano Guardini's chapel at Vienna University in the 1920s, but the real development came with the new churches in Germany and Switzerland after the Second World War. A feature of these churches was that the chancel had disappeared and the separation of priest and people became muted. There was an integrated space symbolizing unity.

The intervention in the Honan Chapel is one which respects the historical origins of the chapel while acknowledging the liturgical need to bring the liturgy closer to the people. Because of this, a moveable wooden altar was introduced to the front of the chancel. This gesture reinforced the integrity of the original design – while at the same time welcoming liturgical renewal.

The significance of the moveable altar was recognized by commissioning Imogen Stuart to carve an altar which relates the two periods of history. The carving of the altar reflects the unity between priests and people and echoes the iconography of earlier times. The magnificent collection of artefacts, the stained glass, etc reflects all that was best in the Hiberno-Romanesque revival. This is the great tradition of Irish sacred art – the visualization of the beautiful. Executed in terms of our own time, it is thus a valid representation of the hidden life.

The hidden life is ephemeral as spirituality changes, and I need only refer to the glories of the Gothic age and the beginnings of what has been symbolized in the liturgical renewal, which will rely more and more on communication and visual representation or presentation. Hiberno-Romanesque revivalism was a subconscious desire to recreate a medieval Church – not understanding the historical development of the Church, which is ongoing to the end of time. Wholesome change embodies recreation which leads us to the Spirit blowing where it will.

'See I create all things new', Rev. 21.5

Acknowledgements

I wish to thank Richard Hurley, F.R.I.A.L., and Fr. Vincent Ryan, O.S.B., Glenstal Abbey, for their help with this paper.

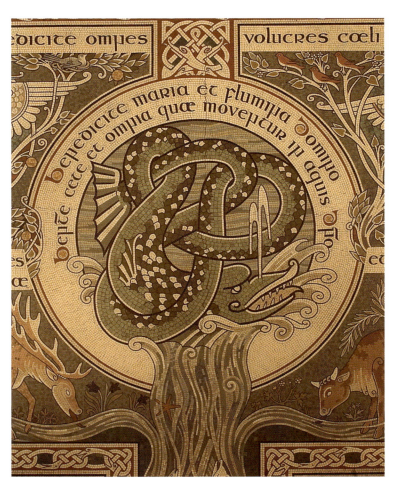

198

The Inventory

The evolution of liturgical practice since Vatican II has resulted in the re-ordering of ecclesiastical spaces and the consequent dislodgement of many sacred items from their earlier places in the practice of worship. In the context of the tightly defined, singular aesthetic, based upon deeply held theological and cultural values, which informed every detail of the foundation and creation of the Honan Chapel, splintering the parts results in an incomplete whole. This inventory is an effort to redress this.

The inventory sets out to record and make publicly accessible details of those items which comprise the Honan Collection as originally commissioned in 1916. The emphasis has been on providing a comprehensive listing of artefacts that are not part of the fabric of the building and which therefore are more vulnerable to being moved or replaced. Visitors to the chapel can still enjoy the wonderful mosaic floor, stained glass windows, stone carvings and other elements that comprise part of the original collection. As many of the items included in the following inventory are now in storage, it is hoped that the publication of this list, coupled with the works still on view in the chapel, will provide the public with an understanding of the full, and impressive, extent of the Honan Collection as it was originally conceived and executed.

FIG. 1: *Processional cross (detail)*
FIG. 2: *Black chasuble (detail)*
FIG. 3: *Altar card (detail)*
FIG. 4: *Mosaic floor beasthead (overview)*

Structure and arrangement

Structurally, the inventory works to bring similar items together into sections. Each section is preceded by a short introduction. The sections are as follows:

Section 1   Metalwork and Enamel
Section 2   Liturgical Textiles and Sanctuary Furnishings
Section 3   Liturgical Manuscripts and Books
Section 4   Chapel Furnishings.

Within the section headings individual items have been grouped together as appropriately as possible. Detailed entries for each item record reference number, title, brief description, names of makers, designers, craftworkers etc. hallmarks and maker's mark (where relevant), materials, maximum dimensions; inscriptions (where relevant) are transcribed and recorded as written.

Section 1

METALWORK AND ENAMEL

Context

The collection of altar plate is extensive. Two firms of silversmiths worked on the Honan pieces, the greater number being by Edmond Johnson Ltd., of Dublin, the rest being by the Cork firm of William Egan & Sons. As is the case with all the other items in the collection, Celtic Revival design and decoration are used to full effect, although it varies from group to group. In the first group the designs are probably by the Johnson and Egan firms who made them, the largest pieces being the processional cross, a full-size facsimile of the twelfth-century Cross of Cong, complete with a large rock crystal and replica enamels. The second and more interesting group comprises the items designed by William Scott, the first professor of architecture at University College Dublin. These are highly original re-inventions of the Celtic style, full of vigour and strength, and include the large silver sanctuary lamp and other related items, as well as the brass candlesticks, the iron gates at the west end and the decorative hinges on the main door.

Structure

This section of the inventory groups items together by maker, designer and media. The final part of this section records the enamels, which are a hugely significant part of the overall collection.

The structure is:

- Items by William Egan & Sons (HCC/1–7)
- Items by Edmond Johnson Ltd. (HCC/8–15)
- Items designed by William A. Scott and made by Edmond Johnson Ltd. (HCC/16–29)
- Items designed by William A. Scott and made by other makers (HCC/30–38)
- Miscellaneous items (HCC/39–40)
- Enamels (HCC/41)

FIG. 5:
Sanctuary lamp (detail,
partially revealing
inscription)

FIG. 6:
Processional cross (detail)

FIG. 7: Incense boat
(detail showing enamel
triskel)

Fig. 8: *Altar card frame (detail)*

Fig. 9:
Ciborium (detail showing crest of University College, Cork in enamel), made by William Egan, Cork

Fig. 10:
Altar card frame (detail)

Items by William Egan & Sons (HCC/1–7)

HCC/1
Chalice (col. illus. p. 68)

Silver-gilt cup with a band of interlace in relief, interspersed with armorial shields in coloured enamels. Cylindrical knop with garnets on a cylindrical shaft, jewelled foot, and conical base engraved with an inscription, recorded below. Part of a set with matching ciborium.

MATERIALS: silver, gilt, enamel, semi-precious stones.
DIMENSIONS: H 24.5 cm, D (base) 13 cm, D (cup) 12.5 cm.
MAKER: William Egan & Sons, Cork, 1916.
HALLMARKED: 1916, Cork, WE.
INSCRIPTION: *Pray for the soul of Matthew, Robert and Isabella Honan of the City of Cork who caused me to be made.*

HCC/2
Ciborium and lid (col. illus. p. 67)

Silver-gilt cup with interlace designs in relief, interspersed with armorial shields in coloured enamels, to match those above. Cushion-shaped knop on the cylindrical shaft. Conical base with engraved inscription, recorded below. The lid has a cross-shaped handle, and is decorated with amethysts.

MATERIALS: silver, gilt, enamel, semi-precious stones.
DIMENSIONS: H 36 cm, D (base) 15 cm, W 15 cm
MAKER: William Egan & Sons, Cork, 1916.
HALLMARKED: 1916, Cork, WE.
INSCRIPTION: *'Sanctus, Sanctus, Sanctus' Pray for the souls of Matthew, Robert and Isabella Honan of the City of Cork by whose Piety and Zeal this chapel of St. Fin Barr was built and furnished RIP.*

HCC/3
Paten

Circular silver-gilt plate with engraved inscription on the convex surface, forming part of the set with the chalice above.

MATERIALS: silver, gilt. Dimensions: D 15.25 cm.

MAKER: William Egan & Sons, Cork, 1916.
HALLMARKED: 1916, Cork, WE.
INSCRIPTION: 'IHS'.

HCC/4
Protective case for chalice and paten

(col. illus. pp. 68, 69)
Oak box with red silk lining.
MATERIALS: wood, silk, metal clasp.
DIMENSIONS: D 17.5 cm, W 20 cm, H 16.5 cm.
MAKER: William Egan & Sons, Cork, 1916.
MAKER'S MARK: William Egan & Sons, Patrick St., Cork.

HCC/5
Protective case for ciborium and lid

Oak box with red silk lining.
MATERIALS: wood, silk, metal clasp.
DIMENSIONS: D 18 cm, W 37.5 cm, H 16.5 cm.
MAKER: William Egan & Sons, Cork, 1916.
MAKER'S MARK: William Egan & Sons, Patrick St., Cork.

HCC/6
Custos and lunette (col. illus. pp. 69, 207)

Custos (host-carrier) with separate lunette (wafer-holder) inside. The silver-gilt custos is in the form of a miniature monstrance with flaring foot, topped with a Celtic cross. The hinged door, with the letters *IHS* in a trefoil, is inset with four garnets. The whole piece is decorated with repousse interlace. The lunette, in the form of a simple silver-gilt ring, is undecorated.

MATERIALS: silver, gilt, semi-precious stones.
DIMENSIONS: H 22.5 cm, D (of Custos) 9.5 cm
MAKER: William Egan & Sons, Cork, 1916.
HALLMARKED: 1916, Cork, WE.
INSCRIPTION: *IHS.*

HCC/7
Oval dish

Simple, undecorated, oval dish.

MATERIALS: silver. Dimensions: L 25 cm, W 18 cm.
MAKER: William Egan & Sons, Cork, 1916.
HALLMARKED: 1916, Cork, WE.

Items by Edmond Johnson Ltd. (HCC/8–15)

HCC/8
Chalice (col. illus. p. 207)
Part of a set with matching ciborium. Jewelled silver-gilt cup, cushion-shaped knop on a cylindrical shaft, and conical base, all decorated with garnets and bands of animal interlace in relief. The Honan chapel arms and motto are engraved on the base, as well as the inscription recorded below.
MATERIALS: silver, gilt, semi-precious stones.
DIMENSIONS: H 20.5 cm, D (base) 12.5 cm, D (cup) 8.5 cm.
MAKER: Edmond Johnson Ltd., Dublin, 1916.
HALLMARKED: 1916, Dublin, EJ.
INSCRIPTION: *Of your charity pray for the souls of Matthew, Robert and Isabella Honan of the City of Cork by whose piety and zeal this chalice was made for St. Fin Barr's Chapel of the Honan Hostel AD 1917.*

HCC/9
Ciborium and lid
Jewelled silver-gilt cup with cylindrical shaft, cushion-shaped knop and conical foot, all decorated with garnets and bands of interlace in relief, to match chalice above. Handle of lid in the form of a Celtic cross. The base is engraved with the inscription recorded below.
MATERIALS: silver, gilt, semi-precious stones.
DIMENSIONS: H 26.5 cm, D (base) 13.5 cm, D (cup) 10 cm
MAKER: Edmond Johnson Ltd., Dublin, 1916.
HALLMARKED: 1916. Dublin, EJ.
INSCRIPTION: *Of your charity pray for the souls of Matthew, Robert and Isabella Honan of the City of Cork by whose Piety and zeal the ciborium was made for St. Fin Barr's Chapel of the Honan Hostel A.D. 1917.*

HCC/10
Protective case for chalice (col. illus. p. 207)
Wooden box with curved top, covered with red leather covering, lined with green silk cloth and gilt clasp fastener.
MATERIALS: wood, leather, metal clasp, gold leaf, silk.
DIMENSIONS: D 19 cm, W 26.5 cm, H (max.) 15 cm.
MAKER: Edmond Johnson Ltd., Dublin, 1916.
MAKER'S MARK: Edmond Johnson, Dublin.

HCC/11
Protective case for ciborium and cid
Wooden box with curved top, covered with red leather covering, lined with green silk cloth and gilt clasp fastener.
MATERIALS: wood, leather, metal clasp, gold leaf, silk.
DIMENSIONS: D 19 cm, W 32 cm, H (max.) 15 cm.
MAKER: Edmond Johnson Ltd., Dublin, 1916.
MAKER'S MARK: Edmond Johnson, Dublin.

HCC/111–118
Altar card frames
Two sets of silver and enamel frames, each set comprising two small and one large, with protective boxes, made by Edmund Johnson Ltd., Dublin, 1916. (For description, see section 3 below, Liturgical Manuscripts and Books, HCC/111–118.)

HCC/ 12
Candlestick (col. illus. p. 60)
Silver-gilt candlestick on a drip-tray with handle, decorated with interlace and enamel.
MATERIALS: silver, gilt, enamel.
DIMENSIONS: overall H 26 cm, W drip-tray 12.5 cm.
CANDLEHOLDER: overall H 5 cm, W 2.5 cm.
MAKER: Edmond Johnson Ltd., Dublin.
HALLMARKED: 1916 Dublin, EJ.

HCC/13

Cruet Set (col. illus. pp. 68,69)

Tray with two cruets. The cruets are a pair of glass vessels with silver-gilt mounts and handles, the mounts form open-work interlacements, supported on solid circular bases with ball feet. The silver-gilt tray, with semi-circular handles, is decorated with engraved interlace patterns and fitted with two pods to hold the cruets in place.

MATERIALS: Tray: silver. Cruets: glass, silver, gilt.

DIMENSIONS: tray: L 35 cm, W 18 cm;

cruets: H 13 cm, D 8.25 cm.

MAKER: Edmond Johnson Ltd., Dublin, 1916.

HALLMARKED: 1916, Dublin, EJ.

HCC/14

Ewer with stand (col. illus. p. 60, 207)

Silver-gilt ewer or pitcher in the shape of an open-beaked bird. Decorated with bands of interlace, intertwined braid designs, open-beaked birds, crosses and a pair of enamel crests.

MATERIALS: silver, gilt, enamel.

DIMENSIONS: ewer: H 29 cm, D 14 cm.

Stand: D 27 cm, H 2.5 cm.

MAKER: Edmond Johnson Ltd., Dublin.

HALLMARKED: 1916, Dublin, EJ.

HCC/15

Processional cross (col. illus. pp. 90, 93)

This cross is a large silver and gilt replica of the twelfth century Cross of Cong, with cast panels of interlace decoration, fitted with numerous blue and white enamel studs of knotwork design and many semi-precious, red, green and blue stones, as well as a large rock crystal in the centre. Attached to the back is a bronze figure of the crucified Christ. It is made to be carried in procession. An engraved inscription, running around the sides of the shaft and arms reads as recorded below.

MATERIALS: silver, gilt, enamels and semi-precious stones.

DIMENSIONS: H 75 cm, W(max) 42.5 cm.

MAKER: Edmond Johnson Ltd., Dublin.

HALLMARKED: 1916, Dublin, EJ.

INSCRIPTION: *Hac cruce crus tegitur qua passus coeditor orbis. Of your charity pray for the souls of Matthew and Isabella Honan by whose zeal and piety the chapel of St. Finn Barr, for which this cross was made, was founded for the Honan Hostel in the City of Cork A.D. 1916. Requiescant in pace. Pray for the good estate here and hereafter of Sir John Robert O'Connell and of Dame Mary O'Connell his wife.*

Items designed by William A. Scott and made by Edmond Johnson Ltd., Dublin (HCC/16–29)

HCC/16–21

Altar Candlesticks (col. illus. p. 75)

Set of six altar candlesticks. Each candlestick is supported on a dome-shaped base, with a group of four large blue enamel studs mid-way on the shaft and a cushion-shaped collar just below the drip-tray. Open-work interlace decoration, in panels, at the top, middle and bottom.

MATERIALS: silver, gilt, enamel.

DIMENSIONS: H 76 cm, D (base) 25.5 cm.

DESIGNER: William A. Scott.

MAKER: Edmond Johnson Ltd., Dublin.

HALLMARKED: 1916, Dublin, EJ.

HCC/22

Altar cross (col. illus. p. 74)

Made of silver gilt, this piece is a larger and more elaborate version of the altar candlesticks, with extra bands of open-work interlace and with the group of blue enamel studs placed three quarters of the way up the shaft. A copper open-work Celtic cross surmounts it, upon which hangs a bronze figure of Christ, backed by a panel of red enamel.

MATERIALS: brass, enamel, copper, bronze.

DIMENSIONS: H c.200 cm, D (of base) c. 112 cm, D (of shaft) c. 7.5cm.

DESIGNER: William A. Scott.
MAKER: Edmond Johnson Ltd., Dublin.
HALLMARKED: Dublin, EJ.

HCC/23, 24

Benediction candlesticks (col. illus. p. 62)

Pair of benediction candlesticks. A mixture of metals including copper, brass and silver plate are used together in these pieces, which are notable for the energetically writhing animal brackets that support the sloping candle-holders. The copper dome-shaped bases are decorated with open-work interlace, and are raised on little brass ball feet.

MATERIALS: brass, copper, silver-plate.
DIMENSIONS: overall H 72 cm, max. L (diagonal shaft) 65 cm, max. W 44 cm, max. diameter (base) 18 cm.
DESIGNER: William A. Scott.
MAKER: Edmond Johnson Ltd., Dublin.
HALLMARKED: 1916, Dublin, EJ.

HCC/25

Incense boat and stoup (col. illus. p. 66)

A boat-shaped container, or jug, with animal-head handle. The hinged lid is engraved with the arms and motto of the Honan Chapel; the vessel is decorated with vigorous animal interlace in relief, and two colourful enamel discs. The handle of the stoup (incense spoon) is formed as open-work, in an interlace pattern.

MATERIALS: silver, gilt, enamel.
DIMENSIONS: boat: L 18 cm, H 12 cm.
Stoup: L 14 cm, W.3.5 cm.
DESIGNER: William A. Scott.
MAKER: Edmond Johnson Ltd., Dublin, 1916.
HALLMARKED: 1916, Dublin EJ.

HCC/26

Missal stand (col. illus. p. 72)

Rectangular brass book-rest, on a flaring circular base, with a band of blue enamel studs encircling the shaft, made to rest on the altar table while supporting an open missal. Both book-rest and base are decorated with open-

work designs: the book-rest with four panels of animal interlace arranged around a Celtic cross; the base with geometric interlace .

MATERIALS: brass, enamel.
DIMENSIONS: H 38 cm , D(of base) 28 cm, Supporting rectangular plate for missal:
H 31.5 cm, W 41 cm.
DESIGNER: William A. Scott.
MAKER: Edmond Johnson Ltd., Dublin 1916.

HCC/27

Monstrance (col. illus. pp. 70,71)

This silver-gilt monstrance, which is used for showing the Blessed Sacrament in church and in procession, is topped by a small Celtic cross with circular head and is supported on an octagonal shaft and base; each section is encircled with blue enamel studs. The circular head has panels of open-work interlace interspersed with Celtic crosses, and the base also has open-work in three large ranges, enlivened with eight colourful armorial shields made of finely detailed enamels. An inscription on the base reads as recorded below.

MATERIALS: silver, gilt, enamel.
DIMENSIONS: H 99 cm, D 36.5 cm,
viewing chamber: D 11.5 cm.
DESIGNER: William A. Scott.
MAKER: Edmond Johnson Ltd., Dublin, 1916.
HALLMARKED: 1916, Dublin, EJ.
INSCRIPTION: *Pray for the souls of Matthew, Robert and Isabella Honan by whose charity and piety this monstrance to show forth the body of the Lord was made for the Chapel of St. Fin Barr of the Honan Hostel Cork, by the order of Sir John Robert O'Connell, Doctor of Law' designed from designs William Alphonsus Scott, Professor of Architecture in the National University of Ireland made by Edmond Johnson Dublin. AD 1916.*

HCC/28

Sanctuary lamp (col. illus. pp. 64, 65)

The lamp consists of a large silver bowl with panels of open-work interlace decoration (some of it engraved) embellished with blue enamel studs. It is suspended on

FIG. 11: *Chalice in original box, made by Edmond Johnson, Dublin*

FIG. 12: *Custos (detail)*

FIG. 13: *Ewer with stand (detail)*

three silver chains. The chains, which are attached to the bowl by animal-head brackets, are held apart at intervals by two large open-work rings or spacers. The whole is suspended from a smaller inverted bowl (or dome), similar in form and decoration to the lamp. An engraved inscription, just below the rim of the lamp, reads as recorded below.

MATERIALS: silver, enamel.

DIMENSIONS: (1) Dome: H c 23 cm, D 15 cm. (2) Small ring: H 7 cm, D 31 cm. (3) Large ring: H 7.5 cm, D 4 cm. (4) Lamp: Hc.60 cm, D 39 cm. (Interior fitting missing).

DESIGNER: William A. Scott.

MAKER: Edmond Johnson Ltd., Dublin.

HALLMARKED: 1916, Dublin, EJ.

INSCRIPTION: *May this lamp be ever burning on the altar of God in the Collegiate Chapel of St. Fin Barr obtain eternal rest and peace for the souls of Matthew, Robert and Isabella Honan of this City of Cork by whose charity and piety this chapel was built and this lamp was made Requiescant in pace. Sir John Robert O'Connell Doctor of Laws ordered me to be made, William Alphonsus Scott first Professor of Architecture of the National University of Ireland designed me, Edmond Johnson of Dublin fashioned me AD 1916.*

HCC/29

Thurible (col. illus. p. 63)

The thurible, or incense-burner, is made up of three silver-gilt pieces, each with open-work interlace decoration, consisting of a bowl, with an inner lid and an outer lid, all joined together by silver chains. The bowl, similar in form to the Ardagh Chalice, has a circular foot with repoussé interlace panels, and six blue enamel studs; the chains are attached to three animal-shaped brackets. The inner lid fits onto a copper bowl within, for burning the incense. The outer lid is onion-shaped.

MATERIALS: silver, gilt, enamel, copper.

DIMENSIONS: H 32 cm, D (bowl) 32.5 cm, D (foot) 11 cm

DESIGNER: William A. Scott.

MAKER: Edmond Johnson Ltd., Dublin.

HALLMARKED: 1916, Dublin EJ.

Items designed by William A. Scott and made by other makers (HCC/30–36)

HCC/30

Hand bell (col. illus. p. 74)

Cast-iron bell of Irish early Christian type.

MATERIALS: iron. Dimensions: H 21 cm, W 12 cm.

DESIGNER: unknown, possibly William A. Scott.

MAKER: possibly J. & G. McLoughlin, Dublin.

HCC/CF/31

Iron grille chapel gates (col. illus. p. 73)

These wrought-iron gates, made to hang outside the great west door, incorporate a large Celtic cross in their design, filled in with elaborate geometric and animal interlace.

MATERIALS: iron.

DIMENSIONS: Each gate: H 288 cm, W 81 cm.

DESIGNER: William A. Scott.

MAKER: J & G McLoughlin, Dublin, 1916.

HCC/CF/32–35

Iron Hinges on west door (col. illus. p. 74)

Four decorative cast-iron strap hinges of neo-Celtic interlace design.

MATERIALS: iron.

DIMENSIONS: H 38 cm, W 68 cm.

DESIGNER: William A. Scott.

MAKER: J. & G. McLoughlin, Dublin, 1916.

HCC/36

Sacristy bell

Cast-iron bell of Irish early Christian type, hanging from an animal-interlace bracket in the sacristy.

MATERIALS: iron.

DIMENSIONS: H 21 cm, W 12 cm.

DESIGN: attributed to William A. Scott.

MAKER: unknown, possibly J. & G. McGloughlin, Dublin, 1916.

Miscellaneous other items (HCC/37–38)

HCC/37

Altar Bell

The altar bell consists of a cluster of three individual bells on one circular stand. One bell is complete, the second lacks a clapper, the third is missing. The base bears the inscription recorded below.

MATERIALS: silver-plate.

DIMENSIONS: H 22 cm, D (base) 15.5 cm.

MAKER: unknown. 1910.

INSCRIPTION: *In usum Capella Sct Antonii apud Corcagiam ex dono Bertrami et Aedithae Windle, MCMX.*

HCC/38

Holy water stoup and sprinkler with rose

MATERIAL: brass.

DIMENSIONS: H 17.5 cm, D 13 cm. Sprinkler: L 24 cm.

MAKER: unknown. 1916.

Enamels (HCC/39)

HCC/39

Tabernacle doors and tympanum

(col. illus. pp. 84–86)

Two silver panels, in bronze frames, with basse-taille enamel. The door panel is rectangular and depicts the Adoration of the Lamb; above it, in the gable, is a triangular panel depicting the Trinity with the sun and moon.

MATERIALS: silver, bronze, enamel.

DIMENSIONS: door panel: H 50 cm, W 42 cm
Tympanum: H 39 cm, W 38 cm.

DESIGNER AND MAKER: Oswald Reeves, Dublin 1916.

Liturgical textiles and Sanctuary Furnishings

Context

The collection of textiles includes a group of chancel furnishings (embroideries, tapestries, a banner and carpets) made by the Dún Emer Guild in Dublin as well as several sets of embroidered vestments made partly by Dún Emer and partly by the Cork firm William Egan & Sons Ltd. A number of wall hangings (dossals) and altar frontals (antependia) in different colours were designed to correspond to the seasonal changes of the liturgical year. Matching vestments were supplied in the same seasonal colours: black, violet, blue and white, green, and red and gold.

Each set of textiles is inspired by liturgical and Catholic spiritual convention. For example, one altar frontal reflects events in the life of the Virgin Mary – the Annunciation, the Nativity and the Assumption – and would have been used for her feast days. Other sets represent the symbols of The Passion and Crucifixion. The dossal used in the chapel on a daily basis represented symbolically the Four Evangelists, Matthew, Mark, Luke and John, drawing on the artistic heritage of the early Irish Church.

The following outlines, in summary form, the relevant ecclesiastical names for liturgical textiles recorded in this inventory.

> BURSE: a flat cloth case for carrying the piece of linen, or corporal, that is used in celebrating the Eucharist. In procession the burse is carried on top of the veiled chalice.
> COPE HOOD: shield shaped embroidered cloth attached to the back of the cope, deriving from the hood that was originally an integral part of the cope.
> MORSE: the fastening, either of cloth or metal, at the neck of the cope.
> ORPHREY: a band of elaborate embroidery decorating certain ecclesiastical vestments.

Structure

This section of the inventory groups items together by liturgical season as represented by the colours designating each season (see above). The final sub-sections deal with linen textiles and carpets.

The Black set (HCC/40–54)

HCC/40

Black altar frontal (col. illus. pp. 142, 143)

Poplin cloth stretched on a wood frame. Silk-thread embroidery in purple and grey in twelve roundels (six on top, six below). In the centre there is an elaborately decorated Celtic cross, based on the grave-slab of Tullylease, Co. Cork. An embroidered label stitched to the back reads as recorded below.

MATERIAL: silk and wool poplin, silk embroidery thread.

DIMENSIONS: H 100 cm, L 208 cm.

DESIGNER: Katherine McCormack [Cáitín nic Cormaic].

MAKER: Dún Emer Guild, Dublin, 1916.

INSCRIPTION: *Pray for Cáitín nic Cormaic who designed this frontal and for Evelyn Gleeson, Kate Dempsey, Josephine Mullhall, Siobáin ní Dilluin, Christina Fanning, Mary Perry, Sheila Stapleton and Mary Kerley who together made it. Dún Emer Guild, Dublin 1916.*

HCC/41

Cover for Black altar frontal

Canvas wrapping to protect altar frontal with brass tacks along the top to seal closure.

MATERIAL: canvas, black ink.

DIMENSIONS: H 100 cm, L 208 cm.

DESIGNER: unknown.

MAKER: Dún Emer Guild, Dublin. 1916.

INSCRIPTION: Honan Hostel, 1914.

HCC/42

Black dossal (col. illus. pp. 143, 155)

Poplin cloth with shades of violet, purple and grey silk embroidery and silver braid. White silk ribbon is used to divide the field into three sections and to outline the large central celtic cross, which is enriched with eight small panels of Celtic design worked in purple thread.

MATERIAL: silk and wool poplin, silk embroidery thread, braid.

DIMENSIONS: H c. 277 cm, W 511 cm.

DESIGNER: Katherine MacCormack.

MAKER: Dun Emer Guild, Dublin. 1916.

INSCRIPTION: *Made at the Dún Emer Guild, Hardwicke Street, Dublin; under the direction of Evelyn Gleeson; by Kate Dempsey, Susan Dillon, Tina Fanning, Sheila Stapleton, Mary Corri and Kathleen MacLoughlin. Designed by Katherine MacCormack. Dún Emer, báile-áta-cliat [sic], 1917.*

HCC/43

Black cope

Poplin cloth with Y-shaped orphrey and cope hood with multicoloured silk and silver-thread embroidery composed of interlace panels and roundels. There is a silver-coloured cross with crown of thorns motif, the central triskel in three shades of purple being embroidered within the orphreys. Fastened with a cloth morse (fastening). The morse is edged with a metal-thread fringe. Embroidered inscription sewn to the lining records the embroiderers' names as listed below.

MATERIAL: silk and wool poplin, silk and metal embroidery thread, braid.

DIMENSIONS: this item is too fragile to measure.

DESIGNER: unknown.

MAKER: William Egan & Sons, Cork, 1916.

INSCRIPTION: *M. Barrett, H. Harte, A. Calnan, K. Allman, M. Desmond, M. Twomey, H. Ahearne, M.Countie, K. Cramer, T. Good, M.E. Jenkins, N. Barry, E.J. Scully (died on 28th July 1915)*

FIG. 16: *Black chasuble*
(detail)

FIG. 18: *White antependium*
(detail)

FIG. 17: *Gold chasuble*
(detail)

FIG. 19: *Black chasuble*
(detail)

HCC/44

Black chasuble (col. illus. pp. 135, 213)

Black poplin cloth used for vestments for funeral masses and the annual Founders' Day Mass. Decorated with multicoloured silk and silver-thread embroidery; Y-shaped orphreys on both front and back, infilled with Celtic-style birds and interlace patterns; the arms of University College Cork on the front and the crown of thorns on the back.

MATERIALS: silk and wool poplin, silk and metal embroidery thread.

DIMENSIONS: L (centre front) 110 cm, L (centre back) 119 cm, W 110 cm.

DESIGNER: John Lees, Cork.

MAKER: William Egan & Sons, Cork, 1916.

HCC/45

Black chalice burse

Burse, of poplin cloth, decorated with silver and grey embroidery and a purple triskel, edged with silver braid.

MATERIALS: silk and wool poplin, silver, grey and purple silk embroidery thread.

DIMENSIONS: L 23 cm W 25 cm.

DESIGNER: unknown.

MAKER: William Egan & Sons, Cork, 1916.

HCC/46

Black chalice veil

Veil, of poplin cloth, used to cover the chalice, decorated with silver and grey embroidery and a purple triskel.

MATERIALS: silk and wool poplin, silver, grey and purple silk embroidery thread.

DIMENSIONS: L 60 cm W 60 cm.

DESIGNER: unknown.

MAKER: William Egan & Sons, Cork, 1916.

HCC/47,48

Black dalmatics

Two black dalmatics in very poor condition.

MATERIALS: silk and wool poplin, silver metal thread, fringes and tassels.

DIMENSIONS: these pieces are too fragile to measure.

DESIGNER: unknown;

MAKER: William Egan & Sons, Cork, 1916.

HCC/49–51

Black stoles

Three stoles (one long, two shorter) of poplin cloth with multicoloured silk embroidery edged with braid and silver fringe on each end. Weft system of braid has slanting pattern of black, purple to silver grey threads, and slanting silver metal bands. HCC/49 is decorated with cross, crown of thorns and triskel interlace patterns and lined with black silk. HCC/50 is decorated with a long panel of embroidery; HCC/51 is decorated with a small cross motif. All three are lined with black silk satin.

MATERIALS: Silk and wool poplin, satin weave silk, silk embroidery thread, metal braids and fringes.

DIMENSIONS: HCC/49: L 272 cm, W 33 cm.

HCC/50: L 246cm, W 22 cm.

HCC/51 L 284 cm, W 15 cm.

DESIGNER: unknown.

MAKER: William Egan & Sons, Cork, 1916.

HCC/52, 53, 54

Black Maniples

Three maniples each decorated with embroidered Celtic cross motifs and silver-metal knotted and fringed silver fringes at each end edged with silver silk braid. A piece of silver braid joins each maniple at one side. Each maniple is lined with black silk cloth.

MATERIALS: silk and wool poplin, multicoloured silk embroidery thread, silver braid and fringe.

DIMENSIONS: (for all): L 120cm, W 14cm.

DESIGNER: unknown.

MAKER: William Egan & Sons, Cork, 1916.

Violet set (HCC/55–67)

HCC/55
Violet altar cloth with frontlet
Poplin cloth used on the altar with cut-outs for the tabernacle and six candlesticks. The frontlet is decorated with a band of embroidery of Celtic interlace in varying shades of purple silk with orange and yellow highlights, edged with purple braid. A central roundel is emblazoned with IHS and decorated with shamrocks. Two side roundels incorporate cruciform and interlace motifs. Lined with violet cotton sateen.
MATERIALS: silk and wool poplin, cotton sateen, silk and gold thread, braid.
DIMENSIONS: W 262 cm (bottom width); 356 cm (total width), L 136 cm.
DESIGNER: unknown.
MAKER: unknown.

HCC/56
Violet altar frontal (col. illus. p. 144)
Poplin cloth stretched on a wood frame. Silk thread embroidery mainly in mauve, plum and orange depicting scenes from the Crucifixion with Celtic interlace patterns, backed with purple cotton cloth. An inscription written on a cotton label stitched to the back reads as recorded below.
MATERIALS: silk and wool poplin, silk embroidery threads, ink.
DIMENSIONS: H 100 cm, L308 cm
DESIGNER: Katherine MacCormack.
MAKER: Dún Emer Guild, Dublin, 1916.
INSCRIPTION: *do cum glóire dé agus ónora na h-eireann do tarraing Cáit nic Cormaic do déin Cáit ní Demsiag, Tína Fanning, Josepin Mulhall, Siobáin ní Dilliun, Sígle Stapleton brat sin, dún emer, at cliat,[sic], 1917.*

HCC/57
Cover for violet altar frontal
Canvas wrapping to protect altar frontal with brass tacks along the top to seal closure.
MATERIAL: canvas, black ink.
DIMENSIONS: H 100 cm, L 308 cm.
MAKER: Dún Emer Guild, Dublin. 1916.
INSCRIPTION: Honan Hostel, 1914.

HCC/58
Violet dossal (col. illus. p. 144)
Poplin cloth with silk embroidery, mainly in violet, depicting symbols of the Crucifixion, i.e. spears, die and scourge; also coat of arms of the Honan Chapel.
MATERIALS: silk and wool poplin, silk embroidery thread, metal-thread braid.
DIMENSIONS: H c. 277cm, W 522 cm.
DESIGNER: unknown.
MAKER: Dún Emer Guild, Dublin, 1916.

HCC/59
Violet cope
Poplin cloth with Y-shaped orphrey and cope hood at the back of multicoloured silk and metal-thread embroidery and gold braid, which are divided into ten interlace panels by small roundels, and an armorial shield. Embroidered cloth morse or fastening.
MATERIALS: Silk and wool poplin, silk embroidery threads.
DIMENSIONS: L 152 cm, W 288 cm.
DESIGNER: unknown.
MAKER: William Egan & Sons, Cork, 1916.

HCC/60, 61
Violet chasubles

Two chasubles in slightly different qualities of poplin
cloth with multicoloured silk and gold-metal embroidery
edged with gold braid. The first (HCC/60) is the earlier
piece which has been relined in violet silk and has
replacement red and gold braid at the neck. There are
Y-shaped orphreys on the front and back of each chasuble
infilled with elaborate animal interlace of constantly
changing rainbow colours; IHS is emblazoned on the
centre of each orphrey. The second piece (HCC/61) is
decorated with the chapel crest and gold-coloured silk
braid. The stitching on this piece is machine embroidery.
It is lined with violet silk.

HCC/60:

MATERIALS: silk and wool poplin, multicoloured silk
and metal-thread embroidery, braid.

DIMENSIONS: L 110 cm (centre front),
L 119 cm (centre back) W 118 cm.

DESIGNER: unknown;

MAKER: William Egan & Sons, Cork, 1916.

HCC/61

MATERIALS: silk and wool poplin, silk, multicoloured
silk and metal-thread embroidery, braid.

DIMENSIONS: L 91.5 cm (centre front),
L 101 cm (centre back), W 134 cm.

DESIGNER AND MAKER: unknown.

HCC/62
Violet chalice burse

Poplin burse decorated with multi-coloured embroidery
in silk and metal threads, edged with gold braid. The
base is relined with violet twill silk; interior lined with
white linen.

MATERIALS: silk and wool poplin, linen, twill weave
silk, multicoloured silk and metal embroidery thread,
metal-thread braid.

DIMENSIONS: L 23 cm, W 23 cm.

DESIGNER: unknown.

MAKER: William Egan & Sons, Cork, 1916.

HCC/63
Violet chalice veil

Veil used to cover the chalice, decorated with
multicoloured and gold-metal embroidery, edged with
gold braid and lined with purple moiré watered silk.

MATERIALS: silk and wool poplin, moiré watered silk
and metal-thread embroidery, braid.

DIMENSIONS: L 60 cm W 60 cm.

DESIGNER: unknown.

MAKER: William Egan & Sons, Cork, 1916.

HCC/64–66
Violet maniples

Three maniples of poplin cloth each decorated with
embroidered Celtic cross motifs and gold metal knotted
and fringed gold fringe at each end, edged with gold silk
braid. They have been relined in purple twill silk with an
elastic loop sewn inside each.

MATERIALS: silk and wool poplin, silk twill,
multicoloured silk embroidery thread, gold braid
and fringe.

DIMENSIONS: L 120 cm W 14.5 cm.

DESIGNER: unknown.

MAKER: William Egan & Sons, Cork, 1916.

HCC/67
Violet stole

Poplin stole with multicoloured silk and gold-metal
embroidery edged with gold braid and fringe at each
end, decorated with celtic cross motifs, relined in purple
twill silk.

MATERIALS: Silk and wool poplin, multicoloured silk
and metal-thread embroidery.

DIMENSIONS: L 274 cm W 14.5 cm.

DESIGNER: unknown.

MAKER: William Egan & Sons, Cork, 1916.

White Set (HCC/68–74)

HCC/68
White and blue altar frontal
(col. illus. pp. 145, 146, 157)

White, blue and gold poplin cloth on a large wooden frame, secured with upholstery tack, and embroidered with silk thread mainly in blue and golden yellow, with multicoloured details. Strips of blue poplin cloth are used to divide the piece into three zones, with a top border of Celtic patterns interspersed with three scenes from the life of the Virgin Mary. A large central roundel below displays the initials MR, flanked by smaller roundels with a golden crown to the right and a *fleur-de-lis* to the left. Edged with gold-coloured silk braid, and on a blue poplin backing.

MATERIALS: silk and wool poplin, silk embroidery threads, braid.

DIMENSIONS: H 240 cm, W 540 cm

DESIGNER: unknown.

MAKER: Dún Emer Guild, Dublin, 1916.

HCC/69
Cover for white and blue altar frontal
Canvas wrapping to protect altar frontal with brass tacks along the top to seal closure.

MATERIAL: canvas, black ink.

DIMENSIONS: H 100 cm, L 308 cm.

MAKER: Dún Emer Guild, Dublin. 1916

INSCRIPTION: Honan Hostel, 1914.

HCC/70
White and blue dossal with blue trim
White poplin with blue silk ribbon delineating panels containing silk and gold-metal embroidery depicting various Marian motifs or symbols linked with couched yellow cord.

MATERIALS: silk and wool poplin, silk ribbon, silk and gold-metal embroidery thread.

DIMENSIONS: H c. 240 cm, W 540 cm.

DESIGNER: unknown.

MAKER: Dún Emer Guild, Dublin, 1916.

HCC/71
White cope
Almost completely destroyed as a result of water damage. This piece cannot be measured, or properly examined.

MATERIALS: silk and wool poplin.

DESIGNER AND MAKER: unknown.

HCC/72
White Humeral Veil
Poplin cloth with fine quality embroidery in blue silk thread, with a clasp.

MATERIALS: poplin, silk embroidery threads.

Poor condition, could not be measured.

DESIGNER AND MAKER: unknown.

HCC/73
Replacement White Humeral Veil
Replacement humeral veil with original silk embroidery sewn onto new cloth.

MATERIALS: Poplin, silk embroidery threads,

Could not be measured.

MAKER: unknown.

HCC/74
Replacement white stole
Replacement stole with original silk embroidery sewn onto new cloth edged with gold metal braid, gold metal fringes on each end, lined with gold silk twill.

MATERIALS: poplin, silk twill, silk thread embroidery threads, braid and metal fringe.

DIMENSIONS: L 220 cm W 19 cm.

MAKER: unknown.

Green set (HCC/75–80)

HCC/75
Green altar cloth and frontlet
(col. illus. p. 150)

Poplin cloth used on the altar with cut-outs for the tabernacle and altar candlesticks. The frontlet is decorated with silk and gold thread embroidery (predominantly red). It is divided into three zones by Celtic interlace panels, in the centre is a slim Celtic cross, to either side are golden roundels with red interlace. A label on the back lists the names of the makers, see inscription below.

MATERIALS: silk and wool poplin, silk and metal embroidery threads.

DIMENSIONS: H c. 240 cm, W 540 cm.

DESIGNER: Katherine McCormick.

MAKER: Dún Emer Guild, Dublin, 1917.

INSCRIPTION: *Made at the Dún Emer Guild, Hardwicke Street, Dublin; under the direction of Evelyn Gleeson, by Kate Dempsey, Susan Dillon, Tina Fanning, Sheila Stapleton, Mary Corri; and Kathleen MacLoughlin. Designed by Katherine MacCormack, Dún Emer, Baile-atha-cliath, 1917.*

HCC/76
Green chasuble (col. illus. p. 134)

Poplin cloth with multicoloured silk and metal-thread embroidery. There are Y-shaped orphreys front and back infilled with elaborate animal-interlace embroidery of constantly changing rainbow colours. Edged in braid.

MATERIALS: silk and wool poplin, multicoloured silk and metal-thread embroidery, braid.

DIMENSIONS: L (centre front) 110 cm, (centre back) 119 cm W (max.) 118 cm.

MAKER: William Egan & Sons, Cork, 1916.

HCC/77
Green chalice burse

Poplin cloth burse decorated with multicoloured embroidery in silk and metal threads, edged with gold braid. The back is relined with green silk taffeta.

MATERIALS: silk and wool poplin, multicoloured silk taffeta and metal embroidery thread, braid.

DIMENSIONS: L 25 cm, W 21 cm.

DESIGNER: unknown.

MAKER: William Egan & Sons, Cork, 1916.

HCC/78
Green chalice veil

Poplin cloth veil used to cover the chalice, decorated with multicoloured and gold-metal embroidery, edged with gold braid and lined with green silk.

MATERIALS: Silk and wool poplin, multicoloured silk and metal threads, braid.

DIMENSIONS: L 60 cm, W 60 cm.

DESIGNER: unknown.

MAKER: William Egan & Sons, Cork, 1916.

HCC/79
Green maniple

Poplin cloth maniple decorated with embroidered Celtic cross motifs and gold metal knotted and fringed gold fringe at each end, edged with gold silk braid. It has been relined in forest green silk with an elastic loop sewn inside.

MATERIALS: silk and wool poplin, multicoloured silk embroidery thread, gold braid and fringe.

DIMENSIONS: L 120 cm, W 15 cm.

DESIGNER: unknown.

MAKER: William Egan & Sons, Cork, 1916.

HCC/80
Green stole

Poplin cloth stole with multicoloured silk and gold-metal embroidery edged with gold braid.

MATERIALS: Silk and wool poplin, multicoloured silk and metal embroidery thread, braid.

DIMENSIONS: L 276 cm, W (max.) 14.5 cm.

DESIGNER: unknown.

MAKER: William Egan & Sons, Cork, 1916.

Red and Gold Set (HCC/81–99)

HCC/81

Red and gold altar frontal

(col. illus. pp. 148, 149, 152–54, 221–2)

Elaborately embroidered canvas ground, predominantly in gold silk thread enriched with multicoloured silk embroidered images, designs and inscriptions. Celtic key pattern panels divide the piece into three zones and also form a lower border interspersed with coats of arms (of the Honan Chapel, University College Cork and Cork City). The middle zone depicts Christ in Glory holding the Book of the Gospels, seated in the central mandorla around which runs the inscription, *Holy, Holy, Holy, Lord God of Sabboath, the Heaven and the Earth are full of thy Glory.* This is flanked by symbols of the Evangelists (in *Book of Kells* style) and by identified Irish saints, Columcille and Patrick to the left, and Bridget and Fin Barr to the right. Below this is the chapel motto, *do chum glóire dé agus onóra na hÉireann.* The kneeling figure of St Colman appears in the outer right-hand zone, and St Ita is in the left one. Across the top there is an inscription requesting prayers for the donors, Matthew, Robert and Isabella Honan. Canvas backing, with the inscription recorded below stitched onto the canvas.

MATERIALS: canvas, silk and metal embroidery threads.
DIMENSIONS: H 91.5 cm, L 304 cm.
DESIGNER: Katherine McCormack.
MAKER: Dún Emer Guild, Dublin, (as noted on the inscription below).
INSCRIPTION: *Pray for Caitín nic Cormack who designed this frontal and for Evelyn Gleeson, Kate Dempsey, Josephine Mulhall, Siobain ní Dilluin, Christina Fanning, Mary Perry, Sheila Stapleton and Mary Kerley who together made it. dun emer guild, dublin 1916 [sic].*

HCC/82

Red and gold altar cloth and frontlet

(col. illus. pp. 153–4, 221)

Beige-coloured poplin cloth used on the altar with cut-outs for the tabernacle and six candlesticks. The frontlet is decorated with silk and gold-thread embroidery, predominantly in gold, bronze and orange. An embroidered cruciform within a central roundel is surrounded by Celtic interlace with repeating triskels.

MATERIALS: silk and wool poplin, silk and metal embroidery thread.
DIMENSIONS: L 132 cm, W 288 cm.
DESIGNER: unknown.
MAKER: [Dún Emer Guild, Dublin, 1916].

HCC/83

Red and gold banner (col. illus. p. 147)

Gold silk embroidery on canvas ground. The main figure is that of St Fin Barr, in bishop's robes worked in multicoloured silk thread with gold-coloured embroidered background. The saint is accompanied by a lamb and his name, *Naomh Barra,* worked in gold thread, appears below him. Panels of multicoloured interlace form borders all around. The banner is lined with crimson cotton poplin, has two gold-thread tassels and a gold fringe along the bottom edge. It is suspended from a wooden pole.

MATERIALS: canvas, cotton poplin, silk and gold-metal threads.
DIMENSIONS: H 64 cm, W 38.5 cm.
DESIGNER: unknown.
MAKER: Dún Emer Guild, Dublin, 1916.
INSCRIPTION: *Naomh Barra.*

HCC/84

Red and gold cushion

Wool tapestry work on canvas ground, depicting the eagle of St John encircled in yellow on a green background. This is attached to a cushion cover of red canvas with a gold cord and tassel stitched around its edge. This figure replicates the eagle on the red dossal.

MATERIALS: canvas, wool tapestry yarn, gold-metal thread.
DIMENSIONS: W 60 cm, D 11 cm.
DESIGNER: unknown.
MAKER: Dún Emer Guild, Dublin, 1916.

HCC/85

Red and gold dossal (wool tapestry dossal)

(col. illus. pp. 150, 222)

Wool tapestry with cotton warp now relined in linen or cotton. Inscription cut from original lining is stitched onto the new cloth backing. The deep red ground is divided into four zones by panels of richly coloured romanesque patterns edged with gold braiding; similar panels also form a top border. Each zone features one of the symbols of the Evangelists (man, lion, ox and eagle, derived from the *Book of Kells*) in a gold-edged roundel.

MATERIALS: cotton, wool.

DIMENSIONS: H 277 cm, W 511 cm.

DESIGNERS: Evelyn Gleeson, Katherine MacCormack, Kate Dempsey and Mary Stapleton.

MAKERS: Dún Emer Guild, as in inscription below, Dublin, 1916.

INSCRIPTION: *Pray for the designers of this dossal Evelyn Gleeson and Cáitlin nic Chormaic: [Kate Dempsey] Mary Stapleton: Dún Emer Guild, Dublin and for the Weavers Tina Fanning, Cissie Burke, May Keegan, Lily Keegan.* 1915-1916.

HCC/86

Cloth of gold cope

Cloth of gold (tabby weave with weft system of gold thread) cope, with Y-shaped orphrey on centre back and embroidery on cope hood of multicoloured silk, mainly green, blue and purple, worked in panels of interlace to form borders and edged with gold braid. The Honan crest is embroidered on one end of the orphrey. The names of the donors, Matthew, Robert and Isabella Honan, and of the embroiderers have been stitched on the back of the lining. The condition of this item is so poor, due to water damage, that it cannot be measured or properly examined.

MATERIALS: silk and wool poplin, silk and metal embroidery thread, braid, metal fringe, silver gilt, amethysts.

DIMENSIONS: this item is too fragile to measure.

DESIGNER: unknown.

MAKER: William Egan & Sons, Cork, 1916.

INSCRIPTION: *M. Barrett, H. Harte, A. Calnan, K. Allman, M. Desmond, M. Twomey, H. Ahearne, M.Countie, K. Cramer, T. Good, M.E. Jenkins, N. Barry, E.J. Scully.*

HCC/87

Cloth of gold humeral veil

Humeral veil, which accompanies cope (HCC/86) fastened by means of an Arts and Crafts style silver-gilt morse, decorated with six amethysts, in each half, one half of which is missing. The scarf is bordered with gold braid and has a gold metal fringe at each end. The condition of this item is so poor, due to water damage, that it cannot be measured or properly examined.

MATERIALS: cloth of gold, gold metal thread fringe, silk embroidery threads.

DIMENSIONS: This item could not be measured.

MAKER: William Egan & Sons, Cork, 1916.

HCC/88

Cloth of gold chasuble (col. illus. pp. 136–40, 213)

Cloth of gold, replacement of original cloth, with the original embroideries in multicoloured silk and gold-metal thread, bordered with gold braid, sewn onto the replacement Y-shaped orphreys on both front and back, with the symbols of the Evangelists worked in roundels formed by Celtic interlace. The crest of University College Cork appears on the front only. The original label identifying the seamstresses has been stitched onto the new lining with the inscription recorded below.

MATERIALS: cloth of gold, silk lining and acetate cloth (modern insertion) silk and metal embroidery thread, braid.

DIMENSIONS: L 110 cm (centre front), L 119 cm (centre back), W 118 cm.

DESIGNER: unknown.

MAKER: William Egan & Sons, Cork, 1916.

INSCRIPTION: *M. Barrett, H. Harte, A. Calnan, K. Allman, M. Desmond, M. Twomey, H. Ahearne, M.Countie, K. Cramer, T. Good, M.E. Jenkins, N. Barry, E.J. Scully (died on 28th July 1915), Michael Barry Egan.*

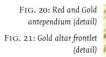

FIG. 20: *Red and Gold antependium (detail)*

FIG. 21: *Gold altar frontlet (detail)*

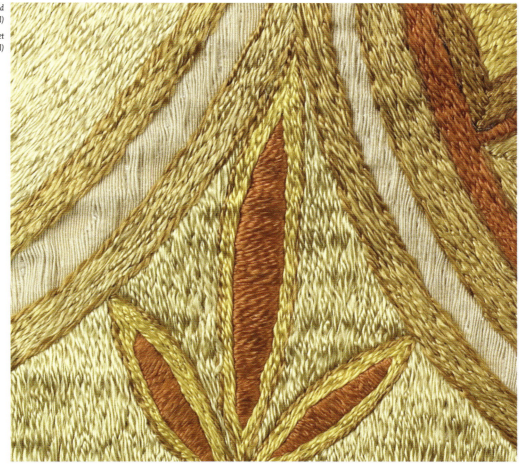

HCC/89, 90

Cloth of gold chalice burses

Two burses of cloth of gold, one of which is original the second being a replacement piece with the original embroidery sewn onto the new cloth, decorated with multicoloured animal-interlace embroidery in silk and metal threads, edged with gold braid. The original burse is lined with silk taffeta, the replacement is lined with twill silk.

MATERIALS: silk and wool poplin, twill silk, silk taffeta, silk and metal embroidery thread, braid.

DIMENSIONS: HCC/89 L 25 cm W 23.5 cm; HCC/90 L 23 cm, x W 23cm.

DESIGNER: unknown.

MAKER: William Egan & Sons, Cork, 1916.

HCC/91

Cloth of gold chalice veil

Cloth of gold veil used to cover the chalice. This is a replacement but with the original embroideries sewn onto it. These are of multicoloured and gold-coloured metal silk thread, edged with gold metal and silk braid. The veil is lined with gold-coloured twill silk.

MATERIALS: cloth of gold, multicoloured silk embroidery thread, braid.

DIMENSIONS: L 54 cm, W 54 cm.

DESIGNER: unknown.

MAKER: William Egan & Sons, Cork, 1916.

HCC/92, 93

Cloth of gold dalmatics

Two cloth of gold dalmatics. These items are in very poor condition.

MATERIALS: cloth of gold, multicoloured silk thread embroidery.

DIMENSIONS: These items could not be measured.

DESIGNER: unknown.

MAKER: William Egan & Sons, Cork, 1916.

HCC/94– 96

Cloth of gold maniples

Three maniples of cloth of gold, one of which is a replacement but with the original embroideries sewn onto it. These are in multicoloured silk and gold-metal thread, and incorporate celtic cross motifs. The maniples have gold metal *passementerie* knotted and fringed at each end and are edged with gold metal and silk braid.

MATERIALS: cloth of gold, multicoloured silk embroidery thread, gold metal braid and fringes.

DIMENSIONS: L 102 cm, W 15 cm.

DESIGNER: unknown.

MAKER: William Egan & Sons, Cork, 1916.

HCC/97–99

Cloth of gold stoles

Three cloth of gold stoles with multicoloured silk and gold-metal embroidery edged with gold braid. One stole is original. This piece is decorated with interlace patterns, a cross in the centre, with embroidery depicting animal heads and a gold fringe at each end.

A tubular gold metal cord is attached to both sides 61cm up from the bottom, with gold toggle and end 'buttons'. The remaining two are replacements but retain the original embroidery sewn onto the new cloth. Lined with yellow silk.

MATERIALS: cloth of gold, multicoloured silk and metal embroidery thread, braid.

DIMENSIONS: HCC/97: L 240 cm, W 22.5 cm; HCC/98: L 256 cm; W 15 cm; HCC/99: L 137 cm, W 14.5 cm.

DESIGNER: unknown.

MAKER: William Egan & Sons, Cork, 1916.

Red Set (HCC/(100–104)

HCC/100
Red altar cloth with frontlet

Poplin cloth used on the altar with cut-outs for the tabernacle and six candlesticks. The frontlet is embroidered with silk and gold thread, in roundels and panels of interlace of various colours.

MATERIALS: silk and wool poplin, silk and gold thread.

DIMENSIONS: H c.240 cm, W 540 cm.

DESIGNER: unknown.

MAKER: [William Egan & Sons, Cork], date unknown.

HCC/101
Red chasuble (col. illus. pp. 132, 135)

Poplin cloth with multicoloured silk and metal-thread embroidery. The Y-shaped orphreys on the front and back are infilled with elaborate animal interlace in constantly changing rainbow colours, edged with gold braid.

MATERIALS: silk and wool poplin, multicoloured silk and metal embroidery thread, braid.

DIMENSIONS: L (centre front and back) 119 cm, W 118 cm.

DESIGNER: unknown.

MAKER: William Egan & Sons, Cork, 1916.

HCC/102
Red chalice burse

Poplin cloth burse decorated with multicoloured embroidery in silk and metal threads, edged with gold braid.

MATERIALS: silk and wool poplin, multicoloured silk and metal embroidery threads, braid.

DIMENSIONS: L 25 cm, W 23 cm.

DESIGNER: unknown.

MAKER: William Egan & Sons, Cork, 1916.

HCC/103
Red chalice veil

Poplin cloth veil used to cover the chalice, decorated with multicoloured and gold-metal embroidery, edged with gold braid.

MATERIALS: silk and wool poplin, multicoloured silk and metal embroidery thread, braid.

DIMENSIONS: L 54 cm, W 54 cm.

DESIGNER: unknown.

MAKER: William Egan & Sons, Cork, 1916.

HCC/104
Red maniple

Poplin cloth maniple with multicoloured silk embroidery of Celtic cross motifs, and gold metal *passementerie* knotted and fringed at each end, edged with gold metal and silk braid. The piece is relined in red silk with an elastic loop sewn inside.

MATERIALS: silk and wool poplin, multicoloured silk embroidery thread, gold braid and fringe.

DIMENSIONS: L 120 cm W 15 cm.

DESIGNER: unknown.

MAKER: William Egan & Sons, Cork, 1916.

Linen Textiles (HCC/105–108)

HCC/105–108
Altar runners

Four linen altar runners.

MATERIALS: Linen;

DIMENSIONS: L 279 cm, W 30 cm.

MAKER: William Egan & Sons, Cork, 1916.

Carpets (HCC/(109–111)

A set of three carpets was provided for use at the front of the altar, on the altar steps and in the sanctuary. They are hand made of knotted wool in muted colours.

HCC/109
Altar steps carpet (col. illus. p. 151)
Hand-tufted wool on a jute ground. Celtic designs in blue, gold and crimson on a light mossy green background; interlace motifs at each corner; geometric borders in Romanesque style echoing those in the red dossal.
MATERIALS: wool, jute.
DIMENSIONS: W c.90 cm, L 498 cm.
MAKER: Dún Emer Guild, Dublin. 1916.

HCC/ 110
Front of altar carpet
Hand-tufted wool on a jute ground. Celtic designs in blue, gold and crimson on a light mossy green background; interlace motifs at each corner; geometric borders in romanesque style echoing those in the red dossal.
MATERIALS: wool, jute.
DIMENSIONS: W c.78 cm, L 202 cm.
MAKER: Dún Emer Guild, Dublin, 1916.

HCC/111
Sanctuary carpet
Hand-tufted wool on a jute ground. Celtic designs in blue, gold and crimson on a light mossy green background;interlace motifs at each corner; squares and roundels decorate the borders.
MATERIALS: wool, jute.
DIMENSIONS: W c.540 cm, L 417 cm.
MAKER: Dún Emer Guild, Dublin, 1916.

Liturgical Manuscripts and Books

Context

The manuscript materials and books of the Honan Collection comprise altar cards, missals and a rite of service. These items are designed and made to complement the altar plate. Conceived and executed according to a holistic aesthetic, each item works in harmony with the others, resulting in a seamless transition from plate to illuminated altar cards to elaborate leather bindings. The fine quality of the calligraphy and bindings, the delicacy of the paper and leather media and the exquisite decorative detail – common to all parts of the collection – make the liturgical manuscripts and books a particularly beautiful achievement.

There are two sets of altar cards, each comprising three cards (two small and one large). Both sets have silver frames with elaborate decoration. The cards are provided with protective leather-covered boxes lined with white satin. The altar cards are rich in colour and ornament. They are elaborately illuminated by the calligraphic artist Joseph Tierney and set in decorated silver frames made by the firm of Edmond Johnson & Sons, who made many of the plate items.

There are three bound volumes. All the bindings are by Eleanor Kelly, in Celtic style and delicately worked in gold tooling on red and black morocco leather; the Roman missal is inlaid with jewels and semi-precious stones.

Structure

This section of the inventory groups items together by format as follows:

• Altar Cards
• Bound Volumes

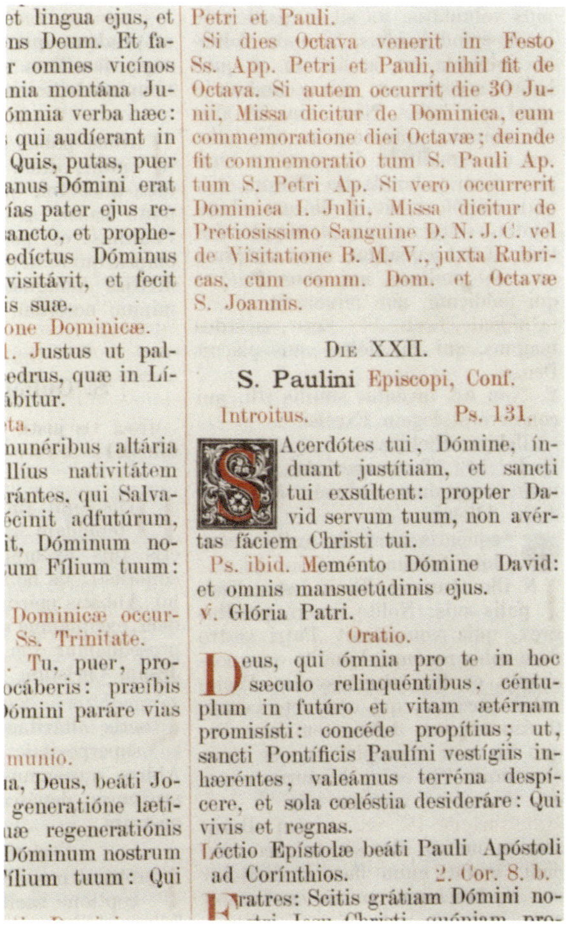

et lingua ejus, et
ns Deum. Et far
r omnes vicinos
nia montána Ju-
ómnia verba hæc:
qui audíerant in
Quis, putas, puer
anus Dómini erat
ías pater ejus re-
ranto, et prophe-
edíctus Dóminus
visitávit, et fecit
is suæ.
one Dominicæ.
Justus ut pal-
edrus, quæ in Lí-
ábitur.
ta.
nunéribus altária
íllius nativitátem
rántes, qui Salva-
écinit adfutúrum,
it, Dóminum no-
um Fílium tuum:
Dominicæ occur-
Ss. Trinitate.
Tu, puer, pro-
ocáberis: præíbis
Dómini paráre vias
munio.
a, Deus, beáti Jo-
generatióne læti-
æ regeneratiónis
Dóminum nostrum
Fílium tuum: Qui

Petri et Pauli.
Si dies Octava venerit in Festo
Ss. App. Petri et Pauli, nihil fit de
Octava. Si autem occurrit die 30 Ju-
nii, Missa dicitur de Dominica, cum
commemoratione diei Octavæ; deinde
fit commemoratio tum S. Pauli Ap.
tum S. Petri Ap. Si vero occurrerit
Dominica I. Julii, Missa dicitur de
Pretiosissimo Sanguine D. N. J.C. vel
de Visitatione B. M. V., juxta Rubri-
cas, cùm comm. Dom. et Octavæ
S. Joannis.

DIE XXII.
S. Paulini Episcopi, Conf.
Introitus.   Ps. 131.
Acerdótes tui, Dómine, ín-
duant justítiam, et sancti
tui exsúltent: propter Da-
vid servum tuum, non avér-
tas fáciem Christi tui.
Ps. ibid. Meménto Dómine David:
et omnis mansuetúdinis ejus.
℣. Glória Patri.
          Oratio.
Deus, qui ómnia pro te in hoc
sæculo relinquéntibus, cén-
plum in futúro et vitam ætérnam
promisísti: concéde propítius; ut,
sancti Pontíficis Paulíni vestígiis in-
hæréntes, valeámus terréna despí-
cere, et sola cœléstia desideráre: Qui
vivis et regnas.
Léctio Epístolæ beáti Pauli Apóstoli
ad Corínthios.   2. Cor. 8. b.
ratres: Scitis grátiam Dómini no-

FIG. 25:
Roman missal (detail) 
FIG. 26:
Altar card (detail)

Sacerd
Saquar
bene
eus,
nitat
mirab
parum aqu
nobis per
ejus divini

rum . Amen.

Altar Cards, first set (HCC/111–114)

HCC/111, 112
Altar cards

(col. illus. pp. 5, 76–77, 78, 80, 227, 229, 230)
Two framed altar cards, written in Latin, the hand
representing the script used in the *Book of Kells*, featuring
red and gold capitals and black lettering. The illuminated
borders are adorned with brightly coloured panels of
modernized spiral patterns and interlacements,
interspersed with figures of saints and biblical scenes.
The frames, with hinged oak supports behind, have
repoussé silver animal-interlace decorations, each
differing from the other, enriched with multicoloured
enamels and rock crystals.
MATERIALS: frames: silver, multicoloured enamelled
panels, rock crystals. Text: vellum, ink, watercolour and
oil paints.
DIMENSIONS: H 40 cm, W 29 cm, max.
D (including stand) 17 cm.
MAKERS: Calligrapher: Joseph Tierney, Dublin;
silversmith: Edmond Johnson Ltd., Dublin.
HALLMARKED: 1916, Dublin, EJ (frames).

HCC/113
Protective box (col. illus. p. 76)

Wooden box covered with gold- tooled black leather with
gilt metal clasp. Box lined with dark green velvet, lid lined
with white satin imprinted with the makers crest:
Edmond Johnson Ltd., Dublin. Key attached to box.
MATERIALS: wood, leather, velvet, satin and
metal clasps.
DIMENSIONS: H 65 cm, W 43 cm D 6.25 cm.
MAKER: Edmond Johnson Ltd., Dublin, c. 1916.

HCC/114
Altar card (col. illus. p. 9)

One framed altar card, twice the size of the previous two,
has the Crucifixion as its central image and is heavily
illuminated with red, silver, purple and orange painted
lettering, ornate initials and pictorial borders in geometric

Celtic designs. The irregularly shaped frame, decorated
with finely detailed Celtic repoussé silver decoration, has
curved edges, each decorated with enamels and rock
crystals, and hinged supports behind.
MATERIALS: frame: silver, enamel, rock crystal. Text:
paper, ink, watercolour and oil paints.
DIMENSIONS: H 54.5 cm, W 62 cm,
max D (including stand) 7 cm.
MAKERS: calligrapher: Joseph Tierney, Dublin, 1916;
Silversmith: Edmond Johnson Ltd., Dublin, 1916.
HALLMARKED: no hallmark visible [1916, Dublin, EJ].

Altar cards, second set (HCC/115–118)

HCC/115, 116
Altar cards (col. illus. pp. 78-79)

Two framed altar cards, illuminated with red lettering and
black initials, within Celtic key pattern borders, by Joseph
Tierney, Dublin. The frames, with hinged oak supports
behind, have projecting rounded corners and projecting
square panels on each mid-side; they are decorated with
chevron decorations in relief and enriched with
multicoloured enamel panels by Edmond Johnson Ltd.,
Dublin. The protective boxes for these cards appear to
be missing.
MATERIALS: frame: silver, enamel. Text: paper; ink,
silver paint, oil paint.
DIMENSIONS: H 54.5 cm, W 62 cm, max D
(including stand) 13.5 cm.
MAKERS: calligrapher: Joseph Tierney, Dublin;
Silversmith: Edmond Johnson Ltd., Dublin.
HALLMARKED: 1916, Dublin, EJ.

HCC/117
Altar card

One framed altar card, twice the size of the previous two by
Joseph Tierney, Dublin. Illuminated with black lettering and
red and black initials, within a Celtic border, beneath a
panel of the Crucifixion. The frame with oak support
behind (which is missing) has projecting round corners
and projecting squares at each mid-side, decorated with

FIG. 27: Altar card (detail)
FIG. 28: Altar card (detail)

Initium
Sancti Evangelii
secundum Joannem.

In principio erat Verbum, et Verbum erat apud Deum, et Deus erat Verbum. Hoc erat in principio apud Deum. Omnia per ipsum facta sunt: et sine ipso factum est nihil, quod factum est. In ipso vita erat, et vita erat lux hominum: et lux in tenebris lucet, et tenebrae eam non

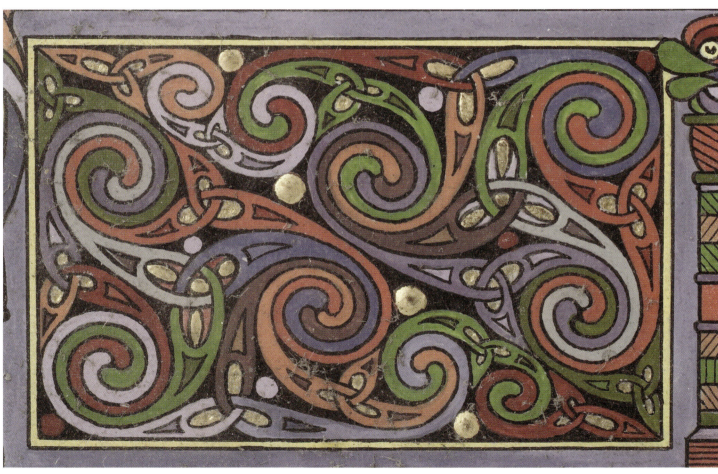

Fig. 29:
*Altar card
(detail)*

Fig. 30:
*Altar card
(detail)*

silver Celtic decoration in relief and enamel panels.

MATERIALS: frame: silver, enamel.

Text: paper, ink, paint.

DIMENSIONS: H 54.5 cm, W 62 cm, D 2.5 cm.

MAKERS: calligrapher: Joseph Tierney, 1917, Dublin; silversmith: Edmond Johnson Ltd, Dublin.

HALLMARKED: 1916,Dublin, EJ.

HCC/118
Protective box

Identical to HCC/113 above, with slightly different dimensions.

MATERIALS: wood, leather, velvet, satin and metal clasps.

DIMENSIONS: H 63.5 cm W 71 cm D 6.25 cm.

MAKER: Edmond Johnson Ltd., Dublin, c. 1916.

Bound volumes (HCC/119–122)

HCC/119
Roman Missal (col. illus. p. 81–3)

Missale Romanum, printed on paper (Augustae Taurinorum: ex typographia Pontificia et Sacror, 1912) in gold-tooled, full red morocco binding. Coloured inlays, front and back; jewels on front cover only (mother of pearl, garnet, amethyst and peridot); a gold- tooled ringed cross, front and back; also other motifs. Illuminated frontispiece with armorial designs depicting the arms of the Honan Hostel surrounded by the arms of the City of Cork, University College Cork, and the O'Connell and Honan families.

MATERIALS: leather, vellum, paper, inks, paints, semi-precious stones.

DIMENSIONS: H 38.5 cm, W 27.5 cm, D 17 cm.

DESIGNERS AND MAKERS: binding: Eleanor Kelly, Dublin, 1916; frontispiece: illuminated by Sangorski and Sutcliffe, London, 1916. Inscriptions record the names of the makers.

HCC/120
Rite of service

This rite of service, printed on paper, is lavishly bound in full red morocco leather with gold-tooled ringed cross on the front cover, and tooled Celtic designs on the back. It was presented to the Honan Chapel by one of the founders, Sir John O'Connell, and bears the inscription recorded below.

MATERIALS: paper, leather, inks.

DIMENSIONS: H 28.5 cm W 22.5 cm 17 cm.

PUBLISHER: Arden Press, Letchworth, 1912.

INSCRIPTION: *Presented for use of St. Fin Barr's Chapel of the Honan Hostel on the occasion of the blessing on 5th Nov. 1916 by Sir John O'Connell as his own gift to the Chapel. Die Novembris V MCMXVI.*

HCC/121
Roman missal

Ordo Missae Defunctorum for use on annual Founders' Day Mass, printed on paper, with full black morocco binding. Inlaid with coloured leathers, front and back, and semi-precious stones on the front only (amethyst and rock crystal); gold-tooled ringed cross (inspired by the grave-slab of Tullylease, Co. Cork) and Celtic motifs on both front and back. There are six bookmarks embroidered with silk thread in a leaf pattern on a black ground attached to the upper spine.

MATERIALS: paper, inks, leather, semi-precious stones.

BOOKMARKS: silk threads.

DIMENSIONS: H 35 cm, W 25 cm D 2 cm.

DESIGNER AND MAKER OF BINDING: Eleanor Kelly, Dublin, c. 1916.

HCC/122
Protective box

Simple board box covered with hand-made paper, lined with white satin.

MATERIALS: board, paper.

DIMENSIONS: H 38 cm, W 26 cm, D 2.5 cm.

MAKER: Eleanor Kelly, Dublin, 1916.

Chapel Furniture

Context

The chapel's furnishings mirror in beautiful detail the Celtic Revival style of the building. Each delicately designed and executed piece, from the circular wrought-iron ventilation panels in the ceiling to the oak President's chair and kneeler, works in harmony so that each piece sits precisely within the overall aesthetic so carefully set out by Sir John O'Connell. Under O'Connell's direction, every individual item, while designed and created in a way that represented the spirit and skill of earlier times, could nonetheless be fully appreciated by contemporary society. The overall effect is one of simplicity and restfulness.

The number of furnishings is small. This reflects O'Connell's desire to create a peaceful, dignified space by limiting the furnishings, free from extravagant ornamentation, to those essential items necessary for the chapel to function as a place of worship. Most of the furnishings recorded in this section are designed by J.F. McMullen, architect of the chapel; many pieces, including the pews, were made by the Cork firm John Sisk & Son, who were its builders.

The practice of liturgy changed after Vatican II. This required that some of the original furnishings be replaced. A short list of replacement furnishings is included below.

Structure

This section groups items together as follows:
- Works designed by J.F. McMullen
- Works by unknown designers
- Works added after Vatican II

Works designed by J.F. MacMullen
(HCC/123–162)

HCC/123
Confessional grille (col. illus. p. 59)
Carved oak panel of open-work interlace design, in a chamfered oak frame and set into wall near vestry door.
MATERIALS: oak.
DIMENSIONS: panel: H 20 cm, W 30 cm.
frame: H 30 cm, W 38 cm.
DESIGNER: uncertain, probably J.F. McMullen, CE., Cork.
MAKER: John Sisk & Son, Cork, 1916.

HCC/124
Credence table
Low table on four square legs, with stretcher; carved chevron decoration in Romanesque style. Carcass of oak, top of pine.
MATERIALS: oak, pine.
DIMENSIONS: H 62 cm, L 62 cm, W 33.5 cm.
DESIGNER: J.F. McMullen, CE., Cork.
MAKER: John Sisk & Son, Cork, 1916.

HCC/125
Music stool (col. illus. p. 54)
Oak stool with concentric bands of chevron and other patterns in Romanesque style. Red leather cushion.
MATERIALS: oak, leather.
DIMENSIONS: stool: H 78 cm, W 74 cm, D 52 cm.
Cushion: 51 cm.
DESIGNER: J.F. McMullen, CE., Cork.
MAKER: John Sisk & Son, Cork, 1916.

HCC/126
Noticeboard
Glass-fronted noticeboard covered with green baize in carved oak frame, raised on two legs, surmounted by a Celtic cross, bearing inscription recorded below. Chevron decoration carved on the frame and legs.
MATERIALS: oak, baize.
DIMENSIONS: H 192 cm W 100 cm B 36 cm.
DESIGNER: J.F. McMullen, CE., Cork.
MAKER: John Sisk & Son, Cork, 1916.
INSCRIPTION: *Pray for the eternal repose of the souls of Sir (later Rev Sir) John O'Connell (1868-1943) Administrator of the Honan estate who caused this chapel to be built and of his wife Mary (1870-1925) who also contributed much to it's beauty Requiescant in Pace.*

HCC/127–154
Pews (col. illus. p. 52)
Twenty-eight long, and three short oak pews, with solid curving ends carved with concentric bands of chevron and other patterns in the Romanesque style.
MATERIAL: oak.
DIMENSIONS: long pews: L 304 cm, H 97 cm, W 53 cm. Short pews: L 180 cm, H 97 cm, W 53 cm.
DESIGNER: J.F. McMullen, CE., Cork.
MAKER: John Sisk & Son, Cork, 1916.

HCC/156, 157
President's chair and kneeler
(col. illus. pp. 56–7)
Carved oak armchair, for use by the President of University College Cork (ex-officio Chairman of the Board of Governors, Honan Hostel), with concentric bands of chevron and other patterns in romanesque style. The arms and motto of the university are carved onto a plaque on the back rail. Red leather cushion. Accompanying carved oak kneeler with decorative carved panel, partly of linen fold design and partly open-work interlacings. At the front are two bronze animal- interlace brackets, used to support the university mace.
MATERIALS: oak, bronze.
DIMENSIONS: chair: H 106 cm, D 60 cm, W 68 cm.
Kneeler: H 101 cm, D 65 cm, W 69 cm.
DESIGNER: J.F. McMullen, CE., Cork.
MAKER: John Sisk & Son, Cork, 1916.

HCC/158
Pulpit (col. illus. p. 57)

Oak reading-desk on a raised stand with steps and
handrail. Carved panel of interlace beneath the lectern
and other panels of Romanesque designs.

MATERIALS: oak.

DIMENSIONS: H 178 cm, D 145 cm, W 88 cm.

DESIGNER: uncertain, probably J.F. McMullen,
CE., Cork.

MAKER: John Sisk & Son, Cork. Date uncertain, c. 1916.

HCC/159, 160
Two ventilator panels

Set in the ceiling, curved animal interlace in circular
frames.

MATERIALS: probably iron;

DIMENSIONS: unable to measure.

DESIGNER: uncertain, probably J.F. McMullen,
CE., Cork.

MAKER: John Sisk & Son, Cork, 1916.

HCC/161, 162
Warden's chair and kneeler

Carved oak armchair and kneeler identical to those above
(HCC/156, 157) but with the arms and crest of the Honan
Chapel on the background. There are no brackets on the
kneeler.

MATERIALS: oak.

DIMENSIONS: chair: H 106 cm, D 60 cm, W 68 cm.
Kneeler: H 101 cm, D 65 cm, W 69 cm.

DESIGNER: J.F. McMullen, CE., Cork;

MAKER: John Sisk & Son, Cork, 1916

Works by unknown designers
(HCC/163–165)

HCC/163
Display cabinet

Oak display cabinet on four square legs, with glass
hinged lid opening upwards, decorated with chevron
carvings and beading. A manuscript volume recording
the names of deceased members of the College is stored
and displayed within.

MATERIALS: oak, glass.

DIMENSIONS: W. 58 cm, L 38.5 cm H 76 cm.

DESIGNER: unknown.

MAKER: Quality Furniture Company, 52 Pope's Quay,
Cork, c. 1930s.

HCC/164, 165
Kneelers (col. illus. p. 58)

Pair of kneelers in carved oak with chamfered chevron
edges, rather different from the Sisk made furniture.

MATERIALS: oak.

DIMENSIONS: W 52.5 cm, D 51 cm, W 52.5 cm.

DESIGNER: unknown.

MAKER: bears label: M.J. Galligan, Upolsterer and
Cabinet Maker, Cork, c. 1920s.

Works Added After Vatican II

A number of items of furniture by the Dublin sculptor Imogen Stuart were added following Vatican II. Designed and made in 1986–7, these include a massive oak altar carved in relief with the Four Evangelists, now placed in the middle of the mosaic floor in front of the sanctuary; a bronze ambo, or lectern, in the form of a fruiting vine; a carved oak credence table, of folding design hinged to the sanctuary wall; an oak presider's chair adapted from the traditional three-legged cottage chair of Connemara, with a high back terminating in a Celtic cross. were supplied to cater for the popularity of the chapel as a wedding venue. A bride's chair and kneeler and a groom's chair and kneeler, the symbolism of their design being explained on labels attached beneath the seats:
The Groom's chair and kneeler are carved in oak. They are angular-masculine in shape. The chair back is based on an evergreen tree. The tree symbolises the life in God's law. It stands for holiness, eternity and everlasting salvation 19IMO/GEN87
The Bride's chair and kneeler are carved in oak. The shapes are soft and mostly curved feminine. The chair back is based on the rainbow which stands for the convenant which God made between Him and man. The rainbow is also a symbol for peace and reconciliation 19IMO/GEN87.
In 1997 Imogen Stuart designed and made a white marble font in the form of a pair of upturned hands, placed directly inside the West door. Also in 1997, the Co. Cork sculptor Kenneth Thompson made a free-standing elm candelabrum to hold the altar candle, carved in relief with the words *Lumen Christi*; and a set of twelve rectangular fumed-oak stools were made by the Co. Cork furniture-maker Eric Pearce. The harmonium was replaced in 1999 with a pipe organ, made by Kenneth Jones and Associates of Bray, Co. Wicklow.